NER
press

Sir Walter Scott's Crusades and Other Fantasies

Sir Walter Scott's Crusades and Other Fantasies

Ibn Warraq

Published by New English Review Press
a subsidiary of World Encounter Institute
PO Box 158397
Nashville, Tennessee 37215
&
27 Old Gloucester Street
London, England, WC1N 3AX

Cover Design by Kendra Adams
Cover Image: *The Abduction of Rebecca* by Eugene Delacroix,
1846, Metropolitan Museum of Art, NYC.

ISBN: 978-0-9884778-5-8

First Edition

NEW ENGLISH REVIEW PRESS
newenglishreview.org

À ma famille raillacaise
À Jacques et Jean

Contents

Preface, Acknowledgements, Caveats and Advertisements for Myself

The essays gathered together here have all been published before on the Internet. I feel decidedly old-fashioned in thinking that a book—a hard copy, in cyberspace parlance—is still the way to go. A book confers dignity and respectability, and will reach a particular audience which values books, and which takes time to ponder their contents in a way not possible in the new cyber medium. A book also seems appropriate since many of the essays here are about books and could be seen as extended annotated bibliographies about Sir Walter Scott, Saladin, or the Crusades in general.

I should like to thank Rebecca Bynum for her discreet, but meticulous editing. I am grateful to Robert Spencer for agreeing to publish many of the present essays on his website, *Jihad Watch*. My main debts are to scholars who have written such magnificent works on the Crusades, and, of course, my essays would not have been possible without them. Hugh Fitzgerald, and Phyllis Chesler made valuable suggestions all of which I adopted, thereby giving some of my essays greater coherence and depth.

Finally, I am forced to address a problem that I have ignored for many years. There are many unscrupulous people on the Internet—on chat rooms, Twitter, and, above all, Facebook—pretending to be Ibn Warraq, speaking as Ibn Warraq, making comments and analyses in the name of Ibn Warraq. May I take this opportunity to state clearly that I, Ibn Warraq, author and editor of *Why I am Not a Muslim, Defending the West, Why the West is Best*, and seven other books, do not have any Facebook or Twitter account, that I have never participated in any discussions in "chat-rooms." I do not have an "official Ibn Warraq Website" either. If you need to know the opinions of Ibn Warraq, read my books, and my occasional articles in the press (*Wall Street Journal, The Guardian, Die Welt, Der Spiegel*, and so on) and even rarer articles on the Internet at *New English*

Review, *National Review Online*, and *Jihad Watch*.

The entry on Ibn Warraq on *Wikipedia* poses problems of another kind: partial quotes, and general tendentiousness. We have all used the *Wikipedia* at one time or another-—it is a useful tool for quick reference. But it is to be used with discretion, and cannot be considered a source for serious works of scholarship, at least not without cross-references, and not without recourse to original or more reputable sources. Unfortunately, far too many people take *Wikipedia* as a scholarly source of information, when, in fact, its various entries, manned by ill-informed and vindictive zealots, are of uneven quality, and many are inaccurate and biased. I hope eventually the public will gain maturity and realise that it cannot believe or rely on everything they read on *Wikipedia*. At any rate, to counter its hostility I assembled, a few years ago, a number of positive reviews of my books from eminent scholars, and they can now be viewed in my book *Virgins? What Virgins? And Other Essays* in the chapter entitled "Apologia Pro Vita Sua." My works have drawn the approval of such intellectuals and scholars as Christopher Hitchens, Roger Scruton, Douglas Murray, Bernard Lewis, Christoph Luxenberg, Chase Robinson, Claude Gilliot, Pierre Larcher, and many others. I shall close with quotes from Paul Berman, Fouad Ajami, and Dr. David Cook of Rice University.

PAUL BERMAN, author of *Terror and Liberalism*:

First, let me mention Ibn Warraq's book *Defending the West*. Fred Siegel said that the book has been described as a "glorious work of scholarship"; I may be remembering incorrectly, but I think that is my own blurb on the back of the book. If it isn't, I wish I had written it.

Ibn Warraq is a major world figure among intellectuals. If you go through his books, you'll be astounded at his erudition. The depth of knowledge that he brings to questions of Islam and Islamic culture in various languages: there is no relation to the depth that Edward Said brought to these topics. Ibn Warraq's *Defending the West* is, in effect, one of the most devastating demolitions of an intellectual giant that I've ever seen. I don't think that the book has so far been fully appreciated; it's a book that will take some time to sink in. But I do think that Ibn Warraq has written a book that will turn out to be of historic importance in demolishing the ideological system that Said created.

FOUAD AJAMI, Professor at the Johns Hopkins University School of Advanced Internal Studies and author of *The Foreigner's Gift: The Americans, the Arabs, and the Iraqis in Iraq*:

> Ibn Warraq has written a brilliant and luminous book [*Defending the West*] of cultural analysis and intellectual history. He reminds us of so many precious things in the West—and of it—that are worth upholding in the face of critics who enjoy Western liberties and denigrate them at the same time. This is more than a demolition of Edward Said's *Orientalism*: In its own right, it is an exquisite inquiry into the great ideas at play in our world.

DR. DAVID COOK, Professor in Religious Studies at Rice University, Texas:

> As a scholar of Islam myself, I find Ibn Warraq's attitude to be very refreshing, and his scholarship for the most part to be accurate and devastating in pinpointing weaknesses in Muslim orthodoxy. His third essay, "Some Aspects of the History of Koran Criticism, 700 CE to 2005 CE," could almost serve as a history of our field, and of its systematic failure to critique the foundational texts of Islam as those of other faiths have been critiqued.[1] It is an embarrassment for Islamic Studies that no critical text of the Qur'an has been produced.[2] However, even were this basic, elemental work done, there would be still a great more to be done in order to counter one of the most fundamental Muslim presuppositions—namely, that the text of the Qur'an has remained absolutely unaltered since the time of the Prophet Muhammad in the seventh century of the Common Era. Ibn Warraq counters this nonsense, which one hears on a regular basis even from educated Muslims who should

---

1 David Cook's footnote: See for a discussion of this failure, F. E. Peters, "The Quest of the Historical Muhammad," *International Journal of Middle Eastern Studies*, 23 (1991), pp. 291-315.

2 David Cook's footnote: Such work was begun in 1980, but stalled in 1989 due to lack of funding; see "Codex San'a I: A Qur'anic Manuscript from Mid-1st Century Hijra," accessed online at: http://www.islamic-awareness.org/Quran/Text/Mss/soth.html.

know better, by demonstrating the prevalence of variant readings of the Qur'anic text.[3] That the existence of these variants,
known as *qira'at*, demonstrates the falsity of the orthodox Muslim position *vis-à-vis* the Qur'an is obvious, and yet bizarrely
rejected even by mainstream scholars.[4]

---

3 David Cook's footnote: It is further ironic that the existence of either seven or fourteen canonical "readings" of the Qur'an is accepted in Islam, and yet the implications of
this fact for the "unaltered" nature of the text are not.

4 David Cook's footnote: See Hamza Andreas Tzortis, "Luxenberg & Puin: Origins &
Revisions: Responding to Dispatches," accessed online at: http://www.theinimitable-
quran.com/respondingtodispacthes.pdf.

1
Ivanhoe, The Jews and Saracens[1], with Digressions on Blacks and Jews in Britain, and Other Sundry Subjects

E dward Said, the late Professor of Comparative Literature at Columbia University, has, in his influential *Orientalism*, a char-acteristically shallow, sneering aside on Sir Walter Scott, and, in particular, on his novel, *The Talisman*:

> In Scott's novel *The Talisman* (1825), Sir Kenneth (of the Crouching Leopard) battles a single Saracen to a standoff somewhere in the Palestinian desert; as the Crusader and his opponent, who is Saladin in disguise, later engage in conversa-tion, the Christian discovers his Muslim antagonist to be not so bad a fellow after all. Yet he remarks:
>
> > 'I well thought...that your blinded race had their descent from the foul fiend, without whose aid you would never have been able to maintain this blessed land of Palestine against so many valiant soldiers of God. I speak not thus of thee in particular, Saracen, but generally of thy people and religion. Strange is it to me, however, not that you should have the de-scent from the Evil One, but that you should boast of it.'

For indeed the Saracen does boast of tracing his race's line back to Eblis, the Muslim Lucifer. But what is truly curious is not the

---

1 Saracen: Collins English Dictionary: HISTORY C13: From Old French *Sarrazin*, from Late Latin *Saracenus*, from Late Greek *Sarakenos*, perhaps from Arabic *sharq* sunrise, from *sharaqa* to rise.

feeble historicism by which Scott makes the scene "medieval," letting Christian attack Muslim theologically in a way nineteenth-century Europeans would not (they would, though); rather, it is the airy condescension of damning a whole people "generally" while mitigating the offense with a cool "I don't mean you in particular."

Not only does Said make the unwarranted assumption that Sir Kenneth is voicing Scott's thoughts [Said would have done well to heed Evelyn Waugh's motto to *Brideshead Revisited*, "I am not I; thou art not he or she; they are not they"], he misunderstands, or at least fails to mention, the entire import of Scott's novel, the contrast between the two cultures, particularly in the early chapters, with the Muslim one emerging to its advantage many times over. We come away from the novel with a sense of the chivalrous superiority of the Saracens.[2] (Incidentally, Said accuses Scott, creator of the historical novel, of "feeble historicism", when he clearly means "historicity").

Sir Walter Scott, under the influence of the Scottish historian William Robertson, who had perpetuated the Enlightenment myth of the superiority of Islamic civilization, continued the theme of the vain and avaricious Christian Crusaders in contrast to the chivalrous and honorable Saracens. Jonathan Riley-Smith summarizes Scott's influence on the entire Romantic movement and their attitude to the Crusades:

> Four of Scott's novels involved crusades and crusaders. *Count Robert of Paris* [1831] was set in Constantinople at the time of the First Crusade; the other three were set during the Third Crusade. *Ivanhoe* [1819] and *The Betrothed* [1825] were concerned with events on the home front, while the plot of *The Talisman* [1825] was set in Palestine and centered on the friendship between a Scottish knight and Saladin, who appeared in a bewildering array of disguises, including that of a skilled physician who cured King Richard of England. The novels painted a picture of crusaders who were brave and glamorous, but also vainglorious, avaricious, childish, and boorish. Few of them were genuinely moved by religion or the crusade ideal; most had taken the cross out of pride, greed, or ambition. The worst of them were the brothers of the military orders, who may have

---

2 Paul Pelckmans, "Walter Scott's Orient: The Talisman" in *Oriental Propects*, edd. Barfoot, D'Haen. Rodopi: Amsterdam & New York, 1998, p. 99.

been courageous and disciplined but were also arrogant, privileged, corrupt, voluptuous, and unprincipled. An additional theme, the cultural superiority of the Muslims, which was only hinted at in the other novels, pervaded *The Talisman*.[3]

Edward Said, in fact, chose the one novel of the crusades which explicitly extolled the virtues of the Saracens and the superiority of their culture, and not the contrary, as he claimed in *Orientalism*. I shall come back to *The Talisman*, once I have gone through the other three novels involving crusades or crusaders.

IVANHOE [1819]

Ivanhoe, set in late twelfth century England, also displays Scott's more general concerns, his commitment to religious and racial tolerance, and his Enlightenment abhorrence of superstition and fanaticism, whether the unreflective kind of the masses, or the more dogmatic variety of the religious bigot.

Scott, though often considered a respectable historian, is quite cavalier with the historical facts in *Ivanhoe*, or as A.N. Wilson put it, "wildly inaccurate."[4] Scott himself admits the unhistorical nature of many of the details in a footnote, "…but neither will I allow that the author of a modern antique romance is obliged to confine himself to the introduction of those manners only which can be proved to have absolutely existed in the times he is depicting, so that he restrain himself to such as are plausible and natural, and contain no obvious anachronism."[5] And yet, Scott does manage to recreate a vivid past which he treats with respect, and, *pace* Riley-Smith, does not dismiss the Age of Chivalry as a total fraud. Scott wrote in his "Essay on Chivalry" that, "from the wild and overstrained courtesies of Chivalry have been derived our present system of manners. It is certainly not faultless.…Yet it has grace and dignity unknown to classic times, when women were slaves, and men coarse and vulgar, or overbearing and brutal as suited their humour, without respect to that of the rest of their society. Such being the tone and spirit of Chivalry, derived from love,

---

3 Jonathan Riley-Smith, *The Crusades, Christianity, and Islam,* New York: Columbia University Press, 2008, p. 65.

4 A.N. Wilson, Introduction, *Sir Walter Scott, Ivanhoe,* Penguin Books: Harmondsworth, 1986, p. viii.

5 Sir Walter Scott, *Ivanhoe,* Penguin Books: Harmondsworth, 1986, p. 552.

devotion, and valour…"[6]

Saracens do not play a significant role in the novel, though a minor controversy was drummed up by those who objected to Scott's introduction of two putatively black Muslim slaves at the beginning of the novel. Here is Scott's description of the two slaves, Hamet and Abdallah, "These two squires [the crusader, Brian de Bois-Guilbert, and his companion] were followed by two attendants, whose dark visages, white turbans, and the Oriental form of their garments, showed them to be natives of some distant Eastern country. The whole appearance of this warrior and his retinue was wild and outlandish; the dress of his squires was gorgeous, and his Eastern attendants wore silver collars round their throats, and bracelets of the same metal upon their swarthy legs and arms, of which the latter were naked from the elbow, and the former from mid-leg to ankle…. They were armed with crooked sabers, having the hilt and baldric inlaid with gold, and matched with Turkish daggers of yet more costly workmanship. Each of them bore at his saddle-bow a bundle of darts or javelins, about four feet in length, having sharp steel heads, a weapon much in use among the Saracens, and of which the memory is yet preserved in the martial exercise called *el jerrid*, still practiced in Eastern countries.

"The steeds of these attendants were in appearance as foreign as their riders. They were of Saracen origin, and consequently of Arabian descent;…."[7]

A few pages later, the Crusader, Brian de Bois-Guilbert, describes the two slaves, rather confusingly, as "our Turkish captives."[8] That he perhaps had blacks in mind rather than Turks, or at least ethnic Turks, is borne out by Scott's footnote on slaves,

> The severe accuracy of some critics has objected to the complexion of the slaves of Brian de Bois-Guilbert, as being totally out of costume and propriety. I remember the same objection being made to a set of sable functionaries whom my friend, Mat Lewis, introduced as the guards and mischief-doing satellites of the wicked Baron in his *Castle Spectre*.[9] Mat treated the objection with great contempt, and averred in reply, that he made the slaves black in order to obtain a striking effect

6 *The Miscellaneous Prose Works of Sir Walter Scott Bart*, Edinburgh: Robert Cadell, 1847 Vol. VI, p. 49.

7 Sir Walter Scott, *Ivanhoe, op.cit.*, pp. 20-21.

8 *Ibid.*,p. 26.

9 Matthew Lewis [1775-1818] *Castle Spectre*, 1796.

of contrast, and that, could he have derived a similar advantage from making his heroine blue, blue she should have been.

I do not pretend to plead the immunities of my order so highly as this; but neither will I allow that the author of a modern antique romance is obliged to confine himself to the introduction of those manners only which can be proved to have absolutely existed in the times he is depicting, so that he restrain himself to such as are plausible and natural, and contain no obvious anachronism. In this point of view, what can be more natural than that the Templars, who, we know, copied closely the luxuries of the Asiatic warriors with whom they fought, should use the service of the enslaved Africans whom the fate of war transferred to new masters? I am sure, if there are no precise proofs of their having done so, there is nothing, on the other hand, that can entitle us positively to conclude that they never did. Besides, there is an instance in romance.

John of Rampayne, an excellent juggler and minstrel, undertook to effect the escape of one Audulf de Bracy, by presenting himself in disguise at the court of the king, where he was confined. For this purpose, he stained 'his hair and his whole body entirely as black as jet, so that nothing was white but his teeth,' and succeeded in imposing himself on the king as an Ethiopian minstrel. He effected, by stratagem, the escape of the prisoner. Negroes, therefore, must have been known in England in the dark ages.[10]

In defence of Sir Walter Scott, there were indeed blacks in Britain before the twelfth century. Ironically, there were Africans in Britain even before the arrival of the English; they were soldiers in the Roman Imperial Army stationed in the South. Among the troops defending Hadrian's Wall was a division of "moors," raised in North Africa, and garrisoned near Carlisle, north of England in the third century C.E.[11] Archaeological finds in Norfolk suggest a black presence in Britain round the year 1000 C.E.[12] When the records are no longer silent, we have further firm evidence of blacks in Britain in the sixteenth century. But, the intervening years—the years of the events in Ivanhoe—must also have had their share of blacks.

---

10 Sir Walter Scott, *Ivanhoe, op.cit.*, pp. 551-552.

11 Peter Fryer, *Staying Power: The History of Black People in Britain*, [3rd Edn.] University of Alberta: 1987, p. 1.

12 *Ibid.*, p. 2.

The real tension in the novel is provided by the antagonism of the Saxons for the Normans—the former determined to preserve their rites, ritual, language, and land from the overwhelming manners and sheer force of arms of the latter. Caught between the two are the fortunes of a Jewish money-lender, and his beautiful daughter, Rebecca. Along the way, Scott praises the original ideals of the Crusaders, but pours scorn on the grubby reality of their actual behaviour. Cedric, the Saxon, father of Crusader Ivanhoe, has this to say about the pilgrims and crusaders: "Palestine! how many ears are turned to the tales which dissolute crusaders, or hypocritical pilgrims, bring from that fatal land! I too might ask—I too might enquire—I too might listen with a beating heart to fables which the wily strollers devise to cheat us into hospitality—but no. . . .The son who has disobeyed me is no longer mine; nor will I concern myself more for his fate than for that of the most worthless among the millions that ever shaped the cross on their shoulder, rushed into excess and blood-guiltiness, and called it an accomplishment of the will of God."[13]

It would be foolish to impute these sentiments of a character in his novel to Scott, but there is good external evidence to think that they do reflect his personal views. He tells us that King Richard's repeated victories in the Holy Land, "had been rendered fruitless, his romantic attempts to besiege Jerusalem disappointed, and the fruit of all the glory which he had acquired had dwindled into an uncertain truce with the Sultan Saladin."[14] In other words, Richard's act may have been "romantic," but ultimately "fruitless," and the result, "an uncertain truce." Again, it is Scott speaking in his own voice, when he contrasts the original shield of Bois-Guilbert which the latter exchanges for one with a more pretentious device, the original high-mindedness giving way to cupidity, "His first had only borne the general device of his rider, representing two knights riding upon one horse, an emblem expressive of the original humility and poverty of the Templars, qualities they had since exchanged for the arrogance and wealth that finally occasioned their suppression."[15]

Scott more generally is concerned with fanaticism; one could even take the motto, usually attributed to Scott himself, to Chapter XXXV as the motto to the entire novel,

Arouse the tiger of Hyrcanian deserts,
Strive with half-starved lion for his prey;

---

13 Sir Walter Scott, *Ivanhoe, op.cit.*, pp. 38-39.
14 *Ibid.*, p. 81.
15 *Ibid.*, p. 81.

Lesser the risk, than rouse the slumbering fire
Of wild fanaticism.[16]

The real heroine of the novel is Rebecca, the beautiful daughter of
Isaac, the Jewish merchant. In describing the attitudes of various characters
to Jews, Scott is able to paint a sympathetic portrait of a despised people
in twelfth century England, and implicitly criticize religious fanaticism as
a source of perpetual strife and instability.

In Part Two, we shall look at the historical reality of the life of Jews
in Medieval England, and Scott's imaginative, empathic evocation of their
plight.

SIR WALTER SCOTT AND THE JEWS

It was argued by Leon Poliakov and others[17] that the portrait of Isaac
the Jew in Ivanhoe is generally an unfavourable one, indeed an unflattering
stereoptype derived from *The Merchant of Venice* and Marlowe's *The Jew of
Malta* of the Jew as a contemptible or comic miser. Scott introduces Isaac
in chapter five which bears the well-known words from *The Merchant of
Venice* as its motto, "Hath not a Jew eyes? Hath not a Jew hands, organs,
dimensions, affections, passions? Fed with the same food, hurt with the
same weapons, subject to the same diseases, healed by the same means,
warmed and cooled by the same winter and summer, as a Christian is?"
However, it seems highly unlikely that an author would choose just such a
passage from Shakespeare if he meant to solely denigrate Jews, or that he
picked this particular passage at random. One has to feel the fine tone of
the entire novel, and its moral nuances before dismissing Scott's portrait of
the Jew as an anti-semitic stereotype.

Cedric, the Saxon father of Ivanhoe, sets the tone when he says, in-
viting Isaac to join them at their meal and refusing to listen to the prejudices of the other guests present, "my hospitality must not be bounded by
your dislikes." One could take that phrase as being addressed to not only
all listeners in his company, but also all the readers of the novel. Isaac and
Rebecca are my guests, Scott tells us, whether you like it or not, and they
deserve all the respect any human being deserves, "Hath not a Jew eyes?....".

---

16 Sir Walter Scott, *Ivanhoe, op.cit.,* p. 387.

17 Leon Poliakov. *History of Anti-Semitism, From Voltaire to Wagner.* Vol.3. New York,
1975, pp. 325-327.
  Edgar Rosenberg. *From Shylock to Svengali: Jewish Stereotypes in English Fiction,*
London, 1961. pp. 73f.

Scott introduces Isaac with a few deft strokes but adds important explanatory notes,

> Introduced with little ceremony, and advancing with fear and hesitation, and many a bow of deep humility, a tall, thin old man, who, however, had lost by the habit of stooping much of his actual height, approached the lower end of the board. His features, keen and regular, with an aquiline nose, and piercing black eyes; his high and wrinkled forehead, and long gray hair and beard, would have been considered as handsome, had they not been the marks of a physiognomy peculiar to a race which, during those dark ages, was alike detested by the credulous and prejudiced vulgar, and persecuted by the greedy and rapacious nobility, and who, perhaps owing to that very hatred and persecution, had adopted a national character, in which there was much, to say the least, mean and unamiable.[18]

Scott here picks out two classes of persecutors of Jews, "the credulous and prejudiced vulgar," and "the greedy and rapacious nobility," to which he, a little later in the novel, adds a third class, the religious bigot. If the Jew has a mean and unamiable look it is because of the role he has been forced into by years of persecution. Scott seems acutely aware of the plight of the Jews in twelfth century England,

> His [Isaac's] doubts might have been indeed pardoned; for, except perhaps the flying fish, there was no race existing on the earth, in the air, or the waters, who were the object of such an unremitting, general, and relentless persecution as the Jews of this period. Upon the slightest and most unreasonable pretences, as well as upon the most absurd and groundless accusations, their persons and property were exposed to every turn of popular fury; for Norman, Saxon, Dane, and Briton, however adverse these races were to each other, contended which should look with greatest detestation upon a people, whom it was accounted a part of religion to hate, to revile, to despise, to plunder, and to persecute. The kings of the Norman race, and the independent nobles, who followed their example in all acts of tyranny, maintained against this devoted people a persecution

---

18 Sir Walter Scott, *Ivanhoe*, *op.cit.*, 1986, p. 50.

of a more regular, calculated, and self-interested kind. It is a well-known story of King John, that he confined a wealthy Jew in one of the royal castles, and daily caused one of his teeth to be torn out, until, when the jaw of the unhappy Israelite was half disfurnished, he consented to pay a large sum, which it was the tyrant's object to extort from him. The little ready money which was in the country was chiefly in possession of this persecuted people, and the nobility hesitated not to follow the example of their sovereign, in wringing it from them by every species of oppression, and even personal torture. Yet the passive courage inspired by the love of gain, induced the Jews to dare the various evils to which they were subjected, in consideration of the immense profits which they were enabled to realize in a country naturally so wealthy as England. In spite of every kind of discouragement, and even of the special court of taxations called the Jews' Exchequer, erected for the very purpose of despoiling and distressing them, the Jews increased, multiplied, and accumulated huge sums, which they transferred from one band to another by means of bills of exchange—an invention for which commerce is said to be indebted to them, and which enabled them to transfer their wealth from land to land, that when threatened with oppression in one country, their treasure might be secured in another.

The obstinacy and avarice of the Jews being thus in a measure placed in opposition to the fanaticism and tyranny of those under whom they lived, seemed to increase in proportion to the persecution with which they were visited; and the immense wealth they usually acquired in commerce, while it frequently placed them in danger, was at other times used to extend their influence, and to secure to them a certain degree of protection. On these terms they lived; and their character, influenced accordingly, was watchful, suspicious, and timid — yet obstinate, uncomplying, and skilful in evading the dangers to which they were exposed.[19]

Obstinate and avaricious, suspicious and timid, the Jews do display such unattractive qualities, but these vices could easily be seen as virtues,

---

19 *Ibid.*, pp. 69-70.

the virtues of patience, vigilance, diligence, and prudence of which they had need after years of mob hysteria, and the rapaciousness of the King and nobility; how else could they have survived? Nor is Isaac always presented as a cringing coward. When he is thrown into a foul dungeon, Isaac reveals further qualities, of resolution, of hope, and dignity:

> The whole appearance of the dungeon might have appalled a stouter heart than that of Isaac, who, nevertheless, was more composed under the imminent pressure of danger, than he had seemed to be while affected by terrors of which the cause was as yet remote and contingent. The lovers of the chase say that the hare feels more agony during the pursuit of the greyhounds than when she is struggling in their fangs. And thus it is probable, that the Jews, by the very frequency of their fear on all occasions, had their minds in some degree prepared for every effort of tyranny which could be practised upon them; so that no aggression, when it had taken place, could bring with it that surprise which is the most disabling quality of terror. Neither was it the first time that Isaac had been placed in circumstances so dangerous. He had, therefore, experience to guide him, as well as hope, that he might again, as formerly, be delivered as a prey from the fowler. Above all, he had upon his side the unyielding obstinacy of his nation, and that unbending resolution, with which Israelites have been frequently known to submit to the uttermost evils which power and violence can inflict upon them, rather than gratify their oppressors by granting their demand.[20]

Moreover, Isaac is not devoid of a deep sense of gratitude, as when he thanks Ivanhoe for protecting him by offering to lend him horses and harnesses even though there was a strong chance Isaac would never see them paid for: "The Jew twisted himself in the saddle, like a man in a fit of the colic; but his better feelings predominated."

Isaac also manifests courage when he refuses to pay Front-le-Boeuf any ransom unless he receives some guarantee that his daughter, Rebecca, will be safe. Remarkable courage since he is threatened with real torture as the Norman's Muslim slaves prepare red-hot irons in a charcoal fire:

---

20 *Ibid.*, pp. 225-226.

"Robber and villain I," said the Jew, retorting the insults of his oppressor with passion, which, however impotent, he now found it impossible to bridle, "I will pay thee nothing— not one silver penny will I pay thee, unless my daughter is delivered to me in safety and honor!"

"Art thou in thy senses, Israelite?" said the Norman, sternly — "has thy flesh and blood a charm against heated iron and scalding oil?"

"I care not!" said the Jew, rendered desperate by paternal affection; "do thy worst. My daughter is my flesh and blood, dearer to me a thousand times than those limbs which thy cruelty threatens. No silver will I give thee, unless I were to pour it molten down thy avaricious throat—no, not a silver penny will I give thee, Nazarene, were it to save thee from the deep damnation thy whole life has merited. Take my life if thou wilt, and say, the Jew, amidst his tortures, knew how to disappoint the Christian."[21]

TWELFTH CENTURY ENGLAND

As remarked earlier, Scott was well aware of the history of Jewish persecution, and knew the plight of Jews during twelfth century England. Scott's contention that the behaviour of the Jews was very much determined by the historical circumstances, their social disabilities pushing them into certain professions, for instance, is borne out by the history of Jewish settlement in England. There seem to have been very few Jews before 1066, and certainly no settlements. William the Conqueror invited the first group of Jews from France, in 1070, wanting to take advantage of their entreprenuerial and financial skills. But, significantly, the Jews were severely restricted as to what they could practice; they were not permitted to own land or to take part in the trades apart from medicine. Since Catholics considered usury a sin, Jews figured largely as money lenders.

Or as Rebecca, Isaac's daughter, tells Ivanhoe, "Heaven in his ire has driven [the Jew] from his country, but industry has opened to him the only road to power and influence which oppression has left unbarred."[22] There one has all the elements of the stereotypes: they practiced medicine, hence the frequent accusations of necromancy and witchcraft that we also witness in *Ivanhoe* as Rebecca, Isaac's daughter, goes on trial; forced to be-

21 *Ibid.*, pp. 233-234.
22 *Ibid.*, p. 444.

ing moneylenders, the Jews were frequently accused of usury, exploitation, avarice. Scott was not inventing the stereotype.

Under Henry II [died 1189], the Jews flourished, establishing themselves as skillful money lenders, and settling in towns such as Norwich, Oxford, Cambridge, Windsor, and of course, London. This situation unfortunately was not to last. There were massacres of Jews between 1189 and 1190 in many towns, such as Thetford, and Colchester, but the most notorious one took place in York, where many Jews killed themselves rather than convert to Christianity as the mob demanded. During Richard I's absence in the Holy Land, the approximate date of the events in *Ivanhoe*, the Jews were harassed by William de Longchamp, the Bishop of Ely. They were forced to contribute huge sums to the king's ransom. On his return, Richard I [died 1199] began the process which led to the establishment of the office of Exchequer of the Jews, making transactions of Jews liable to taxation by the King of England, thereby becoming a tacit partner in all the transactions of Jewish money lending. Moreover, the king demanded two *bezants* in the pound, that is, 10 per cent, of all sums recovered by the Jews with the aid of his courts.[23]

Under King John [died 1216], the lot of the Jews worsened, as he tried to squeeze as much money as possible from them. At first, John treated Jews with much consideration, "But with the loss of Normandy in 1205 a new spirit seems to have come over the attitude of John to his Jews. In the height of his triumph over the pope, he demanded the sum of no less than £100,000 from the religious houses of England, and 66,000 marks from the Jews (1210). One of the latter, Abraham of Bristol, who refused to pay his quota of 10,000 marks, had, by order of the king, seven of his teeth extracted, one a day, until he was willing to disgorge."[24] The latter incident is alluded to by Scott.

Scott was also well aware of the religious dimension in the prejudice against the Jews. Pope Innocent III had written to Richard I and other Christian leaders in 1198,

> calling upon them to compel the remission of all usury demanded by Jews from Christians. This would of course render

---

23 *The Jewish Encyclopedia*, edd. Cyrus Adler, et al. New York 7 London: Funk and Wagnalls Company, 1906, Vol. V, Article, "England", p. 164. See also David A. Carpenter, *The Struggle for Mastery: Britain, 1066-1284*, Oxford: Oxford University Press, 2003, pp. 249-251; *Encyclopaedia Metropolitana*, or *Universal Dictionary of Knowledge*, edd. The Rev. Edward Smedley M.A., *et al.* London, 1845, Vol. XI, p. 685.

24 *The Jewish Encyclopedia*, Vol. V, p. 164.

the Jewish community's very existence impossible.

On July 15, 1205, the Pope laid down the principle that Jews were doomed to perpetual servitude because they had crucified Jesus.[25]

Indeed, the most frightening, and hateful figure in the novel is Lucas de Beaumanoir, the Grand Master, the implacable head of the religious establishment of the Knights Templars. He delighted in tormenting Jews, or as Rabbi Nathan says to Isaac, "to do foul scorn to our people is his morning and evening delight... Specially hath this proud man extended his glove over the children of Judah, as holy David over Edom, holding the murder of a Jew to be an offering of as sweet savor as the death of a Saracen. Impious and false things has he said even of the virtues of our medicines, as if they were the devices of Satan — The Lord rebuke him !"[26]

Here is how Scott introduces the Grand Master, "The Grand Master was a man advanced in age, as was testified by his long gray beard, and the shaggy gray eyebrows, everhanging eyes, of which, however, years had been unable to quench the fire. A formidable warrior, his thin and severe features retained the soldier's fierceness of expression; an ascetic bigot, they were no less marked by the emaciation of abstinence, and the spiritual pride of the self-satisfied devotee. Yet with these severer traits of physiognomy, there was mixed somewhat striking and noble, arising, doubtless, from the great part which his high office called upon him to act among monarchs and princes, and from the habitual exercise of supreme authority over the valiant and high-born knights, who were united by the rules of the Order."[27]

This "ascetic bigot" rails and rants against the Templars for their lax morals, and lack of discipline, and never misses an opportunity to demonize Jews and Saracens, "They [the Templars] are forbidden by our statutes to take one bird by means of another, to shoot beasts with bow or arblast, to halloo to a hunting-horn, or to spur the horse after game. But now, at hunting and hawking, and each idle sport of wood and river, who so prompt as the Templars in all these fond vanities? They are forbidden to read, save what their Superior permitted, or listen to what is read, save such holy things as may be recited aloud during the hours of refection; but lo! their ears are at the command of idle minstrels, and their eyes study empty romaunts. They were commanded to extirpate magic and heresy.

25 *Ibid.*

26 Sir Walter Scott, *Ivanhoe, op.cit.*, p. 389.

27 *Ibid.*, p. 391

Lo ! they are charged with studying the accursed cabalistical secrets of the Jews, and the magic of the Paynim Saracens."[28]

The Grand Master receives Isaac rather unceremoniously, "'Jew,' continued the haughty old man, 'mark me. It suits not our condition to hold with thee long communications, nor do we waste words or time upon any one. Wherefore be brief in thy answers to what questions I shall ask thee, and let thy words be of truth; for if thy tongue doubles with me, I will have it torn from thy misbelieving jaws.'"

When Isaac approaches with extended hand, The Grand Master reacts, "'Back, dog!' said the Grand Master; 'I touch not misbelievers, save with the sword.—Conrade, take thou the letter from the Jew, and give it to me.'"[29]

Isaac's daughter Rebecca is immediately suspected of practising the black arts in curing a Templar of a malady, and the Grand Master is ready to deal with her,

> "There is more in it than thou dost guess, Conrade; thy simplicity is no match for this deep abyss of wickedness. This Rebecca of York was a pupil of that Miriam of whom thou hast heard. Thou shalt hear the Jew own it even now." Then turning to Isaac, he said aloud, "Thy daughter, then, is prisoner with Brian de Bois-Guilbert?"
>
> "Ay, reverend valorous sir," stammered poor Isaac, "and whatsoever ransom a poor man may pay for her deliverance."
>
> "Peace !" said the Grand Master. "This thy daughter hath practised the art of healing, hath she not?"
>
> "Ay, gracious sir," answered the Jew, with more confidence; "and knight and yeoman, squire and vassal, may bless the goodly gift which Heaven hath assigned to her. Many a one can testify that she hath recovered them by her art, when every other human aid hath proved vain; but the blessing of the God of Jacob was upon her."
>
> Beaumanoir turned to Mont-Fitchet with a grim smile. "See, brother," he said, "the deceptions of the devouring Enemy! Behold the baits with which he fishes for souls, giving a poor space of earthly life in exchange for eternal happiness hereafter. Well said our blessed rule, *Semper percutiatur leo*

---

28 *Ibid.*, p. 393.
29 *Ibid.*, pp. 396-397.

varans.—Up on the lion! Down with the destroyer!" said he, shaking aloft his mystic abacus, as if in defiance of the powers of darkness—"Thy daughter worketh the cures, I doubt not," thus he went on to address the Jew, "by words and sigils, and periapts, and other cabalistical mysteries."

"Nay, reverend and brave knight," answered Isaac, "but in chief measure by a balsam of marvellous virtue."

"Where had she that secret?" said Beaumanoir.

"It was delivered to her," answered Isaac reluctantly, "by Miriam, a sage matron of our tribe."

"Ah, false Jew!" said the Grand Master; "was it not from that same witch Miriam, the abomination of whose enchantments have been heard of throughout every Christian land?" exclaimed the Grand Master, crossing himself. "Her body was burnt at a stake, and her ashes were scattered to the four winds; and so be it with me and mine Order, if I do not as much to her pupil, and more also! I will teach her to throw spell and incantation over the soldiers of the blessed Temple.—There, Damian, spurn this Jew from the gate—shoot him dead if he oppose or turn again. With his daughter we will deal as the Christian law and our own high office warrant."[30]

In the above examples, Scott has delineated with consummate skill the terrifying irrationality of religious bigotry, which is able to so easily translate transparent acts of charity, compassion, and care into dark acts of Beelzebub himself, all designed to ensnare Christian souls.

Scott was an accomplished historian and perfectly aware of the wave of antisemitism that the preaching of the First Crusade in 1095 inspired in Europe, especially in the Rhineland where entire communities of Jews were massacred. It is not surprising then to see how critical he is of the Crusades, and Crusaders. He paints severe portraits of several Templars in *Ivanhoe*, their cruelty, rapaciousness and lack of scruples. The abiding impression as one comes to the end of Ivanhoe is not of Scott's antisemitism but the antisemitism of the main actors—their fanaticism, Crusader ideals perverted and channeled into unworthy goals, and the cruelty of the Normans—"The description given by the author of the *Saxon Chronicle* of the cruelties exercised in the reign of King Stephen by the great barons and lords of castles, who were all Normans, affords a strong proof of the

---

30 *Ibid.*, p. 400.

excesses of which they were capable when their passions were inflamed."[31] (Scott, ever the realist, even makes Ivanhoe partake in antisemitism, albeit of a mild kind.) And of course, the almost transcendental goodness and beauty of Rebecca, to whom we shall now turn. Scott does not spare himself in his opening remarks about the true heroine of *Ivanhoe*,

> The figure of Rebecca might indeed have compared with the proudest beauties of England, even though it had been judged by as shrewd a connoisseur as Prince John. Her form was exquisitely symmetrical, and was shown to advantage by a sort of Eastern dress, which she wore according to the fashion of the females of her nation. Her turban of yellow silk suited well with the darkness of her complexion. The brilliancy of her eyes, the superb arch of her eyebrows, her well-formed aquiline nose, her teeth as white as pearl, and the profusion of her sable tresses, which, each arranged in its own little spiral of twisted curls, fell down upon as much of a lovely neck and bosom as a *simarre* of the richest Persian silk, exhibiting flowers in their natural colors embossed upon a purple ground, permitted to be visible—all these constituted a combination of loveliness, which yielded not to the most beautiful of the maidens who surrounded her. It is true, that of the golden and pearl-studded clasps, which closed her vest from the throat to the waist, the three uppermost were left unfastened on account of the heat, which something enlarged the prospect to which we allude. A diamond necklace, with pendants of inestimable value, were by this means also made more congnicuous. The feather of an ostrich, fastened in her turban by an agraffe set with brilliants, was another distinction of the beautiful Jewess, scoffed and sneered at by the proud dames who sat above her, but secretly envied by those who affected to deride them.[32]

Rebecca's moral qualities are equally without blemish—she is devoted to her father, religiously observant without self-righteousness or spiritual pride, generous, compassionate, a ministering angel to those taken ill—all illustrated by Scott with the lightest of touches.

Like her father, Rebecca had learnt much from years of antisemi-

---

31 *Ibid.*, p. 242.
32 *Ibid.*, pp. 82-83.

tism, years of reflection leading her to much wisdom, "Rebecca was now to expect a fate even more dreadful than that of Rowena; for what probability was there that either softness or ceremony would be used towards one of her oppressed race, whatever shadow of these might be preserved towards a Saxon heiress? Yet had the Jewess this advantage, that she was better prepared by habits of thought, and by natural strength of mind, to encounter the dangers to which she was exposed. Of a strong and observing character, even from her earliest years, the pomp and wealth which her father displayed within his walls, or which she witnessed in the houses of other wealthy Hebrews, had not been able to blind her to the precarious circumstances under which they were enjoyed. Like Damocles at his celebrated banquet, Rebecca perpetually beheld, amid that gorgeous display, the sword which was suspended over the heads of her people by a single hair. These reflections had tamed and brought down to a pitch of sounder judgment a temper, which, under other circumstances, might have waxed haughty, supercilious, and obstinate."[33] She bore herself with "proud humility" despite the "arbitrary despotism of religious prejudice."

The most touching and romantic scenes in *Ivanhoe* are those where Rebecca looks after the wounded Ivanhoe with loving care, "[she] lost no time in causing the patient to be transported to their temporary dwelling, and proceeded with her own hands to examine and to bind up his wounds. The youngest reader of romances and romantic ballads must recollect how often the females, during the dark ages, as they are called, were initiated into the mysteries of surgery, and how frequently the gallant knight submitted the wounds of his person to her cure, whose eyes had yet more deeply penetrated his heart." These scenes, where Ivanhoe and Rebecca develop increasing tenderness for each other, turn out to be misleading, and their outcome evidently disappointed countless generations of readers, who were led to believe that the romance would end with Ivanhoe marrying Rebecca. Scott was greatly criticised for making Ivanhoe evenually marry the the rather colourless Saxon princess, Rowena. But on aesthetic grounds, Scott could be defended for his decision. One could argue that moral and historical realism demanded that Ivanhoe, a Saxon, should marry a Saxon, Rowena, however romantic an elopement with Rebecca may have seemed. Neither Isaac, Rebecca's father, nor Cedric, Ivanhoe's father would have allowed such a match for cultural reasons. Besides a careful reading of the scenes where Rebecca tends to Ivanhoe's wounds shows Scott's realism. Ivanhoe had looked on Rebecca with growing tenderness but as soon as he hears that she is a Jewess, his manner changes:

---

33 *Ibid.*, pp. 246-247.

I know not whether the fair Rowena would have been altogether satisfied with the species of emotion with which her devoted knight had hitherto gazed on the beautiful features, and fair form, and lustrous eyes of the lovely Rebecca; eyes whose brilliancy was shaded, and, as it were, mellowed by the fringe of her long silken eye-lashes, and which a minstrel would have compared to the evening star darting its rays through a bower of jessamine. But Ivanhoe was too good a Catholic to retain the same class of feelings towards a Jewess. This Rebecca had foreseen, and for this very purpose she had hastened to mention her father's name and lineage; yet—for the fair and wise daughter of Isaac was not without a touch of female weakness—she could not but sigh internally when the glance of respectful admiration, not altogether unmixed with tenderness, with which Ivanhoe had hitherto regarded his unknown benefactress, was exchanged at once for a manner cold, composed, and collected, and fraught with no deeper feeling than that which expressed a grateful sense of courtesy received from an unexpected quarter, and from one of an inferior race. It was not that Ivanhoe's former carriage expressed more than that general devotional homage which youth always pays to beauty; yet it was mortifying that one word should operate as a spell to remove poor Rebecca, who could not be supposed altogether ignorant of her title to such homage, into a degraded class, to whom it could not be honorably rendered.

But the gentleness and candor of Rebecca's nature imputed no fault to Ivanhoe for sharing in the universal prejudices of his age and religion. On the contrary, the fair Jewess, though sensible her patient now regarded her as one of a race of reprobation, with whom it was disgraceful to hold any beyond the most necessary intercourse, ceased not to pay the same patient and devoted attention to his safety and convalescence.[34]

Surely the above passage is a prime example of Scott's moral and historical realism: Ivanhoe, Rebecca reluctantly acknowledges, shares the prejudices of his age, and acts accordingly. However, despite himself, Ivanhoe retains a certain amount of affection for his nurse. There are other

---

34 *Ibid.*, p. 300.

clues to Scott's reasons for not allowing Ivanhoe and Rebecca to come together. He tells us that Normans and Anglo-Saxons had not managed to come together, and thus it is doubly unlikely historically that his Saxon and Jewess should either, "Four generations had not sufficed to blend the hostile blood of the Normans and Anglo-Saxons, or to unite, by common language and mutual interests, two hostile races, one of which still felt the elation of triumph, while the other groaned under all the consequences of defeat."[35]

Second, in an Introduction written some ten years after the first edition of *Ivanhoe*, Scott tells us why he could not join the fates of Ivanhoe and Rebecca, apart from the prejudices of the Middle Ages,

> The character of the fair Jewess found so much favour in the eyes of some fair readers, that the writer was censured, because, when arranging the fates of the characters of the drama, he had not assigned the hand of Wilfred to Rebecca, rather than the less interesting Rowena. But, not to mention that the prejudices of the age rendered such an union almost impossible, the author may, in passing, observe that he thinks a character of a highly virtuous and lofty stamp is degraded rather than exalted by an attempt to reward virtue with temporal prosperity. Such is not the recompense which providence has deemed worthy of suffering merit; and it is a dangerous and fatal doctrine to teach young persons, the most common readers of romance, that rectitude of conduct and of principle are either naturally allied with, or adequately rewarded by, the gratification of our passions, or attainment of our wishes. In a word, if a virtuous and self-denied character is dismissed with temporal wealth, greatness, rank, or the indulgence of such a rashly-formed or ill-assorted passion as that of Rebecca for Ivanhoe, the reader will be apt to say, Verily Virtue has had its reward. But a glance on the great picture of life will show, that the duties of self-denial, aud the sacrifice of passion to principle, are seldom thus remunerated; and that the internal consciousness of their high-minded discharge of duty produces on their own reflections a more adequate recompense, in the form of that peace which the world cannot give or take away.[36]

---

35 *Ibid.*, p. 8.

36 John Gibson Lockhart. *Memoirs of the Life of Sir Walter Scott*, Black: Edinburgh, 1850, p. 420.

Having allowed Scott his share of realism, I must concede that it is also obvious that Ivanhoe is a romance, where all manner of liberties have been taken with probability, possibility and plausibility. Ivanhoe and Rebecca in reality would never even have met, and since he had already taken such poetic license with sundry scenes and characters, it would have been well-within Scott's authorial privilege to marry off Ivanhoe and Rebecca at the end.

Scott is equally critical of the two, the Saxons and the Normans. He holds Richard the Lion-Heart, the Norman, to be irresponsible, disregarding the needs of his countrymen in pursuit of worthy but ultimately futile ideals, while Cedric, the Saxon, is castigated for holding onto a mythical past, and for refusing to look at the reality of the present.

As A.N. Wilson has pointed out in his Introduction to the Penguin Classic edition of *Ivanhoe*, what Scott wrote in *Letters of Malachi Malagrowther*, 1826, is relevant to the political import of *Ivanhoe*, "For God's sake…let us remain as Nature made us, Englishmen, Irishmen, and Scotchmen, with something like the impress of our several countries upon each."[37] Wilson himself draws the implications of these sentiments for our reading of Ivanhoe, "If the book [*Ivanhoe*] has a political message, it seems to have two very incisive points of view, hard, but necessary to reconcile. One is that there is a wickedness in failing to preserve our racial and ethnic heritages; that Jews and Saxons and Normans are all totally different, and it is grotesquely dishonest to suppose otherwise. At the same time, no society can work without recognizing our interdependence and our common good. Inevitably, this will mean that one racial or social group will have predominance, and it will not necessarily be the oldest inhabitants, or the most morally worthy. But the ruling caste trample on the treasured traditions of the minor ones not merely at their own peril, but at the peril of the nation as a whole."[38]

EDGAR ROSENBERG: FROM SHYLOCK TO SVENGALI[39]

Edgar Rosenberg has a well-argued chapter on Scott in his book on antisemitism in English fiction. Curiously, though he shows with analyti-

---

37 Quoted in A.N.Wilson, Introduction, Sir Walter Scott, *Ivanhoe*, Penguin Books: Harmondsworth, 1986, pp. xxvii-xxviii.

38 *Ibid.*, pp. xxviii-xxix.

39 Edgard Rosenberg. *From Shylock to Svengali: Jewish Stereotypes in English Fiction*, Stanford: Stanford University Press, 1960.

cal clarity the positive role that Scott assigned to the Jews, especially in their role as critics of English society of the twelfth century, Rosenberg insists that Scott's portrait, at least, of Isaac, is a stereotype derived from Marlowe. I have tried to plead the contrary case. However, Rosenberg makes a number of subtle points, particularly of Rebecca's role in the structure of the novel, that are worth considering, and, I think, are totally convincing.

Rebecca's purpose was to plead the ways of the Jews to the Christians. Scott was able to show Isaac's love and loyalty to his daughter despite the threats of torture, and contrast it with the disloyalties of the Saxons, and the fratricidal tendencies of the Normans. It is Cedric, the Saxon, who disowns his own son, Ivanhoe, and John, brother of Richard the Lionheart, who plots his sibling's assassination. In the meeting of Rebecca and Ivanhoe, the chivalric tradition is contrasted with the ideals of the Hebraic-Christian tradition, and it is the the former that is found wanting. Rebecca is able to point out the moral dubiousness of a code that glorifies violence, and makes a virtue of bloodshed.

> "Rebecca," he [Ivanhoe] replied, "thou knowest not how impossible it is for one trained to actions of chivalry, to remain passive as a priest, or a woman, when they are acting deeds of honor around him. The love of battle is the food upon which we live—the dust of the *mêlée* is the breath of our nostrils! We live not—we wish not to live longer than while we are victorious and renowned. — Such, maiden, are the laws of chivalry to which we are sworn, and to which we offer all that we hold dear."
>
> "Alas! " said the fair Jewess, "and what is it, valiant knight, save an offering of sacrifice to a demon of vain glory, and a passing through the fire to Moloch?—What remains to you as the prize of all the blood you have spilled—of all the travail and pain you have endured—of all the tears which your deeds have caused, when death hath broken the strong man's spear, and overtaken the speed of his war-horse?"
>
> "What remains?" cried Ivanhoe; "Glory, maiden, glory! which gilds our sepulchre and embalms our name."
>
> "Glory?" continued Rebecca: "Alas! is the rusted mail which hangs as a hatchment over the champion's dim and mouldering tomb—is the defaced sculpture of the inscription which the ignorant monk can hardly read to the inquiring pilgrim—are these sufficient rewards for the sacrifice of every

kindly affection, for a life spent miserably that ye may make others miserable? Or is there such virtue in the rude rhymes of a wandering bard, that domestic love, kindly affection, peace and happiness, are so wildly bartered, to become the hero of those ballads which vagabond minstrels sing to drunken churls over their evening ale?"

"By the soul of Hereward!" replied the knight, impatiently, "thou speakest, maiden, of thou knowest not what. Thou wouldst quench the pure light of chivalry, which alone distinguishes the noble from the base, the gentle knight from the churl and the savage; which rates our life far, far beneath the pitch of our honor; raises us victorious over pain, toil, and suffering, and teaches us to fear no evil but disgrace. Thou art no Christian, Rebecca; and to thee are unknown those high feelings which swell the bosom of a noble maiden when her lover hath done some deed of emprise which sanctions his flame. Chivalry!—why, maiden, she is the nurse of pure and high affection—the stay of the oppressed, the redresser of grievances, the curb of the power of the tyrant—Nobility were but an empty name without her, and liberty finds the best protection in her lance and her sword."

"I am, indeed," said Rebecca, "sprung from a race whose courage was distinguished in the defence of their own land, but who warred not, even while yet a nation, save at the command of the Deity, or in defending their country from oppression. The sound of the trumpet wakes Judah no longer, and her despised children are now but the unresisting victims of hostile and military oppression. Well hast thou spoken, Sir Knight,—until the God of Jacob shall raise up for his chosen people a second Gideon, or a new Maccabeus, it ill beseemeth the Jewish damsel to speak of battle or of war."[40]

As Rosenberg observes,[41] Rebecca only has to point to herself and her father to refute Ivanhoe's claim that chivalry has been the guarantor of freedom, protector of the oppressed, the redresser of grievances. Indirectly, she does so when she concludes "the argument in a tone of sorrow, which

---

40 Sir Walter Scott, *Ivanhoe*, *op.cit.* pp. 317-318.

41 Edgar Rosenberg. *From Shylock to Svengali. Jewish Stereotypes in English Fiction*, Stanford: Stanford University Press, 1960, p. 91.

deeply expressed her sense of the degradation of her people."[42]

AFTERMATH OF IVANHOE

1. CHATEAUBRIAND

Chateaubriand in his notes on British novelists has an aside on Scott, whom he finds unreadable, undeserving of his high reputation, and who has had an unfortunate influence on the course of English literature. Scott has none of Manzoni's great literary qualities. Scott's creation of the historical novel was equally regretable since it perverted both the novel and history. Scott created a taste for the Middle Ages, not only in literature but architecture, furniture, and books. Though he was able to reach a large public, Scott only dealt with superficial appearances, unlike Samuel Richardson who delved into the inner psychology of his characters. An example of Scott's treatment of the surface, according to Chateaubriand, is his description of Rebecca, "the figure of Rebecca...", etc. which we have quoted above.[43]

When his friend Fontanes[44] asks him why it was that Jewish women were so much more attractive than the Jewish men, Chateaubriand replies as a poet and Christian,

> Jewesses, I told him, have escaped the malediction that their fathers, husbands and sons have been struck with. We do not find a single Jewess joining the crowd of priests and people who insulted the Son of Man, flagellated him, crowned hm with a crown of thorns, submitted him to the ignominies and pains of the Cross. The women of Judaea believed in the Saviour, loved him, followed him, helped him to the best of their ability, and relieved him in his suffering.
>
> A woman of Bethany poured over his head the precious ointment (nard) that she was carrying in an alabaster vase; a fisher woman applied some perfumed oil to his feet, and wiped them with her hair; Jesus in turn extended his compassion and grace over the Jewesses; he resurrected the son of the widow of Naim and brother of Martha; he cured the mother-in-law

---

42 Sir Walter Scott, *Ivanhoe, op.cit.*, pp. 318-319.

43 *Ibid.*, pp. 82-83, quoted above on p. 29.

44 Louis-Marcelin, Marquis de Fontanes (6 March 1757 – 17 March 1821) was a French poet and politician.

of Simon and the woman who touched the bottom of his garment; for the Samaritan woman he was the source of living water,[45] and for the adulteress a compassionate judge; the girls of Jerusalem cried for him; the saintly women accompanied him to Calvary, buying balm and aromatic herbs, looked for him at the sepulchre while crying. Woman, why weepest thou? His first appearance after his resurrection was to Mary Magdalene; she did not recognize him; but he said to her, "Mary!" At the sound of this voice the eyes of Mary Magdalene opened and she replied: "My Lord!" The reflection of some beautiful rays will have remained on the forehead of Jewesses.[46]

2. PLAYS, AND THACKERAY

'twas very few short days ago
Since first in print, appeared Sir Ivanhoe;
How much we've had to do, to think and write,
Compose, rehearse, paint, sew, embroider, and what not to
bring him here tonight

(Opening address, T. John Dibdin, *Ivanhoe, or the Jew's Daughter*, Surrey Theatre, January, 1820).

During 1820, a year after the publication of *Ivanhoe*, four English playwrights placed the Jewish heroes of Ivanhoe on the stage: Alfred Bunn, *Ivanhoe, or the Jews of York*; T. John Dibdin, *Ivanhoe, or the Jew's Daughter*; W.T. Moncrieff, *Ivanhoe, or the Jewess*; George Soane, *The Hebrews*. Moncrieff described such plays as "paste, shears, and a Scotch novel." Dickens mercilessly satirized Moncrieff, thinly disguised as the "literary gentleman" in *Nicholas Nickleby*, as a cultural thief as reprehensible as the pickpocket. But in a sympathetic study of adaptations, Philip Cox pointed out that such adaptations should not be dismissed so summmarily. In a chapter devoted to two such reworkings of Scott's *Ivanhoe*, Cox writes, "Ivanhoe's implicit and explicit exploration of English identity is provided with new meanings through the differing cultural identities constructed through the

---

45 New Testament. John, IV.

46 François-René Chateaubriand, *Oeuvres complètes de M. le vicomte de Chateaubriand: augmentées d'un essai sur la vie et les ouvrages de l'auteur* [*par Delandine de Saint Esprit*]. Paris: F. Didot, 1843, Vol. 5, p. 150. (Another edition: *Oeuvres complètes*, Paris, 1861, Vol. XI, pp. 764-766.)

generic reformulations of Scott's work."[47]   George Soane's adaptation, *The Hebrew* (Drury Lane Theatre, March 1820), "provides a more ambitious reworking of *Ivanhoe* in which questions of race and national identity are dealt with in a more explicit and provocative fashion."[48]

As noted above, readers were disappointed at the unromantic ending of *Ivanhoe*. Thackeray set about correcting this literary wrong in *Rebecca and Rowena, A Romance Upon Romance* [1850]. I doubt, however, that any admirer of Scott's original—except of course its ending—would find much consolation in Thackeray's vulgar farce. Despite extravagant praise for *Rebecca and Rowena* from the likes of Trollope who called it, "of all prose parodies…perhaps the best in the language,"[49] Thackeray's crude burlesque is without wit or invention, and would certainly not please any avid reader of *Ivanhoe*. Hen-pecked Ivanhoe goes off to France to join Richard the Lion-Heart as the latter beseiges some castle. Ivanhoe returns to England to find that Rowena has married Athelstane, thinking that our hero was dead. Both Rowena and Athelstane die, and Ivanhoe returns to his chivalrous ways, makes his way to Spain where he kills hundreds of Saracens, and eventually finds Rebecca, who, in the meantime, has converted to Christianity, and marries her.

The absurdity of such an ending has been well described by Rosenberg, who quite rightly remarks that "any permanent alliance between him [Ivanhoe] and Rebecca was foredoomed from the start; and anyhow it would have turned Scott's novel into the sheerest humbug. Historically the marital problem could have been solved in the way Scott's predecessors solved it, and as Thackeray solved it in his parody, by allowing Rebecca to submit to baptism. In that case she would have compounded the venial sin of bombast with the mortal sin of hypocrisy, and her function in the novel would have lost what meaning it has. She has to stick it out with her father, if only to make good her protests and act out her creeds. The only way in which Scott could have eaten his cake and had it too would have been to recruit Ivanhoe for the synagogue."[50]

47 Philip Cox, *Reading Adaptations: Novels and Verse Narratives on the Stage, 1790-1840*, Manchester (U.K.) Manchester University Press, 2000, p. 90.

48 *Ibid.*, p. 82.

49 A. Trollope, *Thackeray* (English Men of Letters) London, 1925, p. 195.

50 Edgar Rosenberg, *From Shylock to Svengali: Jewish Stereotypes in English Fiction*, Stanford: Stanford University Press, 1960, p. 93.

2

The Talisman, the Crusades, Richard I of England and Saladin: Myths, Legends and History

PART I

GENESIS OF AN IDEA

The present chapter grew out of my inquiries into something that Edward Said wrote about Sir Walter Scott's *The Talisman*. It took on a life of its own, and grew and grew, and led me into the Crusades generally. What follows is not meant as a complete narrative history of the Crusades—some superb new histories of the Crusades have appeared in the last ten years,[1] I do not need to add to these, even if I could—rather I wish to examine some of the myths and legends perpetuated by Sir Walter Scott in his novels on the Crusades, and at the same time I wish to elucidate, if possible, the motives of the Crusaders, and the real origins of the Crusades. I began my studies of Scott's Crusade novels four years ago with an examination of *Ivanhoe* in "Sir Walter Scott, Jews

---

1 Thomas Asbridge, *The Crusades*, New York: Harper Collins, 2010.

Christopher Tyerman, *God's War: A New History of the Crusades*, Cambridge [Mass.]: The Belknap Press of Harvard University Press, 2006.

Jonathan Riley-Smith, *The Crusades: A History*, New Haven: Yale University Press, 2005 [2nd Edn.].

Jonathan Riley Smith, *The Crusades, Christianity, and Islam*, New York: Columbia University Press, 2008.

Thomas F. Madden, *The New Concise History of the Crusades*, New York: Barnes and Noble, 2006.

Peter Frankopan, *The First Crusade: The Call from the East*, Cambridge [Mass.]: The Belknap Press of Harvard University Press, 2012.

and Saracens, and Other Sundry Subjects."[2] While recently researching the historical background of Scott's novel, *The Talisman*, which recounts the exploits of Saladin and Richard the Lionheart during the Third Crusade, I came across Sir Hamilton Gibb's biography—or rather hagiography, as we shall see later—of Saladin. Gibb [1895-1971], born in Alexandria, Egypt, but later educated in Edinburgh, was one of the last great Orientalists or as Albert Hourani described him, "the last of the universal Arabists"; a professor at SOAS, then Oxford, and finally at Harvard. I discovered something that delighted me, since the discovery adds a certain poetic symmetry and brings some kind of justification to my study of Scott's *The Talisman*. Here is the treasure: Sir Hamilton Gibb, not only attended the same school as Scott in Edinburgh, he also immersed himself in Scott's novel at an early age, and Saladin became his hero; and when he became a historian, and university professor, Gibb recommended *The Talisman* to his students as "a work of art from which they could learn much about Islamic history."[3]

Sir Walter Scott wrote four novels that refer in one way or another to the Crusades; the first two were published together in 1825 under the general heading *Tales of the Crusaders* containing *The Betrothed*, and *The Talisman*, the other two novels being *Ivanhoe* [1819] and *Count Robert of Paris* [1832].

THE BETROTHED AND COUNT ROBERT OF PARIS

Although parts of *The Betrothed* were incorporated into Francesco Maria Piave's libretto for Giuseppe Verdi's 1857 opera, *Aroldo*, *The Betrothed* is of little literary interest, and is virtually unreadable; Scott's biographer Hesketh Pearson wrote, "*The Betrothed* was clearly composed in a somnolent if not stertorous condition, and would score high marks in a competition to decide which was the dreariest and stupidest book ever produced by a writer of genius."[4] It has very little to do with the Crusades as such: the tale unfolds in the Welsh Marches during the reign of Henry II after 1187. One of the characters in the tale, Sir Hugo de Lacy, the Constable of Chester, disappears on a crusade for three years, but the Crusades

---

2 See "Sir Walter Scott, Jews and Saracens, and Other Sundry Subjects" *New English Review,* May, 2009 (http://www.newenglishreview.org/custpage.cfm/frm/37551/sec_id/37551).

3 Albert Hourani, *Europe and the Middle East*, Berkeley, CA: University of California Press. 1980, p. 106.

4 Hesketh Pearson, *Walter Scott: His Life and Personality*, New York: Harper & Brothers, 1954, p. 54.

play no part in the plot.

Count Robert of Paris [1832] is a far more interesting novel, and though it is set in Constantinople at the time of the First Crusade, it works best as a novel of ideas since it constantly contrasts the manners, principles, goals and actions of the Frankish knights on their way to the Holy Land, with those of the values and goals of the Greco-Roman Classical society of Byzantium. Along the way, Scott is able to discuss religion, politics, and the internecine squabbles and grievances amongst the Europeans and the dangers the latter pose to the stablilty of the Byzantine Empire.

One of Scott's principal sources for the First Crusade and Byzantium in general, and hence the novel *Count Robert of Paris*, was Anna Comnena or Komnene's *The Alexiad*. One of the foremost authorities on the First Crusade and Byzantium, Peter Frankopan, Senior Research Fellow at Worcester College, University of Oxford, wrote, "*The Alexiad* is perhaps the most famous of all the vast range of Byzantine texts. Written in the mid-twelfth century by a princess, the beautiful and fiercely intelligent Anna Komnene, daughter of Emperor Alexios I Komnenos (reigned 1081-1118), it is a stylish and colourful account of the defining period in the formation of modern Europe. The text covers the time of the First Crusade, the establishment of a Turkish state in Asia Minor, the decisive schism of the eastern and western churches, and ultimately, the separation of the east and west Mediterranean."[5]

In the novel, the Northerners are constantly painted as uncouth— "uncultivated savages," and the Byzantines as sophisticated, and "enlightened." Again, Scott does not follow the Crusaders to the principal theatre of action, the Holy Land and Jerusalem, and the First Crusade is not described though obviously the motives of the Franks are not comprehensible without an understanding of the Crusader movement. We are nonetheless able to gather Scott's attitude to the Crusaders and the Crusades. Scott presents one view of the Crusades through the character Nicephorus, son-in-law of the Greek Emperor of Constantinople, Alexius I Comnenus—though we should be wary of assuming that this is Scott's own view. Nicephorus sings the praises of Godfrey of Bouillon [c.1060-1100], considered one of the heroes of the First Crusade [1096-1099]:

> This Godfrey is one of the wisest, noblest, and bravest of the leaders who have thus strangely put themselves in motion; and among a list of independent princes, as many in number as

---

5 Peter Frankopan, Introduction in Anna Komnene, *The Alexiad*, London: Penguin Books, Revised Edn. 2009, p. ix.

those who assembled for the siege of Troy, and followed, most of them, by subjects ten times more numerous, this Godfrey may be regarded as the Agamemnon. The princes and counts esteem him, because he is the foremost in the ranks of those whom they fantastically call knights, and also on account of the good faith and generosity which he practises in all his transactions. The clergy give him credit for the highest zeal for the doctrine of religion, and a corresponding respect for the church and its dignitaries. Justice, liberality, and frankness have equally attached to this Godfrey the lower class of the people. His general attention to moral obligations is a pledge to them that his religion is real; and, gifted with so much that is excellent, he is already, although inferior in rank, birth, and power to many chiefs of the crusade, justly regarded as one of its principal leaders.

To which the Emperor replies:

Pity that a character such as you describe this prince to be should be under the dominion of a fanaticism scarce worthy of Peter the Hermit, or the clownish multitude which he led, or of the very ass which he rode upon; which I am apt to think the wisest of the first multitude whom we beheld, seeing that it ran away towards Europe as soon as water and barley became scarce.[6]

As we shall see shortly, Scott had expressed his views on the ambiguous legacy of the Crusaders, in his earlier novel *Ivanhoe* [1820], but here we cannot take the Emperor's views as Scott's own. For later in *Count Robert of Paris*, Scott concedes that at least some Crusaders, including Godfrey, were motivated by higher principles: "A better principle determined the celebrated Godfrey, Raymond of Thoulouse [sic][7], and some others, in whom devotion was something more than a mere burst of fanaticism."[8]

In the novel, Michael Agelastes, an old Greek sage, warns the Byzantine Emperor of the avaricious kind of Crusader, "…[T]hese European barbarians are like no others under the cope of the universe, either in the

---

6 Sir Walter Scott, *Count Robert of Paris*, Edinburgh: Edinburgh University Press, 2007, p. 115

7 Now written "Toulouse."

8 Sir Walter Scott, *op. cit.* p.. 158.

things on which they look with desire or in those which they consider as discouraging. The treasures of this noble empire [Byzantium], so far as they affected their wishes, would merely inspire them with the desire to go to war with a nation possessed of so much wealth, and who, in their self-conceited estimation, were less able to defend than they themselves are powerful to assail. Of such a description, for instance, is Bohemond of Tarentum [also known as: Bohemund of Taranto], and such a one is many a crusader less able and sagacious than he; for I think I need not tell your Imperial Divinity that he holds his own self-interest to be the de-voted guide of his whole conduct through this extraordinary war; and that, therefore, you can justly calculate his course when once you are aware from which point of the compass the wind of avarice and self-interest breathes with respect to him."

However there are nobler spirits among the Crusaders, continues the Greek Sage, "But there are spirits among the Franks of a very differ-ent nature. And who must be acted upon by very different motives, if we would make ourselves masters of their actions and the principles by which they are governed....This people—I mean the more lofty-minded of these crusaders, who act up to the pretences of the doctrine which they call chivalry—despise the thirst of gold, and gold itself, unless to hilt their swords, or to furnish forth some necessary expenses, as alike useless and contemptible."[9]

It remains an ambiguous compliment; what does the Greek Sage (Scott, himself?) mean by "act up to the pretences of the doctrine which they call chivalry"—that they are sincere but self-deluded, or even simply insincere?

Again, Nicephorus's harsh judgment of Bohemond accords well with the assessments of some modern historians. For example, Thomas F. Mad-den, a distinguished historian of the Crusades at Saint Louis University, wrote, "More than any other crusading leader, Bohemond was ambitious for personal gain. He had once believed that he would rule in Thessalonica or perhaps even Constantinople. Although his hopes had been dashed, he still looked to the east as his opportunity for power and wealth."[10] For Sir Steven Runciman, "genuine religious fervour was the strongest mo-tive" with all of the leaders of the First Crusade, "except Bohemond."[11]

---

9 *Ibid.* pp. 216-217.

10 Thomas F. Madden, *The New Concise History of the Crusades*, New York: Barnes and Noble, 2007 p. 22.

11 Steven Runciman, *A History of the Crusades. Vol. I The First Crusade and the Foun-dation of the Kingdom of Jerusalem* Cambridge: Cambridge University Press, [1951, 1st

While for Thomas Asbridge, of the University of London, Bohemond was "driven by rapacious ambition,…with at least one eye upon personal advancement."[12]

However other historians are not so convinced of Bohemond's perfidy. As Christopher Tyerman, of New College, University of Oxford, reminds us in his superb one-volume history of the Crusades,[13] "The picture of Bohemond the ruthless schemer derives from *The Alexiad* of Anna Comnena, Alexius's daughter." Certainly, Walter Scott depended heavily on *The Alexiad* for his historical details. Anna's account is vehemently anti-Western, and is a "confused and misleading source for the crusade let alone the motives of the Western leaders." Bohemond proved to be Alexius' staunchest ally, and far from being treacherous "provided a medium of contact between east and west." But Tyerman makes a more general point of the greatest importance: "The traditional view sees [Bohemond's] motives as basely material, in contrast to the supposedly more elevated inspirations of some of his colleagues. This is untenable. The psychologies of the crusade's leaders cannot be reconstructed. Each can be shown to have as much avarice or as little piety as the other. The dichotomy between spiritual and mercenary possesses little meaning. Raymond of Toulouse, whose religious sincerity has been widely accepted, proved both scheming and petulant in his earnest quest for an eastern principality, which he finally achieved in the lands around Tripoli in the south Lebanon. The spiritual agonizing of Tancred of Lecce, Bohemund's nephew, was matched by his alert political opportunism. Godfrey of Bouillon accepted power and lands when offered them in 1099. Baldwin of Boulogne, the most obviously careerist of all, devoted the last twenty years of his life to defending the Holy Places. All the leaders sought to protect their material interests rather than proceed to Jerusalem in the five months after July 1098. Bohemund was not alone in his desire to achieve status, lands and wealth; neither did this ambition automatically contradict the genuineness of his adherence to the cause of Jerusalem. With Baldwin, he undertook a tricky and dangerous journey to fulfil his pilgrimage to the Holy Sepulchre at Christmas 1099, a gesture that, for lack of evidence, cannot be assumed to have been purely for reasons of image or politics."

As for Godfrey of Bouillon, Steven Runciman refuses to accept him as "the perfect Christian knight, the peerless hero of the whole Crusading

---

Edn] p. 112.

12 Thomas Asbridge, *The Crusades*, New York: Harper Collins, 2010, p. 45.

13 Christopher Tyerman, *God's War. A New History of the Crusades*, Cambridge [Mass.]: The Belknap Press of Harvard University Press, 2006, p. 111ff.

epic. A scrupulous study of history must modify the verdict."[14] Runciman points to some distasteful episodes in Godfrey's career: Godfrey raised money for his venture to the Holy Land by blackmailing Jews.[15] And Tyerman also is skeptical of Godfrey of the legend, "Far from the selfless hero of chivalric legend he later appeared, Godfrey struck a number of hard bargains to raise funds for his expedition. Apart from extorting money from the Rhineland Jews, he sold some estates..."[16]

Scott's account, as already remarked upon, is clearly influenced by *The Alexiad*. Here is Anna Komenene's assessment of the first crusaders,

[The Emperor] had no time to relax before he heard a rumour that countless Frankish armies were approaching. He dreaded their arrival, knowing as he did their uncontrollable passion, their erratic character and their unpredictability, not to mention the other characteristics of the Kelt, with their inevitable consequences: their greed for money, for example, which always led them, it seemed to break their own agreements without scruple.[17]

The simpler folk [participating in the Crusade] were led by a genuine desire to worship at Our Lord's tomb and visit the holy places, but the more villainous characters, in particular Bohemond and his like, had an ulterior motive, for they hoped on their journey to seize the capital itself, looking upon its capture as a natural consequence of the expedition. Bohemond disturbed the morale of many nobler men because he still cherished an old grudge against the emperor.[18]

"Peter [the Hermit] had in the beginning undertaken his great journey to worship at the Holy Sepulchre [in Jerusalem], but the other counts, and in particular Bohemond, were nursing an old grudge against the emperor and were looking for a good opportunity to avenge the glorious victory which the emperor had won at Larissa against Bohemond. They were all of one mind and in order to fulfil their dream of taking Constantinople, they adopted a common policy, which I have often

14 Runciman, *op. cit.* vol. I, p. 145.

15 *Ibid.* p. 146.

16 Tyerman, *op.cit.* p. 108.

17 Anna Komnene, *The Alexiad*, London: Penguin Books, Revised Edn. 2009, Book X, p. 275.

18 *Ibid.* p. 277.

referred to before: to all appearances they were on pilgrimage to Jerusalem; in reality they planned to dethrone the emperor and seize the capital.[19]

Let us compare the above to Scott: "In his [Emperor's] first sentences, he treated of the audacity and unheard of boldness of the millions of Franks, who under, the pretence of wresting Palestine from the Infidels, had ventured to invade the sacred territories of the empire."[20]

Anna Komnene describes in great detail of the raids on the Byzantine Empire by the Patzinaks (or Pechenegs), steppe nomads who had established themselves on Byzantium's Danube frontier, and were regularly raiding Imperial territory by the 1070s. She also devotes much attention to the relations with the Turks, campaigns against the Cumans, and Scythians [for example, *The Alexiad*, Book, VIII] throughout Alexius' reign.

Inspired by her, Scott gives a very vivid and accurate picture of the problems besetting the Emperor on all sides, and tells us of his various alliances by which difficult juggling act he was able to play one side off another:

> In different parts of his territory, different enemies arose, who waged successful or dubious war against the Emperor; and, of the numerous nations with whom he was engaged in hostilities, whether the Franks from the west, the Turks advancing from the east, the Cumans and Scythians pouring their barbarous numbers and unceasing storm of arrows from the north, and the Saracens, or the tribes into which they were divided, pressing from the south, there was not one for whom the Grecian empire did not spread a tempting repast. Each of these various enemies had their own particular habits of war, and a way of manoeuvring in battle peculiar to themselves. But the Roman, as the unfortunate subject of the Greek empire was still called, was by far the weakest, the most ignorant, and most timid, who could be dragged into the field; and the Emperor was happy in his own good luck, when he found it possible to conduct a defensive war on a counterbalancing principle, making use of the Scythian to repel the Turk, or of both these savage people to drive back the fieryfooted Frank, whom Peter the Hermit had,

---

19 *Ibid.* p. 285.

20 Sir Walter Scott, *Count Robert of Paris*, Edinburgh: Edinburgh University Press, 2007, p. 131.

in the time of Alexius, waked to double fury, by the powerful influence of the crusades.[21]

Anna talks of the many heresies that Alexius felt obliged to extirpate in order to guard the purity of the Church: the heresy of John Italos [pp.146-52]; Paulicianism [155-6, 424]; of Neilos [260-61]; of Blakhernites [262]; Bogomilism [424, 455-63]; Manichaeanism [424-30].

Here Scott summarizes elegantly, and at the same time, subtly pleads for religious toleration for the heretics:

[Alexius] took a deep interest in all matters respecting the church, where heresy, which the Emperor held, or affected to hold, in great horror, appeared to him to lurk. Nor do we discover in his treatment of the Manichaeans or Paulicians that pity for their speculative errors which modern times might think had been well purchased by the extent of the temporal services of these unfortunate sectaries. Alexius knew no indulgence for those who misinterpreted the mysteries of the church, or of its doctrines; and the duty of defending religion against schismatics was, in his opinion, as peremptorily demanded from him, as that of protecting the empire against the numberless tribes of barbarians who were encroaching on its boundaries on every side.[22]

However, Scott's partly unsympathetic portrait of Alexius, as devious, cunning and treacherous, is derived from hostile western sources, such as the anonymous *Gesta Francorum* or to give its full title, *Gesta Francorum et aliorum Hierosolimitanorum* ("The deeds of the Franks and the other pilgrims to Jerusalem") which is a Latin chronicle of the First Crusade written in about 1100-1101, and was probably as Sir Steven Runciman claims, "a diary [written] by one of Bohemond's followers who went on to Jerusalem with Tancred. It ends with the story of the battle of Ascalon in 1099 and was first published in 1100 or early 1101...The author was a simple soldier, honest according to his lights but credulous and prejudiced and a strong admirer of Bohemond. The wide success of the *Gesta* was mainly due Bohemond's own efforts. He regarded it as his apologia and himself hawked it round northern France during his visit there 1106."[23]

---

21 *Ibid.* p. 35.
22 *Ibid.* p. 37.
23 Runciman, *op cit.*, Vol.1 pp. 329-330.

Equally hostile is Raymond of Aguilers [in the Haute–Loire, France] who "joined the Crusade in the company of Adhemar of Le Puy, and soon became chaplain to Raymond of Toulouse. He began to write his chronicle, the *Historia Francorum qui ceperunt Jerusalem*, [History of the Franks who Captured Jerusalem] during the siege of Antioch and finished it at the end of 1099....Only on one occasion does he mention the Greeks without an unfriendly comment."[24]

Here is Scott's delineation of Alexius: "...if he commonly employed cunning and dissimulation instead of wisdom, and perfidy instead of courage, his expedients were the disgrace of the age rather than his own....Such a mixture of sense and weakness, of meanness and dignity, of prudent discretion and poverty of spirit, which last, in the European mode of viewing things, approached to cowardice, formed the leading traits of the character of Alexius Comnenus, at a period when the fate of Greece, and all that was left in that country of art and civilization, was trembling in the balance, and likely to be saved or lost, according to the abilities of the Emperor for playing the very difficult game which was put into his hands."[25]

Scott ridicules the Byzantine court which was "encumbered with unmeaning ceremonies"—ceremonies described by Anna in *The Alexiad*. However, Scott does concede Alexius's courage in battle, and believes that perhaps Alexius was the right man to lead the Greeks at that moment in history.

THE FIRST CRUSADE: THE CALL FROM THE EAST

Before moving on to *The Talisman* and the Third Crusade, I should like to refer to Peter Frankopan's thesis unfurled in his recent book (published in 2012), *The First Crusade: The Call from the East*.[26] Frankopan argues that the real origins of the First Crusade have not been properly understood. The attention of historians has almost universally concentrated "on Pope Urban II, his rousing speech at Clermont and the galvanising of the knighthood of Europe." But in reality, "the catalyst for the expedition to Jerusalem was not the Pope, but another figure entirely: the call to arms issued by Urban was the result of a direct appeal for help from the emperor of Constantinople, Alexios I Komnenos, in the east....[B]y the

---

24 *Ibid.* p. 328.

25 Sir Walter Scott, *Count Robert of Paris*, Edinburgh: Edinburgh University Press, 2007, pp. 35-38.

26 Peter Frankopan, *The First Crusade. The Call from the East*, Cambridge [Mass.]: The Belknap Press of Harvard University Press, 2012

mid-1090s, [Alexios] was losing his political authority and the Byzantine Empire was reeling from violent incursions on all sides. In 1095, Alexios sent envoys to Urban II, with an urgent message. Finding the Pope at Piacenza, they 'implored his lordship and all the faithful of Christ to bring assistance against the heathen for the defence of this holy church, which had now been nearly annihilated in that region by the infidels who had conquered her as far as the walls of Constantinople.'[27] Urban reacted immediately, declaring that he would head north, to France, to gather forces to aid the emperor. It was this appeal from Alexios that triggered the First Crusade."[28]

The back cover of Frankopan's book has some very impressive endorsements from well-known historians, including Christopher Tyerman, an expert on the Crusades whom I have already cited. Here is Tyerman's blurb, "Peter Frankopan's reassessment of the Byzantine contribution to the origins and course of the First Crusade offers a compelling and challenging balance to traditional accounts. Based on fresh interpretations of primary sources, lucidly written and forcefully argued, [this book] will demand attention from scholars while providing an enjoyable and accessible narrative for the general reader."

Though Anna Komnene's *The Alexiad* makes no direct reference to Alexius' appeal to the Pope, it is clear from her account that the Emperor had already put in place procedures and provisioning plans so that everything was ready by the time the Crusaders reached Byzantium. He was thus not caught by surprise.[29]

Scott does not make any alllusions to Alexius' call for help to the Pope. However, another great historian even though he had perhaps slightly fewer primary sources available to him does, surprisingly, discuss it. Edward Gibbon in Chapter LVIII of his great work writes,

> So popular was the cause of Urban, so weighty was his influence, that the council which he summoned at Placentia was composed of two hundred bishops of Italy, France, Burgundy, Swabia, and Bavaria. Four thousand of the clergy, and thirty thousand of the laity, attended this important meeting; and as

---

27 Frankopan is quoting the contemporary *Chronicle of Bernold of Constance*. Bernold of Constance [c. 1054–1100] was a chronicler and writer of tracts, and a defender of the Church reforms of Pope Gregory VII. The latter part of Bernold's *Chronicon* is a concise record of contemporary events by an intelligent observer in the Papal camp.

28 *Ibid.*, pp. 6-7.

29 *Ibid.*, p. 513 footnote 14.

the most spacious cathedral would have been inadequate to the multitude, the session of seven days was held in a plain adjacent to the city. The ambassadors of the Greek emperor, Alexius Comnenus, were introduced to plead the distress of their sovereign and the danger of Constantinople, which was divided only by a narrow sea from the victorious Turks, the common enemies of the Christian name. In their suppliant address they flattered the pride of the Latin princes; and, appealing at once to their policy and religion, exhorted them to repel the Barbarians on the confines of Asia, rather than to expect them in the heart of Europe. At the sad tale of the misery and perils of their Eastern brethren, the assembly burst into tears: the most eager champions declared their readiness to march; and the Greek ambassadors were dismissed with the assurance of a speedy and powerful succour. The relief of Constantinople was included in the larger and most distant project of the deliverance of Jerusalem; but the prudent Urban adjourned the final decision to a second synod, which he proposed to celebrate in some city of France in the autumn of the same year. The short delay would propagate the flame of enthusiasm; and his firmest hope was in a nation of soldiers, still proud of the pre-eminence of their name, and ambitious to emulate their hero Charlemagne, who, in the popular romance of Turpin, had achieved the conquest of the Holy Land."[30]

THE TALISMAN: SALADIN VS. RICHARD THE LION-HEART

Edward Gibbon in his magisterial history[31] culls this story from Jean de Joinville,[32] "The memory of Coeur de Lion, of the lion-hearted prince, was long dear and glorious to his English subjects; and at the distance of sixty years, it was celebrated in proverbial sayings by the grandsons of the

30 Edward Gibbon, *The Decline and Fall of the Roman Empire*, London: 1788, Vol. VI, Chapter LVIII.

31 Edward Gibbon. *op. cit.*, Chapter LIX

32 Jean de Joinville (1224-1317) wrote "Life of Saint Louis" after having accompanied King Louis IX on his first crusade. He wrote about everything he personally experienced during the reign of Saint Louis, essentially the crusade in Egypt and their stay in the Holy Land.; a lively, humorous account full of anecdotes, said to be an accurate portrayal of the Crusades, and to give insight into the religious and political enthusiasm that led to the fight for the Holy Land.

Turks and Saracens, against whom he had fought; his tremendous name was employed by the Syrian mothers to silence their infants; and if an horse suddenly started from the way, his rider was wont to exclaim, "Dost thou think king Richard is in that bush?"

Major-General Sir Henry Edward Colville (1852–1907) was an English soldier who took a leading part in the Sudan Campaign, and served in South Africa. He wrote two successful travel books, one on Morocco and another on the Holy Land and environs. The latter, titled *The accursed land, or, first steps on the water-way of Edom* recounts this anecdote:

> The memory of our lion-hearted king still lingers and is respected in this country. "Teshoof Rikard?" (do you see Richard?) says the Bedwin if his beast shies; and "I will call Richard" is applied by Syrian mothers to their squalling offspring, with an effect as good, I am told, as that produced by a similar invocation of Cromwell on the lachrymose babies of Ireland.[33]

It is ironical that while Richard the Lionheart [1157-1199], the King of England, and leading Christian commander during the The Third Crusade [1189–1192] is remembered in the Islamic world right up through the nineteenth century, his main rival in the latter conflict, the Muslim Kurd, known in the West as Saladin [c.1138-1193] was largely forgotten in his homeland. Forgotten until he was made known again to the Muslim world largely thanks to the German Emperor Wilhelm II's visit to Saladin's tomb, to pay his respects in 1898, and above all the novel, *The Talisman* [1825] by Sir Walter Scott [1771-1832].

PART II

THE TALISMAN

The Victorian critic Henry Grey provided a useful summary of the Waverley Novels. Here is his entry on *The Talisman*:

> During a truce between the Christian armies taking part in the third Crusade, and the infidel forces under Sultan Saladin, Sir Kenneth, on his way to Syria, encountered a Saracen

---

33 Major-General Sir Henry Edward Colville, *The accursed land, or, first steps on the water-way of Edom*, Sampson Low, Marston, Searle & Rivington, London, 1884, p. 170.

Emir, whom he unhorsed, and they then rode together, discoursing on love and necromancy, towards the cave of the hermit, who was in correspondence with the pope, and to whom the knight was charged to communicate secret information. Having provided the travellers with refreshment, the anchorite, as soon as the Saracen slept, conducted his companion to a chapel, where he witnessed a procession, and was recognised by the Lady Edith, to whom he had devoted his heart and sword. He was then startled by the sudden appearance of the dwarfs, and, having reached his couch again, watched the hermit scourging himself until he fell asleep.

About the same time Richard Coeur de Lion had succumbed to an attack of fever, and as he lay in his gorgeous tent at Ascalon, the Scot arrived accompanied by a Moorish physician, who had cured his squire, and who offered to restore the king to health. After a long consultation, and eliciting from Sir Kenneth his visit to the chapel, the physician was admitted to the royal presence; and, having swallowed a draught which he prepared from a silken bag or talisman, Richard sank back on his cushions.

While he slept Conrade of Montserrat secretly avowed to the wily grand-master his ambition to be King of Jerusalem; and, with the object of injuring Richard's reputation, incited Leopold of Austria to plant his banner by the side of that of England in the centre of the camp. When the king woke the fever had left him, and Conrade entered to announce what the archduke had done. Springing from his couch, Richard rushed to the spot and defiantly tore down and trampled on the Teuton pennon. Philip of France at length persuaded him to refer the matter to the council, and Sir Kenneth was charged to watch the English standard until daybreak, with a favourite hound as his only companion.

Soon after midnight, however, Necbatanus approached him with Lady Edith's ring, as a token that his attendance was required to decide a wager she had with the queen; and during his absence from his post the banner was carried off, and his dog severely wounded. Overcome with shame and grief, he was accosted by the physician, who dressed the animal's wound, and, having entrusted Sir Kenneth with Saladin's desire to marry the Lady Edith, proposed that he should seek the

Saracen ruler's protection against the wrath of Richard. The valiant Scot, however, resolved to confront the king and reveal the Sultan's purpose; but it availed him not, and he was sentenced to death, in spite of the intercessions of the queen and his lady-love; when the hermit, and then the physician, arrived, and Richard having yielded to their entreaties, Sir Kenneth was simply forbidden to appear before him again.

Having, by a bold speech, revived the drooping hopes of his brother Crusaders, and reproved the queen and his kinswoman for tampering with the Scot, Richard received him, disguised as a Nubian slave, as a present from Saladin, with whom he had been induced to spend several days. Shortly afterwards, as the king was reposing in his pavilion, the slave saved his life from the dagger of an assassin secretly employed by the grandmaster, and intimated that he could discover the purloiner of the standard. A procession of the Christian armies and their leaders had already been arranged in token of amity to Richard; and as they marched past him, seated on horseback, with the slave holding the hound among his attendants, the dog suddenly sprang at the Marquis Conrade, who was thus convicted of having injured the animal, and betrayed his guilt by exclaiming, 'I never touched the banner.'

Not being permitted to fight the Teuton himself, the king undertook to provide a champion, and Saladin to make all needful preparations for the combat. Accompanied by Berengaria and Lady Edith, Richard was met by the Saracen with a brilliant retinue, and discovered, in the person of his entertainer, the physician who had cured his fever, and saved Sir Kenneth, whom he found prepared to do battle for him on the morrow, with the hermit as his confessor. The encounter took place soon after sunrise, in the presence of the assembled hosts, and Conrade, who was wounded and unhorsed, was tended by the Sultan in the grandmaster's tent, while the victorious knight was unarmed by the royal ladies, and made known by Richard as the Prince Royal of Scotland. At noon the Sultan welcomed his guests to a banquet, but, as the grand-master was raising a goblet to his lips, Necbatanus uttered the words *accipe hoc*, and Saladin decapitated the templar with his sabre; on which the dwarf explained that, hidden behind a curtain, he had seen him stab his accomplice the Marquis of Montserrat, obviously to prevent him from revealing their infamous plots, while he answered his appeal for mercy in the words he had repeated. The next day the young prince was married to Lady Edith, and presented by the Sultan with his talisman, the Crusade was abandoned, and Richard, on his way homewards, was imprisoned by the Austrians in the Tyrol.[34]

AN ANALYSIS OF THE TALISMAN

Scott's display of his knowledge of Islamic lore, customs and history begins with the title. A talisman, according to the Oxford English Dictionary [O.E.D.], is "A stone, ring, or other object engraven with figures or characters, to which are attributed the occult powers of the planetary influences and celestial configurations under which it was made; usually worn as an amulet to avert evil from or bring fortune to the wearer; also medicinally used to impart healing virtue; hence, any object held to be endowed with magic virtue; a charm." The O.E.D., in fact, quotes Scott's novel for one use of the term, which is thought to derive from the Arabic *tilsam*, in the same sense, as the Greek *telesm*, though the final -an is not accounted for.

Scott also manifests his critical attitude to the Crusades and Crusaders right from the beginning. He makes it clear in the first five pages that not all the crusaders were as chivalrous as the hero, Sir Kenneth, who, "under a calm and undisturbed semblance, had much of the fiery and enthusiastic love of glory which constituted the principal attribute of the renowned Norman line, and had rendered them sovereigns in every corner of Europe, where they had drawn their adventurous swords. It was not, however, to all the race that fortune proposed such tempting rewards; and those obtained by the solitary knight, during two years' campaign in Palestine, had been only temporal fame, and, as he was taught to believe, spiritual privileges. Meantime, his slender stock of money had melted away, the rather that he did not pursue any of the ordinary modes by which the followers of the Crusade condescended to recruit their diminished resources, at the expense of the people of Palestine; he exacted no gifts from the wretched natives for sparing their possessions when engaged in warfare with the Saracens, and he had not availed himself of any opportunity of enriching himself by the ransom of prisoners of consequence. The small train which had followed him from his native country, had been gradually diminished, as the means of maintaining them disappeared, and his only

---

34 Henry Grey, *A Key to the Waverley Novels*, London, 1899, pp. 9-13

remaining squire was at present on a sick-bed, and unable to attend his master, who travelled, as we have seen, singly and alone. This was of little consequence to the Crusader, who was accustomed to consider his good sword as his safest escort, and devout thoughts as his best companion."[35]

Also in the same five pages, Scott presents Saladin, disguised as an emir, as an intelligent, dexterous, brave, and chivalrous warrior, whose words are never to be doubted, "The word of a follower of the Prophet was never broken."[36] The honour of Muslims is constantly stressed, but at their best, the Christians are similarly men of faith, integrity and rectitude; there is little to choose between them, both denominations are guilty of fanatical zeal:

> The distinction of religions, nay, the fanatical zeal which animated the followers of the Cross and of the Crescent against each other, was much softened by a feeling so natural to generous combatants, and especially cherished by the spirit of chivalry. This last strong impulse had extended itself gradually from the Christians to their mortal enemies, the Saracens, both of Spain and of Palestine. The latter were indeed no longer the fanatical savages, who had burst from the centre of Arabian deserts, with the sabre in one hand, and the Koran in the other, to inflict death or the faith of Mohammed, or at the best, slavery and tribute, upon all who dared to oppose the belief of the prophet of Mecca. These alternatives indeed had been offered to the unwarlike Greeks and Syrians; but in contending with the western Christians, animated by a zeal as fiery as their own, and possessed of as unconquerable courage, address, and success in arms, the Saracens gradually caught a part of their manners, and especially of those chivalrous observances, which were so well calculated to charm the minds of a proud and conquering people. They had their tournaments and games of chivalry; they had even their knights, or some rank analogous, and above all, the Saracens observed their plighted faith with an accuracy which might sometimes put to shame those who owned a better religion. Their truces, whether national or betwixt individuals, were faithfully observed; and thus it was, that war, in itself perhaps the greatest of evils, yet gave occasion for display of good faith, generosity, clemency, and even kindly af-

---

35 Walter Scott, *The Talisman*, Harmondworth (UK): 1980 [Ist Edn. 1825], p. 8.
36 *Ibid.*, p. 11.

fections, which less frequently occur in more tranquil periods, where the passions of men, experiencing wrongs, or entertaining quarrels which cannot be brought to instant decision, are apt to smoulder for a length of time in the bosoms of those who are so unhappy as to be their prey.[37]

Scott is not however afraid to point to personal and ultimately cultural differences. Here are some exquisite observations: "The manners of the Eastern warrior were grave, graceful, and decorous; indicating, however, in some particulars, the habitual restraint which men of warm and choleric tempers often set as a guard upon their native impetuosity of disposition, and at the same time a sense of his own dignity which seemed to impose a certain formality of behavior in him who entertained it. This haughty feeling of superiority was perhaps equally entertained by his new European acquaintance, but the effect was different; and the same feeling which dictated to the Christian knight a bold, blunt, and somewhat careless bearing, as one too conscious of his own importance to be anxious about the opinions of others, appeared to prescribe to the Saracen a style of courtesy more studiously and formally observant of ceremony. Both were courteous; but the courtesy of the Christian seemed to flow rather from a good-humored sense of what was due to others; that of the Moslem, from a high feeling of what was to be expected from himself."[38]

Edward Said's conclusions quoted above turn out to be totally absurd when one realises that in the first two chapters the Saracen gives as good as he gets from the Christian. The Emir reproaches Sir Kenneth for feeding "like a dog or wolf." Then as Sir Kenneth exercises his "Christian freedom" by drinking some wine, the Emir contemptuously pronounces, "That, too, you call a part of your liberty, and as you feed like the brutes, so you degrade yourself to the bestial condition, by drinking a poisonous liquor which even they refuse!"

But the Christian Knight has his reply ready, "Know, foolish Saracen that thou blasphemest the gifts of God, even with the blasphemy of thy father Ishmael. The juice of the grape is given to him that will use it wisely, as that which cheers the heart of man after toil, refreshes him in sickness, and comforts him in sorrow. He who so enjoyeth it may thank God for his wine-cup as for his daily bread; and he who abuseth the gift of Heaven, is

---

37 *Ibid.*, pp. 12-13.
38 *Ibid.*, pp. 18-19.

not a greater fool in his intoxication than thou in thine abstinence."[39]

Then follow some delicious exchanges on the relative merits of monogamy and polygamy, the Muslim delighting in the "black-eyed houris of Paradise."

Scott ably summarises the *raison d'etre* of the Crusades, and what he obviously sees as the essential honourableness of the Islamic position on the Holy Land, "for the cruel hand of your people has been red with the blood of the servants of the Lord, and therefore do we come hither in plate and mail, with sword and lance, to open the road to the Holy Sepulchre, and protect the chosen saints and anchorites who yet dwell in this land of promise and of miracle."

"Nazarene," said the Moslem, "in this the Greeks and Syrians have much belied us, seeing we do but after the word of Abubeker Alwakel, the successor of the Prophet, and, after him, the first commander of true believers. 'Go forth,' he said,' Yezed Ben Sophian,' when he sent that renowned general to take Syria from the infidels, 'quit yourselves like men in battle, but slay neither the aged, the infirm, the women, nor the children. Waste not the land, neither destroy corn and fruit-trees: they are the gifts of Allah. Keep faith when you have made any covenant, even if it be to your own harm. If ye find holy men laboring with their hands, and serving God in the desert, hurt them not, neither destroy their dwellings. But when you find them with shaven crowns, they are of the synagogue of Satan! smite with the sabre, slay, cease not till they become believers or tributaries.' As the Caliph, companion of the Prophet, hath told us, so have we done, and those whom our justice has smitten are but the priests of Satan. But unto the good men who, without stirring up nation against nation, worship sincerely in the faith of Issa Ben Marian, we are a shadow and a shield; and such being he whom you seek, even though the light of the Prophet hath not reached him, from me he will only have love, favor, and regard."[40]

Sir Walter ends Chapter Two with a subtle dig at "mullahs and priests," and religion in general, all held responsible for bringing unnatural divisiveness among men of otherwise goodwill, "Slander not him [Muhammad, the Prophet] whom thou knowest not; the rather that we venerate the founder of thy religion, while we condemn the doctrine which priests have spun from it. I will myself guide thee to the cavern of the hermit, which, methinks, without my help, thou wouldst find it a hard matter to reach. And, on the way, let us leave to mollahs, and to monks, to

---

39 *Ibid.*, pp. 19-20.
40 *Ibid.*, pp. 23-24.

dispute about the divinity of our faith, and speak on themes which belong to youthful warriors,—upon battles, upon beautiful women, upon sharp swords, and upon bright armor."[41]

Saladin appears, as Riley-Smith put it, in a bewildering number of disguises, a trait perhaps derived from Harun al-Rashid's habit of roaming the streets of Baghdad disguised in the Arabian Nights. Certainly, "the banner of Death, with this impressive inscription, "SALADIN, KING OF KINGS, SALADIN, VICTOR OF VICTORS; SALADIN MUST DIE" which, in Scott's novel, was displayed among the banners above Saladin's tent was lifted and adapted from *The Sixth Voyage of Sinbad*.[42]

Robert Irwin in a fascinating, all too brief, essay takes Edward Said to task for totally misunderstanding *The Talisman*: "[Said] fastens on the passage in which Sir Kenneth meets Saladin (in disguise). Kenneth praises Saladin as an individual, yet finds it curious that his race and religion boast descent from Iblis (the Devil). Said (*Orientalism*, 1978, p.101) remarks on the airy condescension of damning a whole people 'generally' while mitigating the offence with a cool 'I don't mean you in particular.' Said suggests that the accusation of descent from Iblis was something that Scott took from Beckford or perhaps Byron. In fact the descent of the Kurdish people from Iblis was part of medieval Arab folklore about the Kurds (and historically Saladin was of course a Kurd). More generally, what is missing from Said's somewhat cursory and jaundiced reading of *The Talisman* is any appreciation of just how favourable Scott's portraits of Saladin and his Saracen physician are. Courageous, intelligent and magnanimous, they really come out better than Kenneth, Richard or any of the other protagonists in the story. While one might wish that Sir Kenneth, not long in the Holy Land, would unequivovally express opinions such as that the Arabs are the equal if not the superior of Scotsmen, that Islam is a jolly good religion and the crusades are really just disguised imperialism, in the context of a novel set in the late twelfth century such remarks would strike most readers as anachronistic. Said's reading of Scott's novel is oddly naïve (though hardly more so than his reading of George Eliot's *Daniel Deronda*)."[43]

The Encyclopeadia of Islam, Second Edition,[44] tells us that there were many popular attempts to derive the name "Kurd" from the Arabic root

---

41 *Ibid.*, p. 25.

42 Robert Irwin, "Saladin and the Third Crusade" in ed, Michael Bentley, *Companion to Historiography*, London: Routledge, 1997 p. 141.

43 *Ibid.*, pp. 142-143.

44 *Encyclopedia of Islam*, s.v. 'Kurds, Kurdistan'.

karrada; "the Kurds would thus be the children of young slaves and the demon Djasad ('driven out' by Solomon)."

Saladin is depicted as a virtuous, calm, refined, and sagacious figure much given to uttering what Scott must take to be pearls of Eastern wisdom but which read more like those pseudo-Confucian proverbs to be found in Chinese cookies:

[1] Know, Christian, that when one eye is extinguished, the other becomes more keen—when one hand is cut off, the other becomes more powerful; so, when our reason in human things is disturbed or destroyed, our view heavenward becomes more acute and perfect.[45]

[2] It is better that a man should be the servant of a kind master, than the slave of his own wild passions[46]

[3] The sage fears nothing but Heaven, but ever expects from wicked men the worst which they can do[47]

[4] Fortune may raise up or abuse the ordinary mortal, but the sage and the soldier should have minds beyond her control[48]

[5] Thou canst cut off the head, but not cure the aching tooth[49]

[6] When the rich carpet is soiled, the fool pointeth to the stain, the wise man covers it with his mantle[50]

[7] A valiant camel-driver is worthy to kiss the lip of a fair Queen, when a cowardly prince is not worthy to salute the hem of her garment[51]

[8] Her eye is as the edge of the sword of the Prophet, who shall look upon it? He that would not be burnt avoideth to

---

45 *The Talisman*, p. 42.
46 *Ibid.*, p. 240.
47 *Ibid.*, p. 246.
48 *Ibid.*, p. 249.
49 *Ibid.*, p. 194.
50 *Ibid.*, p. 195.
51 *Ibid.*, p. 307.

tread on hot embers—wise men spread not the flax before a bickering torch—He, saith the sage, who hath forfeited a treasure, doth not wisely to turn back his head to gaze at it.[52]

On the other hand, the character sketch of King Richard is more nuanced; he is painted as a true monarch, a great leader, courageous but impetuous, irritable, haughty, coarse, and contemptuous of his brother sovereigns. He would undoubtedly have triumphantly marched to Jerusalem but for the jealousies of the Christian princes engaged in the same enterprise. However, Richard is unequivocal in his admiration for Saladin,— "my noble Saladin"—considered a man of his words. King Richard listens to some advice, and declares, "yet now this counsel sounds not so strange in mine ear; for why should I not seek for brotherhood and alliance with a Saracen, brave, just, generous,—who loves and honours a worthy foe, as if he were a friend,—whilst the Princes of Christendom shrink from the side of their allies, and forsake the cause of Heaven and good knighthood?"

"It were well," said Richard, "to apply to the generosity of the royal Saladin, since, heathen as he is, I have never known knight more fulfilled of nobleness, or to whose good faith we may so peremptorily intrust ourselves. I speak thus for those who may be doubtful of mishap—for myself, wherever I see my foe, I make that spot my battle-ground."[53] Elsewhere Richard again adduces Saladin's noble qualities, "Noble Saladin, suspicion and thou cannot exist on the same ground."[54]

While he praises the ideals of chivalry: "Sir Kenneth had full leisure to enjoy these and similar high-souled thoughts, fostered by that wild spirit of chivalry, which, amid its most extravagant and fantastic flights, was still pure from all selfish alloy—generous, devoted, and perhaps only thus far censurable, that it proposed objects and courses of action inconsistent with the frailties and imperfections of man,"[55] and though he does not doubt the sincerity of individual crusaders, Scott nonetheless finds the whole crusading project irrational, "But in the Crusade, itself an undertaking wholly irrational, sound reason was the quality, of all others, least estimated, and the chivalric valour which both the age and the enterprise demanded, was considered as debased, if mingled with the least touch of discretion."[56]

---

52 *Ibid.*, p. 321.

53 *Ibid.*, p. 271.

54 *Ibid.*, p. 303.

55 *Ibid.*, p. 143.

56 *Ibid.*, p. 138.

HISTORY

Given that *The Talisman* is a work of fiction, it is startling to read that Sir Hamilton Gibb recommended it to his students as a book from which they could learn much Middle Eastern history. How accurate is Scott in his historical reconstructions? A short answer would be *wildly inaccurate*. Richard and Saladin never met, Saladin never treated the King of England for any illness, and neither of them displayed any clemency if it did not suit them. It was grim warfare, and politics all the way.

Let us begin with the minor actors in the drama. Scott cannot even get the title of Conrad of Montferrat, the main villain in the novel, correct. During his research, he misread the "f" in Montferrat as an "s," and came up with Conrad of Montserrat. Scott wrote of Conrad in this manner:

> Proud, ambitious, unscrupulous, and politic, the Marquis of Montserrat was yet not cruel by nature. He was a voluptuary and an epicurean, and, like many who profess this character, was averse, even upon selfish motives, from inflicting pain, or witnessing acts of cruelty; and he retained also a general sense of respect for his own reputation, which sometimes supplies the want of the better principle by which reputation is to be maintained.[57]

And he accused the marquis of "employing his jealousy of England as the means of dissolving, or loosening at least, the league of the Crusaders."[58]

Extraordinarily enough, Sir Steven Runciman describes Conrad initially in strikingly similar terms: "Harsh, ambitious and unscrupulous…" But adds, significantly, "yet trusted and admired by the native Frankish nobility, would have been a strong and cunning king."[59] Thomas Asbridge describes Conrad as "profoundly ambitious—guileful and unscrupulous as a political operator, competent and authoritative as a general…"[60] Whereas for Thomas Madden, the marquis was "renowned across the Mediterranean for his skill and bravery."[61]

Surely, the most significant act in the life of Conrad, the marquis of Montferrat, was the magnificent and timely defense of Tyre—a feat not

---

57 *Ibid.*, p. 122.
58 *Ibid.*, p. 125.
59 Runciman, *op.cit.*, Vol.III, p. 65.
60 Ashridge, *op.cit.*, p. 394.
61 Madden, *op.cit.*, p. 78.

celebrated in *The Talisman*. He arrived in Palestine in July 1187 just days after the battle of Hattin. Tyre would undoubtedly have fallen to Saladin had not Conrad taken command of its garrison and defences. As Tyerman says, "[a]ccompanied only by a single ship's company of knights, a few score at most, Conrad brought leadersip, determination, energy and optimism to the defence of Tyre."[62] Saladin raised the siege and departed north in early 1188 leaving "a vital Palestinian port in Christian hands, a haven for Frankish refugees and a base for the naval sqaudrons that were beginning to arrive from the west."[63]

Other absurdities and improbabilities include Saladin, in his guise as a physician, carrying Sir Kenneth's wounded dog away to look after it, even though Sir Kenneth recognizes that the dog is "by thy law, an unclean animal." Saladin eloquently defends his gesture, "Where Allah hath deigned to bestow life, and a sense of pain and pleasure," said the physician, "it were sinful pride should the sage, whom he has enlightened, refuse to prolong existence, or assauge agony. To the sage, the cure of a miserable groom, of a poor dog, and of a conquering monarch, are events of little distinction. Let me examine this wounded animal."[64]

Again there are the following noble speeches from the Saracen arguing that he would never contemplate forcing a non-Muslim to convert:

> Saladin makes no converts to the law of the Prophet, save those on whom its precepts shall work conviction. Open thine eyes to the light, and the great Soldan, whose liberality is as boundless as his power, may bestow on thee a kingdom; remain blinded if thou wilt, and, being one whose second life is doomed to misery, Saladin will yet, for this span of present time, make thee rich and happy. But fear not that thy brows shall be bound with the turban, save at thine own free choice.[65]

And,

> Nazarene, thy nation so easily entertain suspicion, that it may well render themselves suspected. Have I not told thee that Saladin desires no converts saving those whom the holy prophet shall dispose to submit themselves to his law—vio-

---

62 Tyerman, *op.cit.*, p. 404.

63 *Ibid.*

64 *The Talisman*, p. 160.

65 *Ibid.*, pp. 162-63.

lence and bribery are alike alien to his plan for extending the true faith. Hearken to me, my brother. When the blind man was miraculously restored to sight, the scales dropped from his eyes at the Divine pleasure—think'st thou that any earthly leech could have removed them? No. Such mediciner might have tormented the patient with his instruments, or perhaps soothed him with his balsams and cordials, but dark as he was must the darkened man have remained; and it is even so with the blindness of the understanding. If there be those among the Franks, who, for the sake of worldly lucre, have assumed the turban of the prophet, and followed the laws of Islam, with their own consciences be the blame. Themselves sought out the bait—it was not flung to them by the Soldan. And when they shall hereafter be sentenced, as hypocrites, to the lowest gulf of hell, below Christian and Jew, magician and idolater, and condemned to eat the fruit of the tree Yacoun, which is the heads of demons—to themselves, not to the Soldan, shall their guilt and their punishment be attributed. Wherefore wear, without doubt or scruple, the vesture prepared for you, since, if you proceed to the camp of Saladin, your own native dress will expose you to troublesome observation, and perhaps to insult.[66]

By contrast here are three passsages of real history that contradict the above noble sentiments. The damning passages are taken from the Arabic life of Saladin by Bahā' al-Dīn Ibn Shaddād [1145-1234], who was permanently enrolled in the service of the Sultan in 1188, and for the rest of Saladin's life was "his intimate and close confidant, being seldom absent for any length of time"[67]

[A] … [A] Frank [a Christian crusader] who had been taken prisoner was brought before him [Saladin]. He ordered his head to be cut off, which was done in his presence, after the man had been offered Islam and had rejected it.[68]

[B] [Saladin] once ordered his son, al-Malik al-Zahir, lord of Aleppo to execute a young man that came forward, called

---

66 *Ibid.*, pp. 254-55.

67 Baha al-Din Ibn Shaddad, *The Rare and Excellent History of Saladin*, Trans. by D. S. Richards, Burlington, VT: 2002 Introduction, p. 2.

68 *Ibid.*, p. 30.

al-Suhrawardi, of whom it was said that he rejected the Holy Law and declared it invalid. His son had arrested him because of reports about him that he heard. He informed the sultan [Saladin] of this, who ordered his execution and his body to be publicly displayed for some days. This was done.[69]

[C] [After the Battle of Hattin, July 1187, Saladin summons the prisoner Prince Reynald of Châtillon] He said to him, "Here I am having asked for victory through Muhammad, and God has given me victory over you." He offered him Islam but he refused. The sultan then drew his scimitar and struck him, severing his arm at the shoulder. Those present finished him off and God speedily sent his soul to Hell-fire. His body was taken and thrown down at the door of the tent.[70]

Here is an example of Saladin's Eastern hospitality. Towards the end of the novel, Scott takes a real incident and uses it to dispatch the villain, Grand Master of the Templars. The latter is about to taste a refreshing drink from a goblet, "but those lips never touched that goblet's rim. The sabre of Saladin left its sheath as lightning leaves the cloud. It was waved in the air,—and the head of the Grand Master rolled to the extremity of the tent, while the trunk remained for a second standing with the goblet still clenched in its grasp, then fell, the liquor mingling with the blood that spurted from the veins." Saladin then explains why he had to decapitate the Grand Master just at that moment, "but had I not hastened his doom, it had been altogether averted, since, if I had permitted him to taste of my cup, as he was about to do, how could I, without incurring the brand of inhospitality, have done him to death as he deserved? Had he murdered my father, and afterwards partaken of my food and my bowl, not a hair of his head could have been injured by me. But enough of him—let his carcase and his memory be removed from amongst us."[71]

The real incident is even more disagreeable, an unpleasant piece of casuistry. The scene takes place soon after Saladin's victory over the Crusaders when he took many prisoners, including King Guy and Prince Reynald of Châtillon. Bahā' al-Dīn Ibn Shaddād continues the story: "Then [Saladin] summoned King Guy, his brother and Prince Reynald. He handed the king a drink of iced julep, from which he drank, being dreadfully thirsty,

69 *Ibid.*, p. 20.

70 *Ibid.*, p. 75.

71 *Ibid.*, pp. 320-330.

and he then passed some of it to Prince Reynald. The sultan [Saladin] said to the interpreter, 'Tell the King, You are the one giving him a drink. I have not given him any drink.' According to the fine custom of the Arabs and their noble ways, if a prisoner took food or drink from whoever had captured him, his life was safe. His intention was to follow these noble ways…. [Saladin] said to [Reynald], 'Here I am having asked for victory through Muhammad, and God has given me victory over you' He offered him Islam but he refused. The sultan then drew his scimitar and struck him, severing his arm at the shoulder. Those present finished him off and God speedily sent his soul to Hell-fire. His body was taken and thrown down at the door of the tent."[72]

Far from showing each other respect, Saladin and Richard, in reality accused each other of bad faith, which led to bloody reprisals on both sides. Here is the historical outcome of the Fall of Acre. After a long siege, a deal was struck on 12 July, 1191 whereby the Muslims surrendered to the Franks the city and its contents, though the lives of the Muslims within were to be spared. Furthemore, "the captive garrison would then be held hostage as guarantors against the fulfilment of further punitive terms: the payment of 200,000 gold dinars; the return of the relic of the True Cross captured at Hattin; and the release of some 1,500 Frankish prisoners 'of common, unremarkable background,' as well as 100 to 200 named captives of rank."[73]

Richard the Lionheart's main concern was to see the terms of Acre's surrender fulfilled, and accordingly began pressuring Saladin for a precise timetable for the implementation of the peace settlement's terms. For Richard speed was of the essence, for various tactical, and military reasons—ultimately, he risked the collapse of the entire crusade. Saladin knew this and so he began delaying tactics. The deadline of the first payment of the money—12 August—passed, and Saladin "began deliberately to equivocate,"[74] and even sought to introduce new conditions into the original deal. Saladin had obviously miscalculated, for Richard marched out of the city with 2,700 Muslim prisoners, who were bound in ropes, and ordered their mass execution in full sight of the Muslim camp.

John Gillingham,[75] formerly professor of medieval history at the London School of Economics, argues that Richard's act was "a reasoned

---

72 *Ibid.* p. 75.

73 Thomas Asbridge, *The Crusades*, New York, 2010, p. 443.

74 *Ibid.*, p. 451.

75 John Gilllingham, *Richard I.* New Haven: Yale University Press, 2002, pp. 166-71; 260-1

decision, driven by military expediency."[76] Here is Christopher Tyerman's assessment: "Richard I's butchery of his Muslim captives was an atrocity not uncommon in war. It was not an act of random sadism, less so, for example, than Saladin's own execution of the Templars and Hospitallers after Hattin.[77] Even [Bahā' al-Dīn] Ibn Shaddād recognized that Richard's action contained logic: revenge for Muslim killing of surrendering Christians during the siege of Acre 'or that the king of England had decided to march on Ascalon and did not think it wise to leave that number in the rear.' Richard and his apologists, and many observers not noted for their sympathy towards him, insisted on the justice of the killings, even their legality. One favourable source declared that, without the agreement with Saladin, the lives of the defeated garrison were forfeit *jure belli*, 'under the rights of war.'"[78]

Here are some examples of Saladin's subsequent reactions taken from the Arabic history of Bahā' al-Dīn Ibn Shaddād:

[1] At this camp, [Saladin] was brought two Franks who had been snatched by the advance guard. He commanded their execution and they were slain. Many of our men fell upon them with swords to vent their anger.[79]

[2] Another two men taken from the fringes of the enemy host were brought before [Saladin] and they were *most cruelly* done to death, as he was still in an extreme rage at what had been done to the prisoners at Acre.[80] [My emphasis.]

What does "cruelly done to death" mean? It means the prisoners were first horribly tortured and mutilated, and then executed. No clemency, humanity, and magnanimity is in evidence here.

[3] Another prisoner is ordered to be executed, but this time "he forbade any mutilation."[81]

---

76 Thomas Asbridge, *op.cit.*, p. 455.

77 To be discussed in part III.

78 Tyerman, *op.cit.*, pp. 456-457.

79 Bahā' al-Dīn Ibn Shaddād, *op.cit.*, p. 168.

80 *Ibid.*, p. 168.

81 *Ibid.*, p. 169.

[4] Two other Crusader prisoners were odered executed.[82]

[5] Six more prisoners were ordered executed.[83]

[6] Fourteen Frankish men and one woman were also executed on Saladin's orders.[84]

[7] In early September, 1191, Saladin ordered that two Franks be beheaded.[85]

[8] On 7th September, one more execution ordered.[86]

[9] On 10th September, two crusaders executed.[87]

[10] On 25 September, Saladin arrived at the town of Ramla. "He viewed the town and viewed its church and the great size of its construction, then ordered its demolition and the demolition of the castle at Ramla."[88]

Scott did make an effort to get the details of the Western costumes, arms and armour right, for which he was aided by the antiquarian researches of Joseph Strutt [1749-1802] and Samuel Meyrick [1783-1848]. Strutt was a distinguished engraver whose meticulous research in the reading room of the British Museum resulted in beautifully illustrated volumes such as *The Regal and Ecclesiastical Antiquities of England*, and *Manners, Customs, Arms, Habits of the People of England*. While Meyrick's *A critical enquiry into antient armour as it existed in Europe, but particularly in England, from the Norman conquest to the reign of King Charles II, with a glossary of military terms of the Middle Ages* [1842] was particularly important for arms and armour. Otherwise Scott's knowledge of the Crusades was derived from Charles Mills [1788-1826], a solicitor turned historian whose works included, *History of the Crusades for the Recovery and Possession of the Holy Land* [1820], *History of Mohammedanism*, and *History of Chiv-*

---

82 *Ibid.*
83 *Ibid.*
84 *Ibid.*, p. 169 -170.
85 *Ibid.*, p. 174.
86 *Ibid.*, p. 176.
87 *Ibid.*, p. 177.
88 *Ibid.*, p. 181.

alry—the latter was much influenced by Scott's novels. Scott also helped Mills with some references from Scottish chronicles for the *History of the Crusades*.[89] I have already mentioned Scott's reliance on Anna Comnene for his novel *Count Robert of Paris*, but he must surely have had access to the same sources as Edward Gibbon the first volume of whose history came out in 1776. And yet Scott got the history wrong, or else consciously took great liberties with it.

Other literary influences on Scott are well summarised by Robert Irwin: "Scott's vision of chivalry was influenced perhaps by the Gothic novel and certainly by [Edmund] Spenser [1522-1599] and [Sir Thomas] Malory [1405-1471]. When in the opening of *The Talisman* Sir Kenneth rides across the desert towards the Dead Sea, he is re-enacting the ride of the Red-Cross Knight in the opening of Spenser's *The Fairie Queene, Canto I* [1590]:

> A Gentle Knight was pricking on the plaine,
> Y cladd in mightie armes and siluer shielde,

Irwin continues, "As for Scott's reading of Malory's *Morte d'Arthur* [1485], this resurfaced in *The Talisman* in such elements as the strange vision of the ladies in the chapel, the dwarf and the samite arm [Chapter V]. George Ellis' *Specimens of Early English Romances in Metre* (1805) fuelled Scott's medievalism. Folklore also played a part in the shaping of the novel and the central device of the talisman was inspired by legends attached to the Luck of the Lockharts of Lee."[90]

The Germans taking part in the Third Crusade come off the worst in Scott's novel. They are described as essentially and irremediably barbaric:

> The Germans, though still possessing the martial and frank character of their ancestors, who subdued the Roman empire, had retained withal no slight tinge of their barbarism. The practices and principles of chivalry were not carried to such a nice pitch amongst them, as amongst the French and English knights, nor were they strict observers of the prescribed rules of society, which among those nations were supposed to express the height of civilisation. Sitting at the table of the Archduke, Conrade was at once stunned and amused with the clang of

---

89 Robert Irwin, "Saladin and the Third Crusade" in ed, Michael Bentley, *Companion to Historiography*, London: Routledge, 1997 p. 141.
90 *Ibid.*

Teutonic sounds assaulting his ears on all sides, notwithstanding the solemnity of a princely banquet. Their dress seemed equally fantastic to him, many of the Austrian nobles retaining their long beards, and almost all of them wearing short jerkins of various colours, cut and flourished, and fringed, in a manner not common in Western Europe.[91]

Given that Scott's focus is on the Crusaders, and their internecine bickering which had a historical basis, and the fact that Saladin is always presented as the reasonable, honorable and cultivated Saracen in contrast to the barabaric Germans, and coarse Franks, Scots and Englishmen, the overall and overwhelming impression can only be that the Crusaders were fanatical, expending needless energy on a futile enterprise, and the Muslims were patient, forbearing, tolerant of other religions, and simply defending their homelands.

PART III

THE THIRD CRUSADE AND SALADIN IN HISTORIOGRAPHY

I shall give the barest outlines of [A] the historical personages in the drama of the life and times Saladin and the Third Crusade, and [B] the Arabic sources of our knowledge of the times, without which it would be impossible to understand the discussions which will follow.

A. DRAMATIS PERSONNAE

1. Zangi [born in Aleppo, 1087-8, died 1146, also known as Zengi, or Zanki], founder of the Zangid dynasty, was a Turkmen commander, governor of Iraq, later ruler of al-Mawsil [Mosul] and Aleppo (1127-1146). He was the last surviving son of the Seljuk commander Aksunkur. On his father's death in 1094, Zangi was brought up at the court of the governors of al-Mawsil and "distinguished himself in the internal warfare of rival [Seljuk] princes and the wars against the Crusaders." He was the first Muslim ruler to fight the Crusader states effectively, though "he never fought them with the same vigour as he did in the case of the strategi-

---

cally much more important Damascus."[92] He was "primarily concerned with affairs further east and the politics of the Seljuk Baghdad sultanate." Nonetheless he did increase "his hold on the eastern frontiers of northern Outremer. In 1137 he captured the Frankish castle of Montferrand (Ba'rin), the important Muslim city of Homs in 1138 and the strategically significant town of Baalbek in the Biqa valley in 1140, where he installed as a garrison commander a Kurdish mercenary, Naim al-Din Ayyub, Saladin's father." Zangi captured Edessa in 1144.[93]

Murdered at the siege of Kalat Jabar in 1146. Father of Nur al-Din.

2. Nur al-Din [died 1174] was successor to his father Zangi. Quickly established himself as ruler of Aleppo. Fought against Raymond of Antioch who laid siege to Damascus unsuccessfully. Within a few years, Nur al-Din with a series of victories was able to transfer the frontier of Dar al-Islam from the Euphrates to the Orontes, which rises in Lebanon and flows north through Syria into Turkey, before turning west to the Mediterranean. He emerged "as Latin Christendom's most feared and respected Muslim adversary in the Near East—a ruler who nurtured and re-energised the cause of Islamic holy war."[94] Nur al-Din thwarted Joscelin II's attempt to recapture his capital, and regained Edessa whose entire male Christian population was put to the sword for having aided Joscelin II, leaving a city "deserted of life: an appalling vision enveloped in a black cloud, drunk with blood, infected by the cadavers of its sons and daughters."[95]

In 1150, Nur al-Din captured the Frankish leader Joscelin II who was imprisoned for the rest of his life in Aleppo where he suffered regular torture. "Nur al-Din emerged as the Near East's foremost Muslim leader in the aftermath of the Second Crusade. Over the course of his career, Nur al-Din would unite Syria, extend Zangid power into Egypt and score a series of victories against the Christian Franks. He became one of the great luminaries of medieval Islam, celebrated as a stalwart of Sunni orthodoxy and a champion of jihad against Latin Outremer."[96] His conquest of Damascus in 1154 allowed Nur al-Din "to claim dominion over almost all Muslim

---

92 *Encyclopaedia of Islam*, 2nd Edn, s.v. Zangi.

93 Christopher Tyerman, *God's War*, Cambridge, Mass.: Harvard University Press, 2006, p. 188-89.

94 Thomas Asbridge, *The Crusades*, New York: Harper Collins, 2010, p. 229.

95 Michael the Syrian, *Chronique syriaque*, edited and translated by J.B. Chabot, 4 Vols. Paris, 1899-1914, Vol. 3., p. 270, quoted by Asbridge, *op.cit.*, p. 231.

96 Asbridge, *op.cit.*, p. 238.

Syria; for the first time since the crusades began, Aleppo and Damascus were united."[97]

3. THE AYYUBIDS

Ayyubid is the name of the dynasty founded by Saladin. Saladin's grandfather, Ayyub b. Shadi, was a Kurd from Armenia, and had been in the service of the Kurdish Shaddadid dynasty. However when the Kurdish princes and lords were slowly eliminated by the Seljuk Turks, Ayyub b. Shadi went to work for the Seljuk commander of Iraq, who made him governor of Takrit. His son Ayyub, the father of Saladin, succeeded him. "It was in this capacity that Ayyub earned the gratitude of the master of Mawsil [Mosul] and Aleppo, Zanki (Zangi), who after being defeated by the Caliph, was able, with the help of Ayyub, to cross the Euphrates and withdraw without a disaster. In the country behind Mawsil, Zanki first of all adopted a systematic policy of subduing and then of recruiting the Kurds. In 532/1138, Ayyub entered his service.

> He was at once used by him in Syria, being appointed governor of Baclbak, opposite Damascus. On Zanki's death, Ayyub placed himself under the Burid prince of Damascus, who gave him the governorship of that town, whilst his brother Shirkuh, [Saladin's uncle] followed Zanki's son, Nur al-Din, the master of Northern Syria, who gave him Hims as an *iqta*. However, the trend of public opinion in Damascus finally led to the unification of Muslim Syria, with a view to the more effective prosecution of the war against the Franks, under the command of the prince with the most power and the greatest enthusiasm for the jihad, Nur al-Din; in the surrender of Damascus the activities of the two brothers Shirkuh and Ayyub played a major role, and Ayyub chose the side of Nur al-Din, the governor of the Syrian capital.[98]

4. THE ACTORS IN EGYPT

The Fatimids of Egypt. From 969 Egypt was ruled by the Shi'ite Fatimid dynasty, having broken free from the Sunni Abbasid rulers of Baghdad. The Fatimids constructed the new city of Cairo ("Conqueror"

---

97 *Ibid.*, p. 249.
98 *E.I.* 2 s.v. "Ayyubids."

in Arabic) and established a rival Shi'ite caliph, challenging the universal authority of the Sunni caliph in Baghdad.

By the twelfth century, Egypt was governed by the caliph's chief administrator, his vizier. By 1163, the nominal power lay in the hands of the eleven year old Caliph al-Adid, while the vizierate was held by the former governor of Upper Egypt, Shawar [executed 1169]. Shawar was overthrown and forced to flee to Syria, arriving in Damascus at the end 1163, and convinced Nur al-Din to help him regain his vizierate. Nur al-Din sent Shirkuh [died 1169], Saladin's uncle, to Egypt, in April 1164, with a sizeable and well-equipped force. Shirkuh won, and re-installed Shawar, who, however, now wanted Shirkuh to leave. When the latter refused, Shawar invited the Franks to come to Egypt's rescue.

Things went badly for Shawar who was eventually forced to appeal to Nur al-Din once more, this time begging for assistance against Frankish attacks. Nur al-Din responded by sending Shirkuh and Saladin. The rest of the story is told in what follows on the life of Saladin.[99]

B. ARABIC SOURCES

As Sir Hamilton Gibb points out, there are five contemporary sources in Arabic, in whole or in part, besides casual references in the writings of travellers and others.

> 1. Bahā' ad-Dīn Ibn Shaddād [1145-1234] "entered Saladin's service in 1188, was made Qadi to the army and remained a faithful member of the Sultan's household until Saladin's death. [His life of Saladin] is an excellent historical and biographical source, dictated by sincere devotion and admiration unmixed with servile flattery and based for the most part on personal observation."[100] Work: *al-Nawadir al-Sultaniyya wa'l-Mahasin al-Yusufiyya.*

Title translated by Francesco Gabrieli as "*Sultanly Anecdotes and Josephly Virtues*" (Joseph [Yusuf, in Arabic] being Saladin's personal name). Translated by D.S. Richards as "*The Rare and Excellent History of Saladin.*" Bahā' ad-Dīn's work was translated into Latin by the Dutch orientalist, Albert Schultens in 1732. It was very influential in forming the views held

---

99 *Ibid.*, pp. 266-274.

100 Francesco Gabrieli, *Arab Historians of the Crusades*, Berkeley, University of California Press, 1984 [Ist Italian Edn. 1957; Ist English Edn. 1969], pp. xxix.

by European historians of Saladin. Gibbon cites him often, referring to him as Bohadin.

2. 'Imād ad-Dīn al-Isfahani [1125-1200] was secretary to Nur ad-Din and then Saladin. Wrote in the most ornate and artificial style imaginable, full of "blank and rhyming verse, uninterrupted sequences of alliteration, metaphors and puns." His history of the Fall of Jerusalem which extends as far as Saladin's death, called *al-Fath al-qussi fi l-fath al-qudsi*—a punning title which Gabrieli translates as *"Ciceronian Eloquence on the Conquest of the Holy City."* Imād ad-Dīn also wrote *Barq ash-Shami* or *Lightning of Syria*, which chronicles Saladin's life from 1175. But style nothwithstanding, he is an important source for events in Syria and Mesopotamia which he "describes circumstantially, accurately and faithfully."[101]

3. Ibn al-Athīr [1160-1233] His most important work is *al-Kamil fi'l-Ta'rikh*, [The Perfect or Complete Work of History] Gibb was very critical indeed of Ibn al-Athir, especially in the use of his sources. Hardly surprising, since Al-Athir passed harsh judgements on Gibb's hero Saladin. By contrast, Francesco Gabrieli [1904-1996], the late Professor of Arabic Language and Literature at the University of Rome, wrote, "One man stands out as a true historian from the ranks of more or less diligent chroniclers: Ibn al-Athir. His reputation among Orientalists has recently diminished, because of the free and tendentious use he makes of his sources, but the qualities that reduce his reliability as documentary evidence are those of an original thinker, outstanding among so many passive compilers of facts."[102] Said to have favoured the Zangid dynasty (Zangi, Nur ad-Din and their successors). For the Crusades, Ibn al-Athir was "an eye-witness, although not always a sympathetic one of Saladin's career."[103]

4. Ibn Abi at-Tayy [c.1160-1235] was a Shi'ite historian of Aleppo who wrote a biography of Saladin but which work is lost. He is quoted by Abu Shama and Ibn al-Furat [1334-

---

101 *Ibid.*, p. xxx.
102 *Ibid.*, pp. xix-xx.
103 *Ibid.*, p. xxvii.

1405].

5. Al-Qadi al-Fadil, [1131-1199] who was Saladin's most trusted adviser and secretary of state. His despatches and letters are
preserved in full or in excerpts in the works of Imad ad-Din,
Abu Shama (see below), and other collections of documents.
Gibb seems to have trusted al-Fadil completely: "The intima-
cy of the relation between them can be felt in the loyal and
affectionate letters addressed by al-Qadi al-Fadil to Saladin,
especially during the Third Crusade, sustaining him in times
of adversity and even admonishing him on occasions. While,
therefore, the historian will treat with all necessary caution, the
more elaborate public dispatches addressed by al-Qadi al-Fadil
on Saladin's behalf to the caliphs and other potentates, yet the
consistency with which certain themes and ideas are expressed
in them must be taken to reflect some at least of Saladin's real
purposes and ideals."[104]

6. Abu Shama [1203-1267] was a philologist and antholo-
gist, whose *The Book of the Two Gardens* [*Kitab ar-Raudatain*]
concerning the the two dynasties of Saladin and Nur ad-Din,
brings together valuable material, for most of which we also
have his original sources. He quotes (giving his references)
from Ibn Qalanisi, Imad ad-Din, Baha ad-Din, Ibn Al-Athir
and others. More important are his quotations from the lost
Shi'ite historian of Aleppo, Ibn Abi Tayy, among other things
the author of a biography of Saladin. The Two Gardens also
reproduces numerous documents from the Sultan's chancellery,
most of them from the chief secretary [Qadi al-Fadil], individual collections of whose letters also exist."[105]

C. HISTORIANS OF SALADIN

C 1. STANLEY LANE-POOLE [1854-1931] worked in the Coin
Department of the British Museum for eighteen years, and compiled a
fourteen volume catalogue on Oriental coins. He was also employed by
the Egyptian government on archaeological research in Cairo. His uncle

---

104 H.A.R. Gibb, *The Life of Saladin*, foreword by Robert Irwin, London: Saqi Books,
2006, [Ist Edn. Oxford University Press, 1973], pp. 161-62.

105 Francesco Gabrieli. *op. cit.* pp. xxx-xxxi.

Edward William Lane [1801-1876] was already famous by the 1860s for his *An Account of the Manners and Customs of the Modern Egyptians* (1860). Lane-Poole helped complete Lane's monumental *Arabic-English Lexicon* which had got as far as the letter *qāf* (the twenty first letter) when Lane died. Lane-Poole himself was to write several books on Egypt and Cairo, such as *Studies in a Mosque* (1883) and *History of Egypt in the Middle Ages* (1901). Between 1898 and 1904, Lane-Poole was professor of Arabic at Trinity College, Dublin. He published *Saladin and the Fall of the Kingdom of Jerusalem* in 1898[106] in the *Heroes of the Nations* series.

Lane-Poole's last chapter in his *Saladin and the Fall of the Kingdom of Jerusalem* is an important survey of "Saladin in Romance" or Saladin in European literature from the Middle Ages onwards. I shall return to Lane-Poole's account of the Medieval romances later in this chapter, but here I should like to look at his assessment of Walter Scott's *The Talisman*, a work he clearly admired, despite it's historical inaccuracies, which Lane-Poole spells out in detail:

> It would be interesting to trace the effect of these medieval tales upon the two great writers [i.e. Scott, and Gotthold Ephraim Lessing (1729 –1781) the latter to be discussed later] who have introduced Saladin among the *dramatis persona* of European classics. Scott, of course, had read the chronicles and romances, as far as they were readily accessible, and incidents in "The Talisman" may be plausibly traced to the legends of the minstrels. Saladin's visit to Richard's camp in the disguise of a *hakim* may have been suggested by the Minstrel's tale of the equally imaginary visit to the Hospital of St. John at Acre. The quarrel over the banner of Austria is found in the "Romance of Richard Coeur de Lion," published at Edinburgh, in Weber's "Metrical Romances," fifteen years before "The Talisman." But his main source was clearly, not the romances, but the chronicles, which he used as far as they suited him, and very properly threw over whenever they did not fit his scheme. As [Scott] wrote himself in the Preface of 1832:
>
> > One of the inferior characters introduced was a supposed relation of Richard Coeur de Lion; a violation of the truth of history, which gave offence to Mr. Mills the

106 Stanley Lane-Poole, *Saladin and the Fall of the Kingdom of Jerusalem*, London: G.P. Putnam, 1898.

author of the *History of Chivalry and the Crusades*, who was not, it may be presumed, aware that romantic fiction naturally includes the power of such invention, which is indeed one of the requisites of the art.

Scott boldly asserts that he "had access to all which antiquity believed, whether of reality or fable," about Richard I.; but he can hardly have gone very thoroughly into the Oriental sources, although some were even then easily accessible in Latin. It is obvious, however, that when he sins against "the truth of history," in regard to his European characters, it is of *malice prepense*. He admits that he knowingly killed Conrad of Montferrat in the wrong way, and the wrong time, and the wrong place, and his other deviations from history are probably no less intentional. He places the scene of the novel at Jaffa, in the autumn of 1192, as various indications prove; and he must have known that Philip of France and Leopold of Austria had both left the Holy Land after the surrender of Acre more than a year before. He sets "the Diamond of the Desert" [a freshwater foutain] close to the Dead Sea, on the road to Jerusalem, half way between the camps of the Crusaders and the Saracens; which would place Saladin's camp, "over against Jaffa," somewhere in Moab on the other side of the *Mare Mortuum* [Dead Sea] Nor could Ilderim have been deceived for a moment by the notion that the Knight of the Leopard [Sir Kenneth] could possibly find himself beside that inhospitable water if he was riding from Jaffa to Jerusalem, since he must have left the Holy City directly behind him. At that time, moreover, no "pilgrimage to the Holy Sepulchre" was to be thought of. But a crusading tale without a desert, no sand, no oasis, no Dead Sea, no pilgrimage, would lack the essential local colour, and Scott very properly put it in. And so all the quarrelling between the rival nations, which was true enough of the French and English, is infinitely more interesting when the absent King of France himself leads his knights; no novel-reader would care a rush for the jealousy of a Duke of Burgundy—unless, of course, he were Charles the Bold.

Scott's treatment of the Oriental side of the picture is marked by fewer liberties, because there was less occasion. He has exercised a judicious caution in bringing practically only one Eastern figure, that of Saladin himself, upon his canvas, and avoiding the temptation to dwell upon anything but his personality. He says nothing definite of the Sultan's history, and by substituting him for his brother "Saphadin" in the story of the proposed marriage, he gets rid of the necessity for individualising a second important Moslem character; but Scott knew very well that it was to be an alliance between "Saphadin," not Saladin, and Joan of Sicily, not Edith. To avoid crowding the canvas with "inferior characters," to say nothing of lowering the dignity of the alliance, a stroke of the pen abolished both Joan and her proposed bridegroom. No one can deny that the story is all the better for it; and a footnote easily propitiates complaisant history.

But if Saladin was to marry Edith there must be a meeting; and so the ordeal by battle and the unhistorical slaughter of Conrad and the Master of the Temple (whose name was not "Sir Giles Amaury") serve also most conveniently to make the chief actors acquainted. It is possible that Scott was really unaware of the fact—somewhat singular, considering their close relations, both hostile and diplomatic—that Richard and Saladin never actually met face to face. The King twice proposed an interview, but in each case Saladin declined. It was "Saphadin" who really met Richard and exchanged much cordial hospitality, and who conducted all negotiations. Equally fictitious are Saladin's visit in the disguise of a *hakim*, and his solitary rides about the plains. The Sultan never travelled unattended; he generally had his guard of mamluks when he was anywhere near the enemy; and the chance encounter with Kenneth, the disguise and the talisman belong to the category of the "Thousand and One Nights." Nor can Scott honestly be justified in his description of Saladin's appearance. He says he was "in the very flower of his age," but Oriental flowers at fifty-four are apt to be faded; and he ventures to paint his portrait, which, to our loss, no contemporary Eastern attempted. All we know definitely about his face is that at fifty he wore a beard, and we only know this because he happened to tug at it during the battle of Hattin. Sir Walter has got the beard right, "a flowing and curled black beard," to boot, "which seemed trimmed with peculiar care"; but when he goes on to work in the nose, eyes, teeth, and forehead, he trusts to that admirable source, his own invention.

Setting aside these natural licences of the romancer, the portrait of Saladin is drawn with remarkable insight and accuracy. His gentleness, courtesy, and nobility of character, his justice, truthfulness, and generosity, which "The Talisman" has made familiar to so many readers who know nothing else in Mohammedan history, are set forth in every contemporary record. His rare bursts of passion, which Scott has finely rendered, were also historically part of his disposition. Unfortunately he seems to have never heard of Saladin's knighthood, and thereby we have probably lost a magnificent chapter. The general manner, dress, and so on are sufficiently Eastern, but show no minute study of the subject. The hatred of the Templars is another true touch. The two Military Orders were the only Christians to whom, as a class, Saladin showed no mercy: and he had his reasons. On the other hand, Scott is altogether wrong when he says that the Sultan "has been ever found" in "the front of battle," "nor is it his wont to turn his horse's head from any brave encounter." Saladin revelled in the sight of battle; "there was nothing he loved so much as a good knight," says Ernoul—witness his hearty admiration of the Green Knight of Spain—but he did not fight in person. He would fearlessly expose himself between the lines of battle, attended only by a groom with a spare horse, whilst the bolts and arrows whistled about his head; he would even make his chaplains read prayers under fire; and he would be seen in all parts of the field. But his duty as general, he conceived, was to lead, encourage, restrain, and order the disposition of the troops, not to engage in personal encounters; and so far as fighting went, a marshal's *bâton*, or Gordon's cane, would be his proper weapon. Conversing with the Bishop of Salisbury, after peace was made, he censured the rashness of the "Inkitar" Richard in mixing personally in the fray. That Scott played tricks with history is really nothing to the point; but that he was able, through the confused and imperfect records he used, to see and depict the true character of Saladin with remarkable accuracy, is but another proof of his genius.[107]

Though he is often accused of romanticising the life of Saladin, a careful reading of Lane-Poole's biography of the Kurd shows that he was perfectly aware of the limitations of Saladin's putative magnanimity. Robert Irwin misconstrues Lane-Poole entirely when he writes what he apparently takes to be a witty put-down of the historian: "In Lane-Poole's view, Saladin's 'chivalry to the crusaders was the good breading of a gentleman.' The Saladin created by Lane-Poole's pen was very gentle gentleman, a rather quiet scholarly figure (not perhaps so very different from Lane-Poole himself)."[108] Ho! Ho! Ho! Except the laughs are on Irwin who fails to read Lane-Poole attentively. First, Lane-Poole criticises Lessing for turning Saladin into a European, "The main defect, however, of Lessing's delineation (considered historically) is that it is too European. His Saladin is no real Saracen, as Scott's is."[109] Thus, Lane-Poole would not have dreamed of depicting Saladin as an Englishman like himself. Lane-Poole continues, "The set purpose of 'Nathan the Wise,' as a motive-drama, to preach toleration, and to silence the bigoted criticism of worthy pastor Goetze, compels Lessing to hold up Saladin as a type not only of a good Moslem, but a tolerant. The former he was, beyond question; *but tolerance was not his virtue* [Ibn Warraq's emphasis]; his chivalry and clemency were in act, not in thought. He could be kind to Christians, but he never doubted that they must eventually go down into the Pit. He had a holy horror of philosophy, free-thought, 'broad views', and all manner of heterodoxy. The only cruel act recorded against him, *outside the retaliations of war*, was the deliberate execution of a 'philosopher'—a mystic Sufi. *Like many fanatics* [I.W.'s emphasis], he could better tolerate the flat opposition of other religions than heresy within the pale of his own creed. His chivalry to crusaders was the good breeding of a gentleman; it did not touch his intellectual appreciation of their errors. He had a gentle soul and a soft heart, but they did not dispel his conviction that Christians were 'fuel for Hell'. He is a type of a true Moslem of the purest breed; Lessing gives him a theological latitude which he would have indignantly disowned."[110]

Earlier in his summing up of Saladin's life and character, Lane-Poole wrote, "his religion was all the world to him. In this alone he was fanati-

---

107 Stanley Lane-Poole, *Saladin and the Fall of Jerusalem*, London: Greenhill Books, 2002 [Ist Edn. 1898], pp. 262-264.

108 Robert Irwin, "Saladin and the Third Crusade" in ed, Michael Bentley, *Companion to Historiography*, London: Routledge, 1997, p. 144.

109 S. Lane-Poole, *op.cit.*, p. 265.

110 *Ibid.*, p. 266.

cal....In nothing did he show his religious zeal more fervently than in the chief and supreme duty of Moslems, the Jihad or Holy War. Naturally averse to bloodshed, even unwarlike, as he was, he was a changed man when it came to fighting the infidels. To wage God's war was a genuine passion with him, his whole heart was wrapped up in it, and to this cause he devoted himself, body and soul."[111] The totalitarian nature of Jihad is nowhere better expressed than in this anecdote that Lane-Poole repeats from Saladin's biographer Bahā' ad-Dīn, "Saladin even dreamed of wider battles for the faith: when the Franks should be driven out of Palestine, he told his secretary [Bahā' ad-Dīn], he would pursue them over the sea and conquer them, till there should not remain one unbeliever on the face of the earth."[112]

In other words, Lane-Poole is saying that to be a true Muslim you must pursue the totalitarian goal of turning the entire world Muslim, with the sword when necessary; that a true Muslim is not tolerant. In his world view, and the world view of all true Muslims, Christians and Jews are inferior, and treated accordingly—as *dhimmis*. But Lane-Poole and all other apologists of Saladin, do not write of the plight of non-Muslims in Islamic society. Certainly Lane-Poole was aware of Saladin's limitations, the necessary limitations of true Muslims, but does not spell out the consquences of such beliefs for non-Muslims. But I shall indeed look at the treatment of Jews and Christians during Saladin's times later in this chapter.

Nonetheless, Lane-Poole's history is written entirely from the Muslim point of view, a perspective that Gibb was also to take. Lane-Poole's account was the first account in English that took the trouble of going to the original Arabic sources, Bahā' ad-Dīn, Imād ad-Dīn, Ibn al-Athir, and for that reason is of historical importance. But Lane-Poole pays little heed to Saladin's early years, especially the Egyptian. And he seems to have been the originator of the view that Saladin, in his younger days, was essentially a shy retiring, unambitious youth who preferred a quiet seclusion to court intrigues, politics and war. His literary tastes were theological, and loved to hear passages from the Koran explained, and the origins of Traditions traced. He longed for nothing more than the discourse of pious men. But then he had greatness thrust upon him. He was dragged to Egypt against his will, but once there he acquired a passion for Jihad, a desire to found a Muslim empire strong enough to drive the infidels out of the land. Lane-Poole concluded, "Thenceforward his career was one long championship

---

111 *Ibid.*, pp. 250-251.
112 *Ibid.*, p. 251.

of Islam. He had vowed himself to the Holy War."[113]

Lane-Poole was, like Walter Scott, a child of the Scottish Enlightenment, brought up on ideas put forth by philosophers like William Roberston[114] who argued that non-European civilizations were at least the equal of, and perhaps even superior to, Western civilization. Lane-Poole clearly considers the Saracens far superior to the Crusaders. He wrote, "But the students of the Crusades do not need to be told that in this struggle the virtues of civilisation, magnanimity, toleration, real chivalry, and gentle culture, were all on the side of the Saracens."[115] This is quite an extraordinary statement. Lane-Poole is willing to overlook, minimize, or justify the acts of cruelty and barbarism of the Saracens under Saladin but not of the Crusaders. He had the Enlightenment contempt for Christianity, which prejudices and pervades his account of the Crusaders. It shows through on other occasions as when he mocks the very notion that anyone could possibly have the True Cross; what of imitations, he asks sarcastically. "There were doubtless several "'True Crosses'—and imitations," wrote Lane-Poole.[116] I cannot imagine him mocking Muslim beliefs in the same way; there were enough examples of absurdities in the Islamic faith had he so wished, including the superstition that Muhammad ascended heaven from Jerusalem on Buraq—a steed with with wings and a "handsome head." Lane-Poole was also writing at a moment in history when Islamic culture and civilization was at a low ebb, and to kick it at a time when it was on its knees, and so degraded was not very gentlemanly. Least of all was Islam a threat to the West, and hence he could quietly disquisit on Jihad without thinking it would ever pose any dangers.

C 2. SIR HAMILTON GIBB

Two biographies appeared within a few months of each other in the early 1970s—Sir Hamilton Gibb's *The Life of Saladin from the works of 'Imād ad-Dīn and Bahā' ad-Dīn* in 1973, and Andrew S. Ehrenkreutz's *Saladin* in 1972. No two works of history could be more different, where Gibb's Saladin is highly idealised, relies largely on two hagiographical primary sources, and where the Muslim leader is seen as an exemplary hero of Islam, Ehrenkreutz paints a critical portrait of a ruthless and ambitious

---

113 *Ibid.*, p. 89.

114 William Robertson, *An historical disquisition concerning the knowledge which the ancients had of India*, Edinburgh, (1791).

115 S. Lane-Poole, *op. cit.*, p. 213.

116 *Ibid.*, p. 211, footnote.

politician, and relies on diverse Arabic primary sources such as Ibn al-Athir who passed some harsh judgements on the Kurd.

Sir Hamilton Gibb was preparing *The Life of Saladin* shortly before his death in 1971. He had already written extensively of Saladin in various learned journals. His biography is terse, well-footnoted, and written entirely from the Muslim perspective. Every Crusader defeat is a triumph, and every Muslim rout is defended as not being as bad as it seems.

I think we need to have some idea of Gibb's general views on religion and on Islam in particular to appreciate what he admired in Saladin, and what he believed was his true achievement. Gibb was an intensely religious man who worried that Islam was exposed to great dangers, and would be attacked by the corroding acids of the twentieth century: "The external pressure of secularism, whether in the seductive form of nationalism, or in the doctrines of scientific materialism and the economic interpretation of history, has already left its mark on several sections of Muslim society." But the greatest danger to Islam was "the relaxation of the religious conscience and the weakening of the catholic tradition of Islam." In modern times, Gibb feared that the Muslims would discard the Sharia, the Sacred Law, with disastrous consequences, "Modern governments,…when they legislate changes in the sphere of the Sharī'a have done so because by influential sections of contemporary Muslims the classical Sharī'a is regarded as no longer adequate and sufficient interpretation of the moral imperative. Yet if the Sacred Law is wholly dethroned the link with the historic Community is broken; and the popular movements have demonstrated that the appeal to the Sharī'a can still be an effective instrument to energize the demand for social justice. Thus the task before the spiritual leadership of Islam today is not to fight a stubborn rearguard action, but to close the widening rifts within the Community by enlisting its creative participation in the effort to reformulate and reactivate the Sharī'a as a valid way of life in the new and changing conditions."[117]

And that is exactly, according to Gibb, what Saladin had achieved several hundred years earlier, he had saved Islam: Saladin reintroduced the Sharī'a, and closed the rifts within the Community: "[Saladin] saw clearly that the weakness of the Muslim body politic, which had permitted the establishment and continued to permit the survival of the crusading states, was the result of political demoralization. It was against this that he revolted. There was only one way to end it: to restore and revive the political fabric of Islam as a single united empire, not under his own rule, but by

---

117 H.A.R. Gibb, *Islam*, Oxford: Oxford University Press, 1978 [1st Edition, 1949], p. 131.

restoring the rule of the revealed law [Sharī'a], under the direction of the Abbassid Caliphate."[118]

Gibb wrote in *Saladin*: "If the war to which he had vowed himself against the Crusaders was to be a real jihad, a true 'Holy War', it was imperative to conduct it with scrupulous observance of the revealed Law of Islam. A government that sought to serve the cause of God in battle must be not only a lawful government, duly authorized by the supreme representative of the Divine Law, but must serve God with equal zeal in its administration and its treatment of its subjects. In brief, Saladin's object was to restore to Islamic politics the reign of law, a concept that had become for the contemporary princes not only an empty phrase but an absurdity."[119]

Thus certain "sections of contemporary Muslims" are one with "contemporary princes" of Saladin's times in their contempt for the Sacred Law, Sharī'a. Saladin was not, says Gibb, a great military general or strategist, nor was he a successful administrator, the real explanation of his success lies elsewhere: "Himself neither warrior nor governor by training or inclination, he it was who inspired and gathered round himself all the elements and forces making for the unity of Islam against the invaders. And this he did, not so much by the example of personal courage and resolution—which were undeniable—as by his unselfishness, his humility and generosity, his moral vindication of Islam against both its enemies and its professed adherents. He was no simpleton, but for all that an utterly simple and transparently honest man. He baffled his enemies, internal and external, because they expected to find him animated by the same motives as they were, and playing the political game as they played it. Guileless himself, he never expected and seldom understood guile in others—a weakness of which his own family and others took advantage, but only (as a general rule) to come up at the end against his single-minded devotion, which nobody and nothing could bend, to the service of his ideals."[120]

Saladin's achievements were moral, religious and spiritual; he was not someone motivated by "personal ambition and lust of conquest, and who merely exploited religious catchwords and sentiments to achieve their own ends," rather, "his career involved distinctive moral elements which gave his initial victory and subsequent struggle with the Third Crusade a qual-

118 H.A.R. Gibb, "The Achievement of Saladin," in *Bulletin of the John Rylands Library*, 35, no. 1 (Manchester, 1952) pp. 44-60.

119 H.A.R. Gibb, *The Life of Saladin*, foreword by Robert Irwin, London: Saqi Books, 2006, [Ist Edn. Oxford University Press, 1973], p. 19.

120 H.A.R. Gibb, "The Achievement of Saladin," in *Bulletin of the John Rylands Library*, 35, no. 1 (Manchester, 1952) pp. 44-60.

ity of its own."[121] His moral and religious convictions resulted in Muslim unity, and a revival of Islamic values.

C.3 ANDREW S. EHRENKREUTZ

Andrew S. Ehrenkreutz's *Saladin* could not be more different. But before I delineate his thesis, and his assessment of Saladin's career, I need to establish Ehrenkreutz's credentials. In the foreward to a new edition of Gibb's biography of Saladin, Robert Irwin refers to Ehrenkreutz's work only to dismiss it with a quotation from a hostile review by D.S. Richards, a very distinguished scholar, expert on the Arabic sources for the Crusades, and Emeritus Fellow of St. Cross College, University of Oxford. Richards wrote, "One approaches Ehrenkreutz's work with ready sympathy, hoping for a satisfactory re-examination of Saladin's career, because, seductive though it maybe, Gibb's view seems just too good to be true. There are, however, such a number of inaccuracies, major and minor mistakes, slanted or unsupportable interpretations of texts, that one's sympathy evaporates and one begins to feel that perhaps Gibb's Saladin is a more acceptable figure after all."[122]

The review is well-worth reading, and well-argued. Significantly, Richards takes issue with Gibb's interpretation as well.[123] Different interpretations of the life of Saladin depend on what we can justifiably assert about his motives—the inner view. Richards tells us that Gibb himself expressed "doubts about the possibility of penetrating the façade of available Muslim historiography into the secret rooms of individual personalities. Hence the basis of Gibb's writings on Saladin was a close analysis of the various sources, and he came to the conclusion that certain contemporaries, above all 'Imād al-Dīn and Bahā' al-Dīn, though recognized at the outset to be favourable, as opposed, say, to Ibn al-Athīr, could be relied upon to give an honest, inside view of Saladin as man and statesman, and to enable us today to form a clear picture of his motives."[124]

But, argues Richards, "It may well be that Gibb went too far in this. For example, with the dispatches and letters of al-Qādī al-Fādil, despite his own caveat, perhaps Gibb drew too close a tie between the public pronouncements and 'Saladin's real purposes and ideals'. Perhaps too he over-

---

121 *Ibid.*, p. 44.

122 D.S. Richards, "The Early History of Saladin" in *Islamic Quarterly*, 17, 9173, pp. 158-159.

123 For example, *Ibid.*, pp. 157, 158.

124 D.S. Richards, *op. cit.*, p. 141.

estimated the concreteness of some elements in the sources."[125]

But then Richards follows with his substantial criticism of Ehren-kreutz's work: "Ehrenkreutz has two interesting passages (pp. 3 and 237) on aspects of the chronicles of the time that link them up with the 'Mirror for Princes' genre, suggesting that historical characters are presented with the attributes, and in the typical situations, of the ideal types of that litera-ture. That the historians of the time had a moralizing, didactic end in view is often made quite clear in their own writings. ... Ehrenkreutz manifestly believes that Gibb did go too far, but, while Gibb's attitude to his sources is clear and consistent, I do not find this to be true of Ehrenkreutz. His criticism of Gibb's view of Saladin[126] implies that he rejects the evaluation of the special nature of the sources that made that inner view possible. On what basis then does Ehrenkreutz proceed to give a radically different in-ner view of Saladin without fresh documentation of the required nature? The sources cherished by Gibb project a vivid picture; if one denies these sources their special insight, and they are left as public pronouncements of policy, propaganda claims, didactic image-making, then they cannot be used to uncover some other 'inner' Saladin, because their special stand-ing has gone. His personality, his 'real purposes and ideals', must remain obscure; and how much the more so if one has frequent recourse to a frankly hostile source, Ibn al-Athir, for whom no one would claim any special standing and whose view of Saladin must remain external—for, in essence, while Gibb takes the twin part of 'Imad al-Din and Baha' al-Din, Ehrenkreutz plays Ibn al-Athir despite Gibb's close, technical criticism of his account. Ehrenkreutz writes of 'using more realistic perspectives' (p. 9), while he gives subjective interpretation of the motives behind the narrative of events, as told by himself, Many may find it hard to accept Gibb's view of Saladin in toto, for it could be argued that his attitude to the sources is fundamentally circular, yet many will find it hard to accept Ehrenkreutz's view, which swings far in the opposite direction and is less accurately based on the texts, however interpreted."[127]

But precisely what is compelling about Ehrenkreutz's account is not his interpretation of Saladin's motives, but the displaying of those acts of the Sultan which had hitherto been relegated to an obscure background—

---

125 *Ibid.*, p. 141.

126 Ehrenkreutz did not have access to Gibb's *Life of Saladin*, under discussion in my essay, since it was published a year after Ehrenkreutz's work. Ehrenkreutz was referring to Gibb's essays such as "The Achievement of Saladin," "The Rise of Saladin," "The Armies of Saladin," etc.

127 D.S. Richards, *op,cit.*, pp. 141-142.

particularly the acts of his years in Egypt. Who is Ehrenkreutz? Andrew Ehrenkreutz [1921-2008] completed his doctorate at the University of London's School of Oriental Studies, under Bernard Lewis. In 1953 Ehrenkreutz accepted a post-doctorate fellowship to Yale University, and in the summer of 1954 he moved to Ann Arbor as a visiting lecturer in Islamic History at the University of Michigan. From 1967-85 he was professor in both the departments of Near Eastern Studies and History. He was a recognized authority on the economic problems of the Near East in the period of the Crusaders.

If Robert Irwin, in dismissing Ehrenkreutz, was using an argument from authority (in this case the authority of D.S. Richards), I can come up with a far greater number of recognized authorities on the Crusades or Islamic history who wrote favourable reviews of Ehrenkreutz's book.

C.3.1. P.M. Holt [1918-2006] was Emeritus Professor of the History of the Near and Middle East at the School of Oriental and African Studies of London University. "He was a historian of the Middle East, broadly interpreted: his main interests, geographically, were in Sudan, Egypt and Syria. Later in life, he concluded, as so many good historians do, that the Middle Ages were far more interesting than the modern period, and he concentrated on Syria and Egypt during the Crusades and in the Mameluke era which began in 1250."[128]

Holt reviewed Gibb and Ehrenkreutz together.[129] He found Gibb more than unjust towards Ibn al-Athir, "The chronicler Ibn al-Athir, although also a contemporary, was a Zangid partisan, and is impugned in [Gibb's] book more severely than any of Gibb's previous writings. This may occasion some demur: granted that Ibn al-Athir can be inaccurate in detail, and that he displays a known bias (which may therefore be discounted), his testimony should not be ruled completely out of court. Even as an *advocatus diaboli*, he may help in the assessment of motive."

Holt continues, "With Ehrenkreutz's book (which was published some months before Gibb's) there appears a reaction against the eulogies of Saladin, of which the 'standard biography' by Stanley Lane-Poole is a notable example. Ehrenkreutz himself has an established reputation for his scholarly work in the monetary and economic history of the medieval Middle East. ... His approach is in accordance with present-day trends in

---

128 Obituary in *The Independent*, 28 November, 2006 by David Morgan.

129 P.M. Holt, Review of: Hamilton Gibb, *The Life of Saladin from the works of 'Imād ad-Dīn and Bahā' ad-Dīn* (1973); *Saladin* by Andrew S. Ehrenkreutz in *Bulletin of the School of Oriental and African Studies*,[London] Vol.36, No.3 (1973), pp. 651-652.

historical writing on the period: the treatment of the Crusader states as one among several military and political factors in the region, the presentation of Saladin and his predecessors, Nur al-Din and Zangi, as Middle Eastern war-lords operating within a complex web of local politics, the concept of jihad less as a motive for their actions than as the content of their propaganda. A balanced reassessment of Saladin is needed, and *Ehrenkreutz makes several contributions to this, particularly on the economic aspects of the period.*" [Ibn Warraq's emphasis.]

However, Holt takes issue with Ehrenkreutz's manner of presentation with its colloquialisms: "Although the work is based on a wide range of both primary and secondary sources, and is very fully and usefully documented in its notes, the author seems to have written for a general rather than an academic readership. He is not averse to colloquialisms."

C.3.2. Dr. Hans Eberhard Mayer [born 1932] was Professor of Medieval and Modern History at the University of Kiel. His research contributed significantly to the shift in modern scholarly understandings of the crusades in the later half of the twentieth-century. Mayer's most influential work was *The Crusades*, first published in English in 1972. He is considered the leading historian of the Crusades writing in German today. A *festschrift*, with articles from all the greatest historians of the Crusades in the West was presented to him in 1997.[130]

In his review of Ehrenkreutz's biography of Saladin,[131] Mayer also finds Ehrenkreutz's manner of presentation grating, and his introduction of modern conceptions into the Middle Ages where they do not apply illegitimate. Mayer thinks Ehrenkreutz's decision to limit the account of Saladin's war against the Crusaders to 29 pages leads to misleading statements. Mayer takes issue with Ehrenkreutz's analysis of the siege of Tyre, and the reasons for Saladin's haste in capturing Jerusalem. So much for Mayer's negative criticisms of Ehrenkreutz's work. Not only does Mayer have substantial praise for certain aspects of Ehrenkreutz's thesis, contradicting D.S. Richards, but also concludes that many others had arrived at similar conclusions before him.

Mayer writes, "The book is an attempt at *Entmythologisierung* [demythologising], of stripping Saladin of the halo with which Lane Poole in his

---

130 Benjamin Z. Kedar, Jonathan Riley-Smith, Rudolf Hiestand (eds.), Montjoie. *Studies in Crusade History in Honour of Hans Eberhard Mayer*, Aldershot. 1997.

131 Hans Eberhard Mayer. Review of *Saladin* by Andrew S.Ehrenkeurtz, in *Speculum* [Published by Medieval Academy of America], Vol. 49, No. 4 (October, 1974) pp. 724-727.

classical biography had suurounded him. In this the book has the merit of assembling what has been done already in this field into one convenient volume, thus presenting to the general public a fairer view of Saladin than did Lane Poole. For the scholar there is not much that is new and has not already been said in the writings of Minorsky,[132] Cahen[133] and Prawer.[134] On the scholarly level, the revision was accomplished by them rather than by Ehrenkreutz."

Mayer continues, "As a consequence of his objectives the author concentrates not so much on the famous wars of Saladin against the Crusaders as on his rise in Egypt and his conquests in Syria and Mesopotamia. There is virtue in this, although basically the shift in emphasis was made by others before. Studying this rise to power inevitably leads to the conclusion that Saladin was not always the gentlemanly enemy he was depicted as being. He could be quite ruthless when he chose to be or when political expediency demanded it."

Mayer even singles out one of Ehrenkreutz's genuinely new viewpoints: "On the other hand, Saladin's dependency on the Egyptian war effort and the growing estrangement from his secretary al-Fadil on this account is well-brought out in this book, and to the best of my knowledge this is a genuinely new viewpoint."

In the last paragraph of his review, Mayer takes issue with Gibb's thesis, "Whether Saladin should really be considered as the champion of Muslim unity, as Sir Hamilton Gibb suggested, and whether this was his prime objective rather than the aggrandizement of the Ayyubid family, or whether the expulsion of the Crusaders from the Holy Land was for Saladin an end in itself, to which the power buildup in the Muslim world was only a prelude, is hard to tell, although Ehrenkreutz is probably correct in echoing Prawer's sentiments that Saladin was a clever politician rather than a hero of the faith....In support of Ehrenkreutz's views one would also wish for more emphasis on the fact that Saladin is not always eulogized in Muslim sources; the Mosul chroniclers are highly critical of him."

---

132 Vladimir Minorsky [1877-1966], *Studies in Caucasian History*: I. New light on the Shaddādids of Ganja. II. The Shaddādids of Ani. III. Prehistory of Saladin, London: Taylor's Foreign Press, 1953.

133 Claude Cahen, *La Syrie du Nord a l'époque des croisades et la principuaté franque d'Antioche*, Paris, 1940; "Ayyubids" s.v. in *The Encyclopaedia of Islam*, 2ed. I: 796-807, Leiden, 1960.

134 Joshua Prawer. *Histoire du royaume latin de Jérusalem*, Traduit de l'hébreu par G. Nahon. Revu et complété par l'auteur. Imprint Paris, Éditions du Centre National de la Recherche Scientifique, 1969-70.

C.3.3. Ira Lapidus [born c. 1935] is an Emeritus Professor of History, Islamic Social History at The University of California at Berkeley, and the author of *A History of Islamic Societies*, and *Contemporary Islamic Movements in Historical Perspective,* among other works.

As an undergraduate at Harvard, he took a course in Middle Eastern history taught by none other than Sir Hamilton Gibb. Lapidus wrote a very positive account of Ehrenkreutz's work,[135] praising his biography of Saladin from the opening lines of the review, "The subject of Saladin is fun, and Professor Ehrenkreutz gives an attractive and interesting account of his political career. In the main, Saladin's career is well known, but Professor Ehrenkreutz nonetheless presents new information carefully culled from the Arabic sources. Saladin's family background and early life are embellished with fresh and illuminating detail…. Professor Ehrenkreutz gives us an amplified account of Saladin's succession to the generalship of the Syrian forces in Egypt, his accession to the Fatimid wazirate, his consolidation of power, and the return of Egypt to Sunni and Abbasid allegiance."

Lapidus continues, "Saladin's subsequent career as ruler of Egypt is well known. Professor Ehrenkreutz confirms that his ambition in the main, was to recapture the former Zengid [Zangid] domains in Syria and Mesopotamia, while his interest in the jihad and war against the Crusaders was clearly secondary, despite his constant propaganda to the contrary. However Professor Ehrenkreutz takes a new and dim view of Saladin's final struggle with the Crusaders. The great battle of Hattin is only partly to his credit, for Christian mistakes seem to have been decisive. His campaigns against Tyre and Acre, Professor Ehrenkreutz sees as failures and, indeed, disasters…. The protracted sieges of Tyre and Acre, which Gibb interprets as a moral triumph frustrated by circumstances, Professor Ehrenkreutz sees as a failure of political will, and indeed, as a moral failure in a man whose conquests were without moral and ideological purpose."

However Lapidus' main criticisms of his work are that (1) Ehrenkreutz overstates the case against Saladin, whose priority has to have been the conquest of Muslim states before he could even contemplate the liquidation of the Crusaders, and (2) Ehrenkreutz fails to put Saladin into the context of the society of his times, and thus cannot adequately evaluate Saladin's person and career.

But Lapidus agrees with Ehrenkreutz that "Saladin, as he emerges in Lane Poole and Gibb, heroic and pure, is surely a product of roman-

---

135 Ira M. Lapidus, Reiview of *Saladin* by Andrew S. Ehrenkreutz in *Journal of the American Oriental Society,* Vol. 94, No. 2 (Apr.-Jun., 1974), pp. 240-241. Published by American Oriental Society.

tic imagination. Professor Ehrenkreutz makes it clear that Saladin, from youth to old age, was a ruthless, ambitious and energetic seeker after power, a pragmatist rather than an idealist in politics."

Then, irony of ironies, Lapidus accuses Ehrenkreutz of also harbouring a streak of romanticism about Saladin: "Yet the temptation to hagiography lives on. Ehrenkreutz himself speaks of the '...valor, determination, and inspiring leadership of Saladin....'(p.43)." Ehrenkreutz also wrote, "[Saladin] revealed himself not only as a competent and courageous field commander, but as an inspiring leader of men...." (p.44).

Lapidus continues, "In little ways, Professor Ehrenkreutz shows that he too has a streak of romaticism about Saladin—albeit a reverse romanticism about Saladin attracted by political and military adventure, which maybe amoral and surely leads to disaster, but fascinating nonetheless. Saladin wasn't a good good-guy, he was a bad good-guy."

The final assessment is that though there is still place for a new contextual biography of Saladin, "[Ehrenkreutz's] contribution to a meticulous and precise biographical account of the events of Saladin's life is much appreciated."

C.3.4. Wilferd Madelung [born 1930] was a professor of Islamic history at the University of Chicago, and Laudian Professor of Arabic at the University of Oxford from 1978 to 1998. He is the author of many works including, *Religious Trends in Early Islamic Iran*, 1988 and *Religious and Ethnic Movements in Medieval Islam*, 1992. Madelung wrote a joint review of Gibb and Ehrenkreutz.[136]

Madelung wrote, "Gibb's treatment of the Ayyubid sultan [i.e. Saladin, son of Ayyub] in many respects followed the precedents set by S. Lane-Poole who, in 1898, wrote the first well-documented biography of Saladin as an enthusiastic admirer of his chivalrous virtues. It is against this romantic view of the Ayyubid that Professor Ehrenkreutz proposes to offer a more sober, realistic assessment of his aims and accomplishments. While his earlier biographers concentrated most of their attention on Saladin's struggle with the crusaders in the last phase of his life, Ehrenkreutz carefully investigates his youth and early career. Against Lane-Poole's characterization of Saladin as a naïve and retiring youth who against his will was thrust by events into a position political and military leadership, [Ehrenkreutz] shows that Saladin's early training, his ambition, and various posi-

---

136 Wilferd Madelung, Review of *Saladin* by Andrew S. Ehrenkreutz; Hamilton Gibb, *The Life of Saladin from the works of 'Imād ad-Dīn and Bahā' ad-Dīn* in *Journal of Near Eastern Studies*, Vol. 34. No. 3 (Jul., 1975), pp. 209-212.

tions of responsibility held earlier made him a most suitable candidate for the succession of his uncle Shirkuh as leader of the Syrian troops in Egypt and Fatimid vizier. Against Gibb's view that Saladin's campaigns against the Zangids in Syria and Mesopotamia were necessitated by their hostility and willingness to cooperate with the crusaders, whose expulsion always was his primary aim, Ehrenkreutz argues that Saladin was rather motivated by insatiable ambitions of territorial expansion against his Muslim neighbours for which he squandered the resources of Egypt while showing little concern for jihad against the infidels except for propaganda purposes."

Madelung is very skeptical of Gibb's reliance on Bahā' al-Dīn and 'Imād al-Dīn which "is generally justified as far as their account of events is concerned for they had the advantage of being eye witnesses. But does this mean that they are exempt from the pervading partisan commitment characteristic of the historiography of this age? 'Imād al-Dīn's history of the Saljūqs is known to conceal a strong Shāfi'ite bias. There is good reason to think that his accounts of Saladin's career, though generally accurate, does at times contain less than the full truth. The accounts of Ibn Abī Tayyi' and Ibn al-Athīr, though the latter is manifestly often inaccurate in factual reports, deserve serious consideration as a corrective taking into account their particular bias."

Madelung argues that "Gibb in relying solely on 'Imād al-Dīn and Bahā' al-Dīn failed to undertsand the roots and nature of Saladin's conflict with Nūr al-Dīn and his Zangid heirs." Then Madelung endorses Ehrenkreutz whose "criticism of this [i.e. Gibb's] interpretation appears basically sound." Madelung does take issue with some of Ehrenkreutz's own interpretations, but, concludes, "Despite such flaws, Ehrenkreutz's book deserves full credit for having put the biography of Saladin on a realistic historical basis."

C.3.5 Other Reviews of Ehrenkreutz's Work

Professor Michael Dols of California State University wrote,[137] "Scholarly and immensely thorough, Professor Ehrenkreutz's work is a persuasive revision of the interpretation of Saladin presented primarily by Stanley Lane-Poole and Sir Hamilton Gibb." Dols places himself between the two poles: Saladin was neither so naïve as Gibb as would have us believe nor as unscrupulous as Ehrenkreutz contends.

Dr Harris Nierman (Flushing, New York), an expert on the Crusades

---

137 Michael W. Dols, Review of Andrew S. Ehrenkreutz's *Saladin* in *International Journal of Middle East Studies*, Vol. 4, No. 4, (Oct., 1973), pp. 489-491.

and Medieval Islam wrote[138] that Ehrenkreutz's work was welcome and a much needed corrective to Gibb (Lane-Poole). He also thinks Ehrenkreutz thesis was anticipated by Emmanuel Sivan in his *L'Islam et la croisade: Idéologie et propagande dans les réactions musulmanes aux croisades* (1969) but concludes: "Professor Ehrenkreutz's work both revises our conception of Saladin and propounds a meaningful thesis concerning the sultan's role in Egyptian history. This is a highly readable portrait that should become familiar to all those interested in Middle Eastern or medieval history."

C.3 ANDREW EHRENKREUTZ'S *SALADIN*

At last, we come to Ehrenkreutz himself. In his introduction, Ehrenkreutz immediately sets out his thesis, and lays out his differences with Lane-Poole and Gibb, at the same time giving a survey of the field singling out historians who had anticipated his own conclusions. For example, in his article on the "Ayyubids" in the Second Edition of the *Encyclopaedia of Islam*, distinguished French historian Claude Cahen [1909-1991] wrote, "[Saladin] adopted the idea (of the holy war), though it is not possible to discern to what extent ambition was combined with undoubtedly sincere conviction." While Joshua Prawer in his magnum opus, *Histoire du Royaume Latin de Jérusalem*, Paris, 1969, complained that, "Modern historians, seduced by Arabic sources, have sometimes been misled by their tendentious character....There prevails among historians a tendency to attribute a single, dominating idea (*une pensée directrice*) to all of Saladin's actions from the day he seized power in Egypt (1169) to his death, twenty-four years later (1193)....A critical biography of the hero of Islamic history is still lacking."

For Ehrenkreutz, it is obvious that "the political, social, and economic climate prevailing in the Near East in the second half of the twelfth century was not conducive to seeking power through the exercise of tolerance, magnanimity, chivalry, or any altruistic behavior. Besides suffering from the intrusion of the Crusaders, the Byzantines, and the Turkomans, Near Eastern society was torn asunder by factional infighting at all levels of the political hierarchy. In the merciless struggle—whether between the Sunni caliphate of the Abbasids and the Shiite caliphate of the Fatimids, the Saljuqid sultans and the Arab emirs, or between local dynasts and ambitious atabegs—all means were employed to achieve victory. Ideologi-

---

138 Harris Nierman, Review of *Saladin* by Andrew S. Ehrenkreutz; Hamilton Gibb, *The Life of Saladin from the works of 'Imād ad-Dīn and Bahā' ad-Dīn* in *The American Historical Review*, Vol. 79, No. 2 (Apr., 1974), pp. 501-502.

cal or religious principles were readily compromised; the presence of the Crusaders primarily furnished an opportunity for expanding diplomatic intrigues, or for promoting selfish propaganda, rather than uniting the leaders in a sincere effort to defend Islam. Hence one finds Sunni viziers and jurists in the service of the Shiite Fatimids, military assistance rendered by Arab tribes to the Crusaders, or an alliance between Muslim Damascus and and the Latin Kingdom of Jerusalem. In this dangerous political game there was no place for people lacking ambition or leadership qualities. To become a contender one needed the support of a family or a faction; to overcome other contenders one required proper military training, political and diplomatic skills, as well as a natural talent of charismatic leadership. Above all, one needed a lot of luck!" [pp. 7-8.]

SKEPTICISM OF THE LANE-POOLE - GIBB ACCOUNT OF SALADIN'S YOUNGER DAYS

First, Ehrenkreutz carefully dismantles the idea that Saladin was a shy, retiring, unambitious goody-goody. We know from Bahā' al-Dīn and Abu Shama that early in 1169, Saladin "renounced wine, gave up vain pastimes and donned the garments of seriousness and pious endeavour."[139] Ehrenkreutz draws the obvious conclusion: "that until he turned thirty-one, Saladin had not always been averse to drinking and other wordly temptations. And it would indicate that the young officer was not too strongly influenced by the moral example of Nur al-Din, who was well known for his ardent attachment to religion and for his scrupulous ob-servance of Islamic precepts. In any event, Saladin never performed the piligrimage to Mecca, in spite of the fact that in 1157 Ayyub [his father] and 1160 Shirkuh [his uncle], each led a caravan of pilgrims from Damas-cus. In 1161 Shirkuh once again served as the leader of the pilgrim caravan which included the mighty Nur al-Din himself. In spite of these examples set by father, his uncle, and his influential superior, Saladin did not avail himself of those opportunities to fulfill the fundamental religious obliga-tion incumbent on every Muslim." [pp. 32-33.]

Lyons and Jackson go even further and quote Western sources which tell us that Saladin, "that patron of prostitutes whose power was among stews, his campaigns in taverns, his studies among dice and garlic, is sud-

---

139 Bahā' al-Dīn Ibn Shaddād, *The Rare and Excellent History of Saladin or al-Nawādir al-Sultāniyya wa'l-Mahāsin al-Yūsufiyya*, trans. D.S. Richards, Ashgate: Aldershot, 2002, p. 45.

denly lifted up; he sits among princes and is even greater than princes."[140]

As for the putative lack of ambition on the part of Saladin, Ehrenkreutz argues that such a picture is very unlikely: "In view of Saladin's intimate association with his immediate family it is difficult to imagine him unaffected by their military and political ambitions....Had he resented the atmosphere of political pressures and intrigues, he need not have entered military service in Aleppo. As it was, his meritorious performance attracted the eye of the stern sultan, who set him right on the same path taken by other members of his family." [p. 33.]

Saladin was sent on the Egyptian expedition. "The intervention in Egypt was not regarded as a minor operation but as a hazardous campaign with no place for novices or lukewarm participants. Only experienced officers and troops deserved the distinction of taking part in the expedition. Had Saladin shown any aversion to military and political activities, he need not have joined the expeditionary force. Had Saladin not been militarily and politically competent, he could hardly have been included in the officer staff. The selection of Ayyub's son [Saladin] to participate in that difficult and dangerous military operation suggests that at age twenty-six, Saladin enjoyed the reputation of a trustworthy and competent warrior." [p. 33.]

SALADIN IN EGYPT

According to Ehrenkreutz it did not take Saladin long to establish, in Egypt, a reputation as "a man of trust, of intrepid action, who accepted bloody extermination as a political tool." Saladin's promotion to the vizirate of Egypt involved "a series of political maneuvers among a number of pressure groups." The political scene in Cairo was complicated and dangerous, thus "the elevation of Saladin to the vizirate once again revealed his reputation of being an experienced, trustworthy, and ambitious leader of men." Essentially, Saladin's poltical behaviour, *pace* Lane-Poole and Gibb, "did not differ in spirit and methods from that of other medieval military leaders."

SALADIN'S BLOODY SUPPRESSION OF THE REBELLION OF THE BLACK SUDANESE SOLDIERS

140 Malcolm C. Lyons and D.E.P. Jackson, *Saladin: The Politics of the Holy War*, Cambridge: Cambridge University Press, 1982 [Canto (Paperback) Edition, 1997], p. 32.

When Sudanese soldiers rose in arms against the new vizir, that is, Saladin, and his people, Saladin suppressed the rebellion with a ferocity that is breathtaking, and belies his later reputation as a man of generosity and clemency:

> While the battle was raging in the Bain al-Qasrain area [of Cairo, between the Sudanese and Saladin's troops], Saladin proceeded with a gruesome measure against the mutinous Sudanese. With only women and children left in the Sudanese barracks outside the Zuwayla Gate, Saladin's soldiers suddenly appeared and set fire to the entire area." When the Sudanese started to retreat, Saladin's troops burned house after house sheltering the fleeing Sudanese. After two days of fighting the Sudanese agreed to surrender "if Saladin would offer them a safe-conduct. Their request was granted on condition that they promise to leave Cairo. The defeated and disarmed Sudanese marched out and set up their camp in Giza, where—in cynical violation of the safe-conduct pledge—they were massacred in cold blood by Shams al-Dawlah, Saladin's brother. Only a small fraction of the original slave guard regiments survived the blood bath, and escaping to Upper Egypt, they were hunted down by Shibab al-Din al-Harimi who was assigned that mission by Saladin himself.
>
> Outside the Zuwayla Gate, the smoldering ruins of the Sudanese barracks poignantly illustrated the kind of retaliation Saladin would mete out to those who dared to challenge his authority, Indeed to erase all vestiges of the long predominance of the Sudanese guards in Cairo, the barrack area of al-Mansura was ploughed over and later turned into a garden." The property of the Sudanese was seized all over the country, thus, "Not only was Saladin's authority decisively affirmed, but the task of financing his new army was made easier by this quick if bloody elimination of some 50,000 Fatimid soldiers."

Not bad for a shy retiring scholar who preferred the discourse of pious men.

To show that Ehrenkreutz is not exaggerating, I shall quote from Ibn Al-Athir's account in his celebrated history, *al-Kamil fi'l-Ta'rikh*:

The black slaves in old Cairo were angry at the killing of Mu'tamin al-Khilāfa out of loyalty and because he had been strong in their support. They assembled their forces, which numbered more than 50,000, with every intention of making war on Saladin's troops. His force gathered together and met the blacks in Bayn al-Qasrayn. On both sides many were killed. Saladin sent to their quarter, known as al-Mansūra, and burned it down about their possessions, *children and women-folk* [Ibn Warraq's emphasis]. When they received intelligence of this, they turned their backs in flight and were harried by the sword. The mouths of the alleys were blocked against them, so they asked for terms after great slaughter had been done on them. Terms were granted and they were sent out of Old Cairo to Giza. Then Shams al-Dawla Tūranshāh, Saladin's brother, crossed over to them with a detachment of the army and annihilated them by the sword. Only the rare fugitive escaped. God Almighty dealt with their wickedness—God knows best."[141]

Saladin took control, suppressed the Shiite (Fatimid) caliphate, and became the new master of Egypt. But as Ehrenkreutz concludes, "As a result of his suppressing the Shiite caliphate, Saladin became known as an idealistic leader dedicated to the cause of Islamic unity—a reputation which has influenced some of his modern admirers. In reality, Saladin was a pragmatist pursuing power-oriented self-serving ambitions. This motivation guided his policy towards Nur al-Din, which pushed the Muslim forces of Egypt and Syria to the brink of bloody confrontation." [p. 97.]

When in March 1174, Saladin heard of a pro-Fatimid, *i.e.*, Shiite, conspiracy, he took careful steps to put it down with characteristic ruthlessness. In April, mass arrests began, and one after another the chief conspirators were sought out, brought before Saladin. A special panel of Sunni jurists was set up, and it sentenced the principal culprits to death by crucifixion, and their followers to banishment. "For several days beginning 6 April, Cairo residents witnessed a gruesome spectacle, where much of Egypt's former elite were crucified one after another. The first to go was the brilliant poet, Umarah. ... Also executed in Cairo were Abd al-Samad, Shubruma and his accomplices, a number of Saladin's commanders and

---

141 Ibn al-Athir, *The Chronicle of Ibn al-Athir for the Crusading Period from al-Kamil fi'l-Ta'rikh*, Part 2, trans. D.S. Richards, Surrey [U.K.]: Ashgate Publishing Ltd., 2007, p. 180.

regular soldiers, and some slaves and followers of the conspirators....By this well-planned, bloody operation, Saladin destroyed the last remaining nerve center of Fatimid opposition and averted the outbreak of new fighting and internal disorder in Egypt and her capital." [pp. 114-115.] Again, these events are vividly chronicled in Ibn al-Athir.[142]

OTHER EXAMPLES OF SALADIN'S VINDICTIVENESS, AND CRUELTY

Saladin did not show much mercy to the Crusaders taken prisoner after the latter's unsuccessful attack on the town of Hama in August 1178. As Ehrenkreutz says, "The prisoners of war were delivered to Saladin. If some of them expected magnanimity from the Muslim leader, they were in for tragic disappointment. Saladin still smarted from his last confrontation with the Crusaders; the prisoners furnished a convenient outlet for his vindictiveness. They were brought into his presence and summarily executed, one after another, by members of his retinue. The preacher Diya al-Din al-Tabari began the bloodbath by personally decapitating a few of the defenceless captives. Another divine, Sulayman al-Maghribi, followed his example, then emir Aytghan ibn Yaruq and others did so. Only chancellor [and historian] Imad al-Din al-Isfahani refused to join in the butchery." This account is based Ibn Al-Athir,[143] Ibn Wasil,[144] and 'Imad al-Din al-Isfahani.[145]

Lane-Poole and Gibb, on the whole, chose to ignore Saladin's early years which were spent in fighting fellow Muslims. They concentrated on Saladin's struggles against the Crusaders. But the reality is that from the beginning of his independent reign in 1174 to his death in 1193, Saladin spent twelve years fighting Muslims (mainly the family and partisans of the Zangids), and only five years in pursuing Jihad, the Holy War against the Latin Kingdom and the Third Crusade.[146]

Saladin seems at times to have little control over the excesses of his troops, and at other times seems to allow that they had every right to booty and plunder. Here is how Ehrenkreutz characterises the comportment of

---

142 *Ibid.*, pp. 218-220.

143 *Ibid.*, p. 260.

144 Ibn Wāsil, *Mufarrij al-Kurūb*, Cairo, 1953-60, 2:71.

145 'Imad al-Din al-Isfahani, *Al-Barq al-Shami*, vol. III, ed. Mustafa al-Hiyari, Amman, 1986, pp. 130-131.

146 P.M. Holt, *Saladin and His Admirers: A Biographical Reassessment*, in BSOAS, Vol. 46, No. 2 (1983), pp. 235-239.

Saladin's troops after the surrender of Sinjar in December, 1182:

> the defenders must have given the Ayyubid army a lot of
> trouble, because once they entered the city, the population
> had to endure the wild excesses of Saladin's enraged soldiers,
> who broke all discipline in greed of plunder. That Sinjar was
> captured during Ramadan demonstrated the lack of concern
> Saladin and his followers had about restrictive religious injunc-
> tions.[147]

BURNING OF CHURCHES

There are indeed other examples of Saladin's willingness to fight, kill, or burn churches during Ramadan. Let us look at the town of Lydda. Here is how the *Encyclopaedia of Islam*, Second Edition, describes the town of Lydda [under "Ludd"] and its magnificent cathedral: "the Byzantine church [of Lydda] is described by all the early Christian travellers. On the eve of the invasion of the Crusaders in 1099, the Muslims destroyed it again. The Crusaders found Ludd [Lydda] and Ramla deserted, and thus were easily able to establish a corridor from Jaffa to Jersualem, whence they could mount their attack on the Holy City as well as widen their hold on central and southern Palestine. In Ludd [Lydda] they built in 1150 a new cathedral with much splendour and magnificence, over the remains of the previous Byzantine church and the Saint's tomb." In September 1191, Wednesday 3 Ramadan, Saladin, as Bahā' al-Dīn tells us, "viewed the town and viewed its church and the great size of its construction, then ordered its demolition and also the demolition of the castle at Ramla."[148] If that were not sacrilege enough, two days later, *i.e.*, Friday 5 Ramadan, Saladin had some local Christians executed because they were found to be carrying letters to the "enemy" on them.

Saladin also ordered the destruction of another beautiful church, that of the Church of the Virgin in the town of Tartus, or Tortosa (also known as Antartus), which he captured in July 1188. Here is Bahā' al-Dīn Ibn Shaddād's description: "[Saladin] pressed on with the demolition of the city wall until it was all done, and then he demolished the church, an important one in their [Crusaders'] eyes and the object of of piligrimage from all over their lands. He ordered the city to be torched and everything

---

147 Ehrenkreutz, *Saladin, op.cit.*, p. 178.
148 Bahā' al-Dīn Ibn Shaddād, *op.cit*, p. 181.

was burnt. Fire roared through the palaces and houses, while our voices were raised in cries of "There is no god but God" and "God is Great." He stayed there, carrying out this destruction until 11 July, then he left for Jabala."[149] The Church was either rebuilt later in the same year 1188, or just possibly survived the holocaust.[150]

FURTHER EXECUTIONS: HUMAN SACRIFICE

After their successful naval attack on the Crusaders' flotilla off Aidhab, on the west coast of the Red Sea in 1183, Muslims killed most of the Crusaders on the spot, while one hundred and seventy others were captured and taken to the capital where Saladin specifically instructed that they be paraded in the major Egyptian cities and then decapitated. Ibn al-Athir[151] adds the horrific detail that some of the prisoners were sent to Mina, a place five kilometers to the east of Mecca. It plays an important part in the rituals associated with the pilgrimage to Mecca. The Christian prisoners were to be sacrificed—ritually slaughtered by having their throats cut—in place of goats or sheep.

EHRENKREUTZ'S ASSESSMENT OF THE LIFE AND ACHIEVEMENTS OF SALADIN

Ehrenkreutz vehemently disagrees with the Lane-Poole and Gibb thesis, and is not happy with their "focusing on Saladin's Crusader struggle nor with attributing to him lofty devotion to 'the true faith'" which is not borne out by the historical facts. And contrary to what some of his critics accused him of, Ehrenkreutz does not concern himself with Saladin's "motives" of which we "cannot be too certain," but rather of "his actual activities and accomplishments."[152] Ehrenkreutz is even convinced that the rank and file of his armies was not "overwhelmingly inspired by the jihad ideal which Saladin publicly publically embraced."[153] We know that in June 1191 some of Saladin's men mutinied: "they refused to attack the Christians and accused him of 'ruining Islam'. Succumbing to defeatism, three leading amirs in the garrison of Acre deserted their posts in panic, and finally, the garrison itself disobeyed the sultan's orders and

---

149 *Ibid.*, p. 83.
150 Van Berchem, *Journal Asiatique*, 1902, pp. 424-425.
151 Ibn al-Athir, *op.,cit.*, p. 290.
152 Ehrenkreutz, *Saladin, op.cit.*, p. 197.
153 Ehrenkreutz, *Saladin, op.cit.*, p. 211.

surrendered to the Crusaders....Saladin's anti-Crusade cause evoked little active support outside his own dominions....[The] grievous failure of Islam during the Third Crusade must be attributed to lack of enthusiasm for the holy war."[154]

> Saladin's ruthless policy of military suppression...did realize his immediate personal ambitions, but lack of a sincere moral or ideological motivation prevented consolidation and preservation of his dynastic heritage. His authority over the leading members of his family was at best tenuous....By the middle of the thirteenth century—only fifty-six years after Saladin's death—the Ayyubid [*i.e.* Saladin and family] domination in Egypt and Syria came to an abrupt end with the brutal seizure of power by the Mamluk commanders in Egypt.

> Viewed as a whole, Saladin's policy towards Egypt is a depressing record of callous exploitation for the furthering of his own selfish political ambitions....Quite obviously Saladin subordinated Egypt's interests to his expansionist dynastic ambitions in Syria.

> Saladin did not eliminate the Crusaders. His incredible indolence in handling Tyre led to the hardening of Christian resistance. His inability to hold his commanders in the field long enough to crush the early contingents of the Third Crusade led to the disaster of 1191, the humiliations at the hands of Richard the Lionhearted, and the armistice of 1192. To be sure Islam retained Jerusalem, but Acre and almost the entire Syrian littoral remained in Christian possession....[Saladin's] failure gave a new lease of life to the Crusader kingdom, which continued for another century to aggravate the political and economic difficulties of Egypt and Syria.[155]

> Most of Saladin's significant accomplishments should be attributed to his military and governmental experience, to his ruthless persecution and execution of political opponents and dissenters, to his vindictive belligerence and calculated oppor-

---

154 Ehrenkreutz, *Saladin, op.cit.*, pp. 215-217.

155 Ehrenkreutz, *Saladin, op.cit.*, pp. 234-236.

tunism, and to his readiness to compromise religious ideals to political expediency.

….Rather than the alleged attractiveness of his romantic personality, it was the potent spell of his tendentious biographers which has clouded the perceptions of most modern writers retelling the story of the great sultan."[156]

Since Ehrenkreutz's iconoclastic biography in 1972, there have been, perhaps, three major works on Saladin. I shall quickly look at the first two, by Lyons and Jackson (1982), and Lev (1999), and then concentrate on Anne-Marie Eddé's superb history (2011).

C.4. MALCOLM C. LYONS AND D.E.P. JACKSON

Malcolm C. Lyons and D.E.P. Jackson's[157] work met with universal approval on its publication in 1982. For example, P. M. Holt[158] in his review of their work quotes Ehrenkreutz's conclusions (see above), and then writes, "The revision of the historical role of Saladin and the reassessment of his personal qualities is carried a stage further by the work under review, which surveys the whole of his life in the context of his period.…It is an important biography in two respects. In the first place, it gives a very detailed narrative of Saladin's career, which is a most useful assemblage of political and military data. In the second place, it draws on two sources which have not been exploited by previous writers."

Saladin in the pages of Lyons and Jackson is not the dedicated champion of Islam. "The ambiguity of his policy as the self-appointed champion of Islam is brought out at various points in his career."[159] For example, in 1182, after the death of al-Sālih Ismā'īl, "The policy of Ayyubid expansionism," write Lyons and Jackson, "that had been blocked by the peace of treaty of 1176 was about to be renewed. Saladin was laying claim not only to Aleppo, but to any other town whose troops could be shown to be needed for the Holy War. This could not be accepted either by 'Izz al-Din in Mosul or by Zangi in Aleppo and Saladin's sincerity in turning his

---

156 Ehrenkreutz, *Saladin*, *op.cit.*, p. 238.

157 Malcolm C. Lyons and D.E.P. Jackson, *Saladin: The Politics of the Holy War*, Cambridge: Cambridge University Press, 1982.

158 P.M. Holt, "Saladin and His Admirers: A Biographical Reassessment" in *BSOAS*, Vol. 46 No. 2 (1983), pp. 235-239.

159 *Ibid.*, p. 238.

back on the Franks to fight his fellow-Muslims was bound to be called in question."[160]

Their conclusion leans towards Ehrenkreutz rather than Lane-Poole and Gibb.

"To his admirers, Saladin …can be seen as the hero of Islam, the destroyer of the Latin Kingdom and the restorer of the shrines in Jerusalem. Eulogy, however, must accommodate itself to the fact that such a view was not accepted by numbers of his Muslim contemporaries. He can be pictured by his detractors as manipulating Islam to win power for himself and his family…"[161]

Saladin's military successes are off-set by his defeats: "As a war leader, Saladin has to his credit two decisive victories in field actions against Muslim troops, at the Horns of Hama and at Tell al-Sultan, as well as his defeats of the Franks [Crusaders] at Marj 'Uyun and Hattin.…while his reverses included the battle of Ramla, the loss of Acre, the battle of Arsuf and the debacle of Jaffa. His defeat at the battle of Ramla was caused primarily by his carelessness, but elsewhere his tactics and strategy were marked by caution against the Franks and daring against the Muslims."[162]

As to the Holy war, "Saladin blurred the distinctions of the Holy War by adding Muslims, such as the Almohades, to the list of possible enemies and, instead of being confined to the recovery of the Coast, the concept was thus almost infinitely extendable."[163]

Finally, Saladin "cannot be thought of as an innovator, but as a man who was content to act on ideas supplied him. He was a good but not great strategist and tactician, an open-handed but not far-sighted administrator and a man with his share of faults, mixed motives and weaknesses."[164]

C.5 YAACOV LEV

Yaacov Lev, professor in the Department of Middle Eastern Studies, Bar-Ilan University, Israel, devotes a considerable amount of space to a discussion of the sources in his work on Saladin.[165] For Lev, the outlook of the historian-admirers of Saladin was influenced by the Kurd's "later achievements; the victory at Hattin and the conquest of Jerusalem. In retrospect,

160 Lyons and Jackson, *op.cit.*, p. 172.

161 *Ibid.*, p. 365.

162 *Ibid.*

163 *Ibid.*, p. 370.

164 *Ibid.*, p. 373.

165 Yaacov Lev, *Saladin in Egypt*, Leiden: Brill, 1999.

they tended to idealize the personality of the man who became a hero of the Holy War. The events of Saladin's early life were remodelled and censored to fit in with his later fame."[166] There are all sorts of contradictions among the sources, the differences are a result of different perspectives which are mutually exclusive.

Lev is convinced that Saladin had a clear objective in early days in Egypt: to put an end to the Fatimid state, "And to that end he was preparing the necessary legal and religious justification. The war that Saladin waged on the Blacks was an aggressive act. However, Saladin himself and his historian-admirers deny any worldly motives on his part. Therefore the Battle of the Blacks had to be justified and presented as an [sic] defensive act. The complex story of the plot, …served that purpose and the story itself is, in my view, a literary invention."[167]

Lev's conclusion is hard to decipher since on the one hand he thinks that the concept of the Holy War was manipulated by Saladin for political ends, and yet, at the same time, Lev seems to argue that Saladin was totally committed to the ideology of the Holy War. Lev writes, "As a large number of scholars have already established—notably Emmanuel Sivan, Andrew S.Ehrenkreutz, R. Stephen Humphreys, Malcolm C. Lyons, D.E.P. Jackson and Hannes Möhrig—the concept of Holy War was manipulated by rulers in the twelfth century for their political ends. They presented themselves as champions of the Holy War, a presentation supported, propagated if not invented sometimes by members of the civlian elite. In this context Qadi al-Fadil rendered to Saladin a tremendous service: he presented Saladin's war against Nur al-Din's heirs as having an ulterior motive—Holy War and the conquest of Jerusalem"[168]

But a little later, Lev argues, "Undoubtedly, at the beginning of the battle of Acre, Saladin was confident of his ability to win this war. But as the battle dragged on and the challenge of the Third Crusade intensified, Saladin's continuous war effort must also be seen as a reflection of his commitment to the ideology of the Holy War."[169]

C.6 ANNE-MARIE EDDÉ

---

166 *Ibid.*, p. 1.
167 *Ibid.*, p. 84.
168 *Ibid.*, pp. 195-196.
169 *Ibid.*, p. 197.

At last, we come to Anne-Marie Eddé's magisterial history, *Saladin*[170] which covers so much more than all the other biographies reviewed here, especially the social, geographical, political and historical backgrounds often neglected by the others.

Ms. Eddé explains in great detail why and how the image of Saladin was created. The "search for exemplarity and for models, whether ancient and prestigious such as the prophets of Islam, or much closer in space and time, was an essential characteristic of the elaboration of Saladin's image. ...The message to be transmitted was political as well as religious. Above all, there was a need to legitimate the authority of Saladin—considered by some to be usurper—by emphasizing his personal virtues and his qualities as sovereign, one who had concern for the good of his subjects and especially for the interests of Islam, a defender of orthodoxy, an architect of Muslim unity."

It is possible that the portraits painted of Saladin by his Muslim biographers, particularly Bahā' ad-Dīn Ibn Shaddād contained a kernel of truth. "But beyond what might have been based in reality, the way his actions are presented, the qualifiers applied to them, the virtues attributed to him, the praise heaped on him, and the bonds that link him to illustrious figures in the biblical and Islamic tradition stem from a dual legacy: that of the holy man and that of the ideal sovereign. In Islamic hagiographical literature, the Manāqib, or Saints' Lives, were often composed by a disciple of a saint or someone close to him, and were intended to perpetuate his memory. The saint's virtues and miracles were described in a series of narratives that retraced his path, from his conception to after his death. The biographies of Saladin bear a strong resemblance to that type of narrative."[171]

There is also the influence of literary genre known as the Mirrors for Princes which offers "sovereigns a great deal of advice on good government and drew the portrait of the ideal monarch: God-fearing, righteous, just toward his subjects, one who surrounded himself with good advisers and honest administrators, one who knew how to conduct diplomacy and war....The influence of that tradition on Saladin's biographers is obvious....[His biographers] found in such works all the criteria for good governance, which then allowed them, by emphasizing and sometimes exaggerating one character trait or another, to make Saladin's image correspond to that presented in the Islamic tradition as exemplifying the ideal

---

170 Anne-Marie Eddé, *Saladin*, Trans. by Jane Marie Todd, Cambridge, Mass.: The Belknap Press Harvard University Press, 2011.

171 *Ibid.*, p. 149.

sovereign."[172]

We are far from Gibb's idealised portrait. Ms. Eddé is less starry-eyed, "Saladin was also not always the just, kind, and magnanimous sultan whose image has come down to us....Saladin also knew how to be ruthless in the punishments he meted out to his enemy prisoners, and on certain occasions he did not recoil from the use of violence."[173]

The violence committed within his own territory against prisoners, rebels, or heretics was legitimated by the ulemas, the jurists, whose convenient fatwas allowed him to execute the pro-Fatimid poet al-'Umāra and the Iranian mystic al-Suhrawardī, and many others.[174]

Ms. Eddé points out Saladin's tactical errors in his military campaigns but above all his lack of authority over the troops, as for example in July 1192 in Jaffa when he failed to mobilize his troops—"they were too busy looting the city—to seize the citadel before Richard the Lionheart came to its aid."[175]

Instead of going on about his generosity and magnanimity after the taking of Jerusalem, Ms. Eddé offers us this sobering assessment: "Let us refrain, however, from projecting onto him our modern conceptions of openness and tolerance. For Saladin, delivering Jerusalem, the third holy city of Islam, from the authority of the 'infidels' was a religious obligation. He had to defeat, subjugate the enemy, enslave those from whom he could draw no profit, tear down the crosses, and 'assure the triumph of truth over error', in order to prove the superiority of one religion over another, consistent with the ideals of his time. Political and religious interests were thus intimately linked and were served by generosity, natural no doubt, but not devoid of calculation."[176]

Another point that Eddé brings out well is the strange nature of the battles that Saladin was enagaged in since they did not always break down along confessional lines, Christians against the Muslims: "It follows that, in the East at least, the battles in preparation in no way constituted a religious war, despite what the discourse would have us believe. It was not Islam and Christianity facing off, but rather sovereigns confronting internal and external difficulties, who attempted to find allies—whatever their religion—against those threatening them. Hence the Byzantine Christians sought Saladin's alliance against other Christians, Sicilian or

172 *Ibid.*, pp. 149-151.
173 *Ibid.*, p. 162.
174 *Ibid.*, p. 163.
175 *Ibid.*, p. 165.
176 *Ibid.*, p. 221.

German; Saladin was ready to support the Byzantines or the Christian rebel of Cyprus if they supported him in a battle against the Franks; and the Seljuks did not hesitate to offer their services to the Germans to combat the same man they had just congratulated for taking Jerusalem from the Franks."[177] In the middle of all these alliances were the Bedouins who provided their services to the Franks, so long as they were well paid they had no scruples about betraying the Muslims.[178] "It was also fairly common to find Frankish mercenaries in the Muslim armies, since they were not asked to renounce their faith…. Conversely, the Franks used Muslim converts to Christianity, called *turcopoles*, in their army. Saladin was merciless toward these renegades. When he took them prisoner at the castle of Bayt al-Azhan, he had every last one of them executed. It is also known that renegade Aleppine [Muslims from Aleppo] sappers provided their aid to Richard the Lionheart during the assault of the fortress of Darum in 1192….Without entering the service of the Franks, other Muslims, including some important ones, did not hesitate to sell them provisions during times of famine. The lord of 'Azaz in northern Syria, for example, made a fortune selling cereals to Antioch [in Frankish hands] at exorbitant prices, at a time when Saladin was about to conquer the castle of Baghras a few kilometers away."[179]

Eddé is also very realistic, and fair when chronicling Saladin's treatment of prisoners. The Latin sources talk of Saladin's generosity in releasing prisoners without compensation. However the Latin sources also talk of the tortures inflicted on Reginald of Sidon at the foot of the castle of Beaufort, and "the torments imposed on Baldwin of Ibelin, whose teeth were supposedly pulled out, to compel him to gather together his ransom. ….[M]ost of the Arab and Latin authors mention Saladin's initial desire to seize Jerusalem by force and by blood, in order to avenge the Muslims who had died in 1099 during the taking of that city by the Franks. Later, however, Saladin came to understand that such an attitude risked bringing on the destruction of the holy places and the death of Muslim prisoners. It is also known that Saladin showed no pity toward the Knights Templar and the Knights Hospitaller—except when he could extract a high ransom from them—and had almost all of them executed after the Battle of Hattin, believing they were the worst enemies of Islam. Two days after the victory, he sent for them and ordered them beheaded before his eyes. The

---

177 *Ibid.*, pp. 243-244.
178 *Ibid.*, p. 276.
179 *Ibid.*, pp. 309-311.

ulemas actively participated in the massacre [Here is Imād ad-Dīn al-Isfa-hani's account]: 'Each of them asked to be granted the favor of executing a prisoner, unsheathed his saber, and bared his forearm. The sultan [Saladin] was seated; he had a smile on his face, while those of the miscreants were somber. The troops having lined up, the emirs were standing in two rows. Some of these religious sliced and cut well, and were thanked; the sabers of others hesitated and leapt back up, and they were forgiven; still others were mocked and replaced. And there was I, watching the sultan smile at the massacre; I saw him as a man of his word and of action."[180] Such was the cruel circus watched by the smiling Saladin.

THE OTHER

In a fascinating chapter on "The Gaze of the Other," Eddé describes with many humorous anecdotes what the Muslims thought of the Franks, quoting from the journal of the eminent Syrian emir, Usāma ibn Munq-idh [1095-1188],[181] Eddé wrote, "The Franks, good and courageous war-riors, were noted for their coarse manners, their lack of hygiene, and their slow-wittedness. Some Muslim authors go so far as to associate them with the animal kingdom. For Ibn Abi l-Ash'ath, a tenth century doctor living in Mosul, the Franks, like animals, had only generic characteristics and completely lacked individuality. Two centuries later, Usāma ibn Munqidh wrote: 'Mysterious are the works of the Creator, the author of all things! When one comes to recount causes regarding the Franks he cannot but glorify Allah (exalted is He!) and sanctify him, for he sees them as animals possessing the virtues of courage and fighting, but nothing else; just as animals have only the virtues of strength and carrying loads.'"[182]

The Muslim is often compared to the lion while the Franks are re-

---

180 Anne-Marie Eddé, *Saladin*, p. 306. Her references are: 'Imād al-Dīn, *Kitāb al-Fath al-qussī fi-l-fath al-qudsī*, ed. C. Landberg, Leiden, 1888. Translated into French by Henri Massé as *Conquête de la Syrie et de la Palestine par Saladin*, Paris, 1972, p. 31; Lyons and Jackson, *Saladin*, p. 265; Lev, "Treatment of Prisoners of War during the Fatimid-Ayyubid Wars with the Crusaders," in *Tolerance and Intolerance: Social Con-flict in the Age of the Crusades*, edd. M. Gervers & J.M. Powell, Syracuse, NY., 2001, pp. 11-27; P.V. Claverie, "Le statut des templiers capturés en Orient durant les croisades," in G. Cipollone, ed. *La liberazione dei 'captivi' tra cristianità e islam. Oltre la crociata e il Gihad: Tolleranza e servizio umanitario*. Vatican City, 2000, pp. 501-511.

181 Available in English: Usāma Ibn Mumqidh, *The Book of Contemplation: Islam and the Crusades*, Trans. by Paul M. Cobb, New York: Penguin Classics, 2008.

182 Eddé, *op.cit.*, p. 313. The quote from Usāma Ibn Mumqidh can be found on page 144 of the Penguin edition (see note above).

ferred to as the wolf, fox, hare, dragon, jackal, vulture, dog, ape, snake, pig, hyena, fly, and wasp.[183] "The Franks are also often associated with darkness, night, garbage, and filth, in opposition to the light of dawn, daybreak, and purity of Islam. An entire vocabulary with polemical religious connotations was used to spread that negative image of the Franks. 'Imād al-Dīn has no dearth of qualifiers in that register: seditious, polytheistic, impious, idolatrous, people of depravity, Sunday idlers, faithless demons or demons of error, infernal beings, maleficent counts, corrupt barons, bands gone astray, champions of deception, worshippers of human and divine nature, who, upon death, will populate hell, in opposition to the martyred believers who populate paradise."[184]

It is not clear if, at first, the Muslims had any clear idea of the motivations of the Crusaders. By the twelfth century, Muslims began to understand the nature and objectives of the Crusades. As for their knowledge of Christian doctrine and practice, it was a strange mixture of truth and error, and clichés.

The apparent lack of modesty and jealousy of the Franks was a source of wonder for the Muslims. Here is another anecdote from Usāma Ibn Munqidh,

> We had with us a bath-keeper named Salim, originally an inhabitant of al-Ma'arrah, who had charge of the bath of my father (may Allah's mercy rest upon his soul!). This man related the following story:

>> 'I once opened a bath in al-Ma'arrah in order to earn my living. To this bath there came a Frankish knight. The Franks disapprove of girding a cover around one's waist while in the bath. So this Frank stretched out his arm and pulled off my cover from my waist and threw it away. He looked and saw that I had recently shaved off my pubes. So he shouted, 'Salim!' As I drew near him he stretched his hand over my pubes and said, 'Salim, good! By the truth of my religion, do the same for me.' Saying this, he lay on his back and I found that in that place the hair was like his beard. So I shaved it off. Then he passed his hand over the place and, finding it smooth, he said, 'Salim, by the truth of my religion, do the same to madame

183 *Ibid*, p. 319.
184 *Ibid.*, pp. 319-320.

> [al-dama](al-dama in their language means the lady), re-
> ferring to his wife. He then said to a servant of his, 'Tell
> madame to come here'. Accordingly the servant went and
> brought her and made her enter the bath. She also lay on
> her back. The knight repeated, 'Do what thou hast done
> to me!' So I shaved all that hair while her husband was
> sitting looking at me, At last he thanked me and handed
> me the pay for my service.'

> Consider now this great contradiction! They have neither jeal-
> ousy nor zeal but they have great courage, although courage is
> nothing but the product of zeal and of ambition to be above
> ill repute.[185]

Muslims were generally astonished at the relative independence of Western women, in contrast to the sequestered lives of women in Islam. The Frankish women who participated in battles elicited amazement but also admiration. Eddé quotes 'Imad al-Din, "Among the Franks there are lady knights who wear breastplates and helmets. In that male clothing, they leap into the fray, and these mistresses of the gynoecium [The women's apartments in a household; any building set apart for women. O.E.D.] conduct themselves like the stronger sex. In their eyes, that is an act of devotion, by virtue of which they believe they are assuring their salvation, and that is why they dedicate themselves to that life….On battle days, these women can be advancing with the knights, whom they take as their example. They are as ruthless as the men despite the weakness of their sex. These women have no costume other than a coat of mail and are recognizable only when undressed and stripped bare; several of them were taken and sold as slaves."[186] Muslim writers picked out various Frankish individuals for praise for their valor. Saladin had a particular regard for Reginald of Sidon, who is described as someone cultivated, who spoke Arabic, and who took a sincere interest in Islam and its history and doctrines.[187] Henry of Champagne was also looked on kindly by the historian Ibn al-Athir, "who describes him as a good, wise, and tolerant man, a friend to the Muslims." For Ibn Al-Athir, Richard the Lionheart was "an outstanding man of

---

185 *Ibid.*, pp. 320-321. Usama ibn Munqidh, Penguin edition, p. 149. (The Penguin translation differs very slightly from the one given by Eddé.)

186 *Ibid.*, pp. 323-324.

187 *Ibid.*, p. 326.

his time for his bravery, cunning, steadfastness and endurance."[188]

CHRISTIANS AND JEWS

Anne-Marie Eddé is the only one of Saladin's biographers to devote a whole chapter on the Sultan's treatment of non-Muslims, particularly Christian and Jews. The situation in the twelfth century was highly complex and requires sensitive and subtle analysis that can read every nuance. Eddé accomplishes a difficult task with grace and skill.

In twelfth century, Egypt Jews and Christians were still numerous. "In 1175 Burchard of Strasbourg, Frederick Barbarossa's ambassador, was surprised by the large number of churches in Alexandria and Cairo, where Muslims, Jews, and Christians freely practiced their faiths. Some time later, in the thirteenth century, the Coptic author of *The Churches and Monasteries of Egypt* counted thirty-seven churches and five monasteries for the single city of al-Fustat and its outlying area, plus four churches and a monastery in the Fatimid city of Cairo. Christian buildings were also very numerous in the region of Giza, southwest of Cairo, on the other side of the Nile. [Some fifty churches and the same number of monasteries] Also according to that source, in Egypt there were at least 707 churches and 181 monasteries, most of which collected large revenues from the lands granted to them by the former Fatimid caliphs. Large non-Muslim communities also continued to live in Syria-Palestine, in large cities such as Damascus and Aleppo but also in the countryside, where some villages were still entirely populated by Christians. Under Saladin's reign, then, the church played a not insignificant role in the economic life of his states."[189]

However, Saladin, in order to gain the goodwill of the radical *ulemas* re-instated the obligations bearing on the non-Muslims, *i.e.* the *dhimmis*, that is, he demanded a strict application of the Sharia concerning them. These rules had not been followed with any rigour by the Fatimids, and their re-introduction made the lives of the *dhimmis* difficult. The status of *dhimmi*, or protected person, "gave them the right, in exchange for a capitulation, to practice their religion freely and to keep their religious institutions. The *dhimmis* were also obliged to respect a certain number of restrictive and often discriminatory rules: not to insult Islam, not to attempt to convert a Muslim, to refrain from assisting the enemies of Islam, not to build new religious buildings or even restore any, to avoid all contact be-

---

188 *Ibid.*, p. 328.
189 *Ibid.*, p. 397.

tween a male *dhimmi* and a Muslim woman, to wear distinctive hairstyles and clothing, to possess neither weapons nor horses, and so on."[190] Thus *dhimmis* were second-class citizens, subject to whims of the ruler, and the crowds, who were easily swayed, and could take matters into their own hands. Thus we have examples of sporadic looting of churches.[191]

Theoretically, *dhimmis* could not work in the administration, but not all of them were driven out since that would have seriously disrupted the proper running of the government. These restrictions prompted many *dhimmis* to convert to Islam; one source puts the figure as high as fourteen thousand conversions.

Saladin was under the influence of the radical *ulemas*. Qadi al-Fadil urged the Sultan to purge the financial administration of all Christians. The Shafite jurist, al-Khubushani, was a fanatic, who "said he wanted to kill all the *dhimmis* he happened to see on horseback, Once, when he ran into one of Saladin's Jewish doctors, al-Muwaffaq ibn Shu'a, riding a horse, he threw a stone at him, hitting him full in the face and taking out an eye." While, the leader of the Egyptian Shafites, Shibab al-Din al-Tusi, contented himself by extorting money and gifts from the Christians. He also had two churches shut down, and looted the great al-Basatin church.[192]

However, Saladin seems to have been sincere in his desire to protect the non-Muslims. In Aleppo in 1183, Saladin decreed that he was "reaffirming his will to protect the non-Muslim communities."[193] He urged emirs and governors to protect them against hoodlums, guarantee them against injustice, expressing a desire to see non-Muslims live in peace on his territories.

"…The Christians authors, who lament the many destructions and exactions at the beginning of Saladin's reign, also recognize that his governance was that of a just and generous prince who ensured his subjects' well-being by eliminating the illegal taxes and lowering prices."[194]

Saladin's tolerance toward the Jews is attested to in several Christian and Jewish sources. Joshua Prawer argues that the catalyst for Jewish immigration to the East in the thirteenth century was their preception of Saladin's victories over the Franks, victories that allowed the Jews to resettle in Jerusalem, from which they had been banished by the Christians. But behind the "policy of relative tolerance, economic interests were being played

---

190 *Ibid.*, p. 398.
191 *Ibid.*, p. 403.
192 *Ibid.*, pp. 401-402.
193 *Ibid.*, p. 402.
194 *Ibid.*, p. 404.

out as well, since Saladin knew that the Christians and Jews were needed to cultivate the surrounding lands and to maintain the region's economy."[195]

Eddé concludes, "During his reign, although all was not peace and quiet for the *dhimmis*, who no doubt lost some possessions and positions permanently, overall they were not prevented from maintaining their place and influence in society."[196]

EDDÉ'S CONCLUSIONS

Saladin was a man "endowed with strong political instincts; an indefatigable warrior; a man truly interested in religious life, anxious to restore Sunnism and to apply Muslim law strrictly. ...On the list of his successes, we must include his domination of a vast territory extending from the Nile to the Euphrates and from Yemen to northern Mesopotamia, as well as the reconquest of a large portion of the Latin states, Jerusalem in particular.... Saladin actively contributed toward strengthening Sunnism throughout his territory and thereby earned the the solid support of men of religion. In the economic realm, despite the conflicts, commerce continued to develop in the Mediterranean and the Indian Ocean."

"On the negative side, there was, first, Saladin's incapacity to build a state....He constituted an empire but did not impose any centralized state structure; used the resources of his territories to finance his wars without concerning himself about the future of those territories; and sought justice while privileging a patronage system rather than an effective administration. The emirs continued to govern as they wished in the territories entrusted to them, with the sole condition that they fulfill their military obligations. All that explains the financial difficulties at the end of Saladin's reign, the heterogeneity and demobilization of his troops; it explains as well why his empire, too closely associated with his person, did not survive his death. In conflict with the Franks, Saladin succeeded in saving his chief conquest—Jerusalem—but did not manage to eliminate the Latin states. No doubt he committed a few strategic errors....It would be inaccurate, however, to attribute to him sole responsibility for that failure. In addition to the unwillingness of the caliph of Baghdad and the eastern princes to come to his aid, the superiority of the Crusaders' fleet was such that he could not on his own have prevented it from controlling the seas and, as a consequence, from dominating the coast."[197]

---

195 *Ibid.*, p. 411.
196 *Ibid.*, p. 417.
197 *Ibid.*, pp. 504-505.

And finally, "Is it truly by chance that, to evoke Saladin, the figure of a wise man such as Solomon was preferred to that of a conqueror such as Alexander [the Great]?"[198]

SALADIN IN WESTERN ART: THE GENESIS OF A MYTH

The first accounts of Saladin in Western literature are hostile, beginning in 1187, while Saladin was still alive (he died on March 4, 1193), with an anonymous Latin poem, "Carmen de Saladino," a scurrilous attack on Saladin, and his rise to power. He is presented as someone who rose to power from nowhere, and by criminal means.[199] The chronicle of the Third Crusade, *Itinerarium Peregrinorum et Gesta Regis Ricardi,* the earliest parts of which were written between 1191 and 1192, tells us what Saladin's activities were in Damascus, "Saladin collected illgotten gains for himself from a levy on the girls of Damascus: they were not allowed to practise as prostitutes unless they had obtained, at a price, a licence from him for carrying on the profession of lust. However, whatever he gained by pimping like this he paid back generously by funding plays. So through lavish giving to all their desires he won the mercenary favor of the common people…The pimp, who had a kingdom of brothels, an army of taverns, who studied dice and rice, is suddenly raised up on high."[200] On the whole, "Saladin is presented as an ignominious upstart, immoral, opportunistic and murderous."[201] The late thirteenth-century or early fourteenth century Continuations of the epic poem *Chanson de Jérusalem* also present Saladin in a hostile light, as someone malicious, cunning, and murderous. But as Vladimir Minorsky summarized, "Very few political and military leaders—Napoleon being a notable exception—have been the object of such appreciation by their adversaries as was Saladin on the part of the Crusaders. The earliest of European contemporaries may have deliberately blackened his reputation[202] but this was only a passing tendency for in the

---

198 *Ibid.*, p. 509.

199 Gaston Paris, 'Un poème latin contemporain sur Saladin', *Revue de l'Orient latin*, 1, 443-44. 1893; and Margaret Jubb, *The Legend of Saladin in Western Literature and Historiography*, Lewiston, N.Y.: The Edwin Mellen Press, 2000, p. 6.

200 Helen J. Nicholson (translator), *The Chronicle of the Third Crusade: Itinerarium Peregrinorum et Gesta Regis Ricardi*, Aldershot, UK: Ashgate Publishing Ltd., 1997, pp. 27-28.

201 Margaret Jubb, *The Legend of Saladin in Western Literature and Historiography*, Lewiston, N.Y.: The Edwin Mellen Press, 2000, p. 9.

202 Minorsky's footnote, page 107, fn.1, "They invented stories about his intrigue with the wife of his protector Nur al-Din and misrepresented his relations with the Fatimid

end the element of Saladin's 'chivalry' eclipsed any other impressions and recollections.[203] Side by side with the generosity which Saladin showed, for example, after the capture of Jerusalem, there were more brutal moments in his life, as when he cut down Reginald Chatillon with his own hand. However, the European memory retained chiefly such features as his sending a charger to his enemy unhorsed in the thick of the battle of Jaffa (1192). Even Dante in his vision of the limbo whose dwellers suffer no punishment and are only deprived of beatitude, saw Saladin standing 'alone and aside' among the ancient patriarchs, illustrious women and Greek philosophers."

Minorsky continues, "Collective memory is often an unreliable source of information, but as a rule it is less inaccurate about general impressions than about facts. The question of good or bad, pleasant or unpleasant, is easier to answer than the problem of the ground for the conclusions drawn."[204]

William of Tyre (c. 1130 – 29 September 1186), Archbishop of Tyre, grew up in Jerusalem but spent twenty years studying the liberal arts and canon law in European universities. He is now known as the author of a history of the Kingdom of Jerusalem, with the title *Historia rerum in partibus transmarinis gestarum* (*"History of Deeds Done Beyond the Sea"*) or *Historia Ierosolimitana* (*"History of Jerusalem"*), written between 1170 and 1184. It was translated into French soon after his death, and many other languages. It is a valuable source for the history of twelfth-century Jerusalem especially as it is written by a native. He is considered the greatest chronicler of the crusades, and one of the most elegant writers of the Middle Ages. Saladin first appears in his pages in this manner, "Saladin was a man of keen intelligence. He was vigorous in war and unusually generous" [*Vir acris ingenii, armis strenuus et supra modum liberalis*]. But William later portrays him "as an ambitious enemy treacherously bludgeoning the [Fatimid] caliph to death and running through all his progeny with a sword, and as a usurper devoid of all human feeling. The same author also points to the sultan's humble origin and attributes his political

---

caliph ("La Meule", Arabice Maulana). See Gaston Paris, in *Journal des Savants*, 1893; S. Lane-Poole, *Saladin*, 1898, pp. 376-40: "Saladin in romance." See now F. Gabrieli, *Storia della civiltà musulmana*, Napoli, 1947, pp. 1-21: "Storia e leggenda di Saladino."

203 Minorsky's footnote, page 107, fn.2: Speaking of the western lore G.Marçais says with understatement: "le rôle que (Saladin) y joue n'a rien d'odieux", Glotz, *Histoire du Moyen Age*, 1936, p. 594.[*i.e*, there is nothing unpleasant about the role that Saladin plays in the western tradition.]

204 Vladimir Minorsky, "Prehistory of Saladin" in *Studies in Caucasian History*, Cambridge Oriental Series 6, London, Part III, 1953, pp. 107-108.

ascent to chance rather than inheritance. William speaks of Saladin as of a tyrant, primarily because the danger the sultan represented for the Franks in William's time was real (whence his fear), but also because the portrayal corresponded to the medieval conception of history, in which tyrants are sent by God to punish the Christians for their sins. And for William, one of the explanations for the Frankish defeats lay in the fact that the sins of men—especially those of the Eastern Franks—had elicited God's wrath. God therefore punished them by sending Saladin, who now reigned without rival over a reunified Muslim territory."[205]

The text known as *The Old French Continuation of William of Tyre*, or the *Lyon Eracles*, has a highly complex history, but a simplified version goes something like this: the Latin work by William of Tyre was translated into French in the early decades of the thirteenth century, and "many of the manuscripts of the French translation have continuations tacked on to the end."[206] The text translated by Peter W. Edbury, to be quoted below, is to be found in a single manuscript now in the municipal library in Lyon, France, though there are, in fact, a number of other recensions. The *Lyon Eracles*, as our text is also sometimes called, gives examples of Saladin's noble qualities: "I must not omit to tell you about an act of courtesy of Saladin's during the siege of Jerusalem. When Baldwin of Ibelin left the kingdom he entrusted his own small son who was named Thomassin to the care of his brother Balian. There was also another child called Guillemin, the son of Raymond of Jubail. Both children were in Jerusalem, and when their fathers heard that Saladin was besieging the city, they sent asking him to let their children come to them so that they would not be taken into captivity. When Saladin heard this request he was happy to do what he could to comply. He immediately sent word to Balian, who was governor in Jerusalem, telling him to send him his nephew Thomassin, the son of his brother Baldwin, and Guillemin, the son of Raymond. As soon as Balian received this message he sent them to him most gladly. When the children came before Saladin, he received then honourably as the children of free men, and had them taken off and given robes and jewels and ordered them to be given something to eat."[207]

Again at the siege of Jerusalem, the *Lyon Eracles* gives further evidence for Saladin's honorable comportment: "I shall now tell you how Saladin had the city of Jerusalem protected so that the Saracens would do

---

205 Eddé, *op.cit.*, p. 472.
206 Peter W. Edbury, *The Conquest of Jerusalem and the Third Crusade: Sources in Translation*, Aldershot, UK: Ashgate Publishing Ltd., 1998, p. 3.
207 *Ibid.*, p. 57.

harm to the Christians there. He placed two knights and ten sergeants in each street to guard the city, and they guarded it so well that I never heard of any wrong being done to a Christian. When the Christians came out of Jerusalem they camped less than a bow-shot away from the Saracen host. Saladin had his troops guard the Christians day and night so that no one could do them any harm and no robbers could fall on them."[208]

Saladin is also praised by our text for his acts of charity in releasing hundreds of poor people of Jerusalem who could not pay the ransom to free themselves.[209] He was equally generous towards the ladies of Jerusalem: "Now I shall tell you of a great act of courtesy that Saladin did for the ladies of Jerusalem. The women and daughters of the knights who had been killed or taken in the battle had fled to Jerusalem. After they had been ransomed and had left the city, they came before Saladin and craved mercy. …[The ladies told him who they were]. ..They explained that he had their husbands and fathers in prison and that they had lost their lands, and they called on him for the sake of God to have mercy on them and give them counsel and aid. When Saladin saw them weeping, he had great pity on them and said they would be informed as to which of their husbands were alive and he would have them all freed. They made enquiries and found some of them, and they freed all those who were in Saladin's custody. Then he ordered that the ladies and maidens whose fathers and lords had been killed in the battle should be provided for generously from his goods, more to some and less to others according to who they were. He gave them so much that they praised God and man for the kindness and honour Saladin had shown them."[210]

Then the *Lyon Eracles* contrasts the generosity of Saladin with the rapaciousness of the Christians of Nephin and Tripoli who robbed their fellow Christians leaving Jerusalem, "[The Christians] of Nephin and Tripoli treated [the Christians of Jerusalem] worse than the Saracens. For the Saracens, …escorted them to safety and provided them with food in plenty, but they robbed them and refused to let them find refuge." Some of the Christians of Jerusalem ended up in Alexandria, where "they were better received in the land of the Saracens than the others who had gone to the land of Tripoli."[211] Similarly, the *Lyon Eracles* recounts how the Christian pilgrims on their way to Jerusalem were shipwrecked on Cyprus where Isaac, the lord of Cyprus, in an act of wanton cruelty had them all decapi-

---

208 Peter W. Edbury, *op.cit.*, p. 62.

209 *Ibid.*, p. 63.

210 *Ibid.*, p. 64.

211 *Ibid.*, p. 65.

tated. The chronicle adds, "[These Christian pilgrims] encountered greater cruelty among those who called themselves Christians than they would have found with the unbelieving Saracens."[212]

As the Christians came to see Saladin in a more favorable light, they accounted for his chivalrous virtues by claiming that he had Christian noble blood flowing through his veins, as in the fourteenth century Crusade epic poem, *Baudouin de Sebourc*, and the fifteenth century prose, *Saladin*, both of which belong to the body of work referred to as the second crusade cycle. Other works with the same theme include the 15th century romance, *Jean d'Avesnes*. Equally numerous are stories reporting Saladin's generosity, such as *Novellino*, a collection of short stories composed in the late thirteenth century. In Boccaccio's *Decameron* [composed 1370-1371], on Day One, Story Three, and Day Ten, Story Nine, Saladin makes his appearance: "Boccaccio's Saladin is no less lavish: in the story of the three rings, he thanks the Jew who lent him money by showering him with gifts; and in the tale of "Torello, gentleman of Pavia," he is able to appreciate his guest's largesse and even rival it at the proper moment, when he sends him home covered in jewels."[213] Another Italian, Busone da Gubbio, a friend of Dante, wrote *L'Avventurosa Ciciliano* in 1311, and in the additional *Osservazioni* which follow Book III, gives examples of Saladin's magnanimity.[214]

"Loyalty to his oaths, prowess, largesse, magnanimity, and courtesy: Saladin possessed all the virtues of a good knight. But he is also praised for his austerity and humility, virtues that had some basis in truth."[215] Voltaire, in chapter 56 of his *Essai sur les mœurs et l'esprit des nations*,[216] makes allusions to these virtues of Saladin, "[Saladin] died three years later in Damascus, admired even by the Christians. In place of the flag raised outside his door, during his last illness he displayed the sheet in which he was to be buried. The person holding that standard of death cried out loud: 'Here is everything that Saladin, conqueror of the East, takes away from his conquests.' It is said that, in his will, he left alms to be distributed equally to the Mohammedan, Jewish, and Christian poor, wishing to make clear by that provision that all men are brothers, and that to help them, one must not seek to know what they believe but rather what they suffer. Few of our Christian princes have had that magnanimity; and few of the chroniclers

---

212 *Ibid.*, p. 101.

213 Eddé, *op.cit.*, p. 481.

214 *Ibid*, p. 481, Jubb, *op.cit.*, p. 79.

215 Eddé, *op. cit.*, p. 484.

216 Voltaire, *Essai sur les mœurs et l'esprit des nations*, 1756.

with which Europe is overburdened have known how to do him justice."[217] In the nineteenth century, Chateaubriand repeats the story, "Saladin died soon after the taking of Ptolemais: he directed that, on the day of his funeral, a shroud should be carried on the point of a spear, and herald proclaim in a loud voice: 'Saladin, the conqueror of Asia, out of all the fruits of his victories, carries with him only this shroud.'"[218]

The above story was widely disseminated in collections of exempla to serve as models for sermons to be used by Christian preachers.

The Parable of the Three Rings, which attempts to settle the question of which of the three rival religions is the authentic and true religion, probably originated in the eleventh-century, and is found in a developed form in the Jewish collection, *Schebet Jehuda,* composed in the fifteenth century. Etienne de Bourbon [died c.1261] developed a version; another version is the *Dit du vrai anneau* composed between 1270-1294. In the *Gesta Romanorum,* a source for many writers such as Chaucer, Boccaccio, and Shakespeare, which was probably composed between the end of the thirteenth and the beginning of the fourteenth, "One son (Judaism) inherits the Promised Land, one (Islam) wordly treasures and the third (Christianity) healing faith." Boccaccio in *The Decameron* [I. 3] develops the story further: Saladin tries to trick a Jew called Melchisedech into lending him money. "The Jew tells the Parable of the Three Rings, and the three virtuous sons, each of whom thinks he has the true ring. It proves impossible to tell the rings apart, and so the story concludes that it is impossible to determine which of the three religions is the true one."[219]

Gotthold Lessing borrowed this story from Boccaccio and incorporated it into his play, *Nathan the Wise* [written in 1778–79]—a work that exemplifies the Enlightenment's openness to the Other, and its universalism and tolerance. The two themes—"it suffices to be a man" and "be my friend"—run through the play and give it its humanity. Preaching friendship among the three monotheistic religions (Saladin, the great Muslim leader who defeated the Christian Crusaders, is one of the three main characters), Lessing recounts the allegory of the father (God) who gives each of his three sons (representing Islam, Christianity, and Judaism) a ring (representing religion):

---

217 Voltaire, quoted by Eddé, *op. cit.,* pp. 484-485.

218 Chateaubriand, *Itinéraire de Paris à Jérusalem,* 1811, English translation by Frederic Shoberl, *Travels in Greece, Palestine, Egypt, and Barbary, during the years 1806 and 1807,* New York: Van Winkle and Wiley, 1814, p. 318.

219 Jubb, *op.cit.,* p. 96.

The judge went further on to say:
If you will have my judgment, not my advice,
Then go. But my advice is this:
You take the matter as it stands.
If each one had his ring straight from his father,
So let each believe his ring the true one.
'Tis possible your father would no longer tolerate
The tyranny of this one ring in his family,
And surely loved you all—and all alike,
And that he would not two oppress
By favouring the third.
Now then, let each one emulate in affection
Untouched by prejudice. Let each one strive
To gain the prize of proving by results
The virtue of his ring, and aid its power
With gentleness and heartiest friendliness,
With benevolence and true devotedness to God;
And if the virtue of the ring will then
Have proved itself among your children's children,
I summon them to appear again
Before this judgment seat,
After a thousand thousand years.
Here then will sit a judge more wise than I,
Who will pronounce. Go you.
So said the modest judge.
Saladin.[220]

Many writers used the theme of Saladin converting or almost converting to Christianity as a means to criticize what they thought were the abuses in the Christian Church, a Medieval equivalent of the eighteenth century craze of exotic visitors observing, and mocking European customs. Gilles de Corbeil [died first quarter 13th Century], for example, in his poem, *Ierapigra ad purgandos prelatos* (roughly, *"Laxative for Purging Prelates"*[221]) a satire in nine books and 5,929 verses, targets Guala Bicchieri, a cardinal and papal official, and satirizes rather ferociously the abuses

---

220 Gotthold Ephraim Lessing, *Nathan the Wise*, trans. William Jacks, Glasgow: James Maclehose & Sons, 1894, p. 134.

221 A Salerno glossary explains *yerapigra* literally as "sacred and bitter medicine," *sacrum amarum*, from Greek ἱερός, often used for a special pharmacological recipe, and πικρός masculine (*pikrós*) feminine πικρή, neuter πικρό, = bitter.

prevalent among ecclesiastical officials. In the poem, Saladin has instructed himself in the Christian religion, and is about to convert but decides
against it being put off by the behaviour of the clergy, who were wallowing
in lust, dishonesty, envy, wickedness and pillage. In yet other accounts,
Saladin criticises the coarseness of the Christians; their uncharitable attitude to the poor, the offertory, "the worship of the Pope," and so on.

Moving onto the nineteenth century, we have Sophie Cottin's novel
Mathilde, published in 1805, in which the eponymous heroine, sister of
Richard the Lionheart, falls in love with Saladin's brother, Malek-Adel [i.e.
al-'Ādil]. Saladin plays a secondary role, it is his brother who is the para-
gon of the chivalrous knight: noble, courageous, tender, full of fire and
melancholy, physically and morally beautiful. Mathilde, torn between her
religion and her profane passion, dare not confess she loves a Muslim until
Malek-Adel agrees to convert to Christianity. Saladin is reluctant to fight
King Guy in single combat, when he does he fares badly, and is only just
saved by his brother Malek-Adel.

The novel was a great success, and led to six librettos being written
between 1828 and 1863 for the music of Pacini, Bergonzi, Costa, Ponia-
towski, Ventura-Sanchez, and Loewe.

The historical novels of G.A. Henty, written between 1867 and
1902 and aimed at young people, were immensely popular right up to the
1950s, in England, at least. He wrote over 120 works of historical fiction,
which were frowned upon from the 1960s onwards, for their imperialism,
xenophobia, racism, and reactionary views. But these works written during the heyday of British imperialism are making a surprising comeback
among conservative homeschoolers, looking for texts that will build character, courage, resourcefulness, and faith, and teach history at the same
time. Historian, A.J.P. Taylor, a Fellow of Magdalen College, Oxford, lec-
tured in modern history at Oxford from 1938 to 1963, wrote that "true
history began with Sir Walter Scott; he felt himself back into time," and
also confessed to a passion for the historical fictions of G.A. Henty. He
claimed that it was the reading of Henty that gave him confidence to give
tutorials on the Thirty Years War.[222]

A glance at some of the titles of his novels indicate their sweep and
range: With *Clive in India: The Beginnings of an Empire* [1884]; *With Wolfe
in Canada: The Winning of a Continent* [1887]; *Through Russian Snows:
A Story of Napoleon's Retreat from Moscow* [1896]; *In Greek Waters: A Story
of the Grecian War of Independence* (1821–1827) [1893], and of course

---

222 Robert Irwin, *op.cit.*, p. 143, referring to A.J.P. Taylor. *A Personal History*, London,
1983, p. 25.

the work that concerns us here, *Winning His Spurs: A Tale of the Crusades* (aka *Boy Knight*) [1882]. The influence of Sir Walter Scott on the latter work is evident—both the influence of *Ivanhoe* and *The Talisman*. Henty begins the Crusader novel in England and borrows Scott's themes of the rivalry between the Saxons and the Normans, developed in *Ivanhoe*. Young Cuthbert accompanies Sir Walter (a homage to Scott?) and Richard the Lionheart to the Holy Land on the Third Crusade. Though accused of, above all, imperialism, Henty in this work does not take an imperialistic or a jingoistic position but adopts rather a realistic or critical attitude towards the Crusades and Crusaders. Father Francis explains to young Cuthbert what the Crusades were all about: "When the followers of the evil prophet took possession of the land, they laid grievous burdens upon the pilgrims, heavily they fined them, persecuted them in every way, and treated them as if indeed they were but the scum of the earth under their feet....This first attempt to rescue the holy sepulchre was followed by others equally wild, misguided, and unfortunate. Some of them [the Crusaders] indeed began their evil deeds as soon as they had left their home. The last of these bodies fell upon the Jews, who are indeed enemies of the Christian faith, but who have now, at least, nothing to do with the question of the holy sepulchre. As soon as they entered into Germany the Crusaders put them to death with horrible torture. Plunder and rapine indeed appeared to be the object of the crusaders. On this as well as on most other preceding bands, their misdeeds drew down the vengeance of the people. At an early period of their march, and as soon as they reached Hungary, the people fell upon them, and put the greater portion to the sword."[223]

Father Francis then repeats a common explanation for the lack of success of the Crusades, "Doubtless the great misfortunes which have fallen upon the Christian armies have been a punishment from heaven, because they have not gone to work in the right spirit. It is not enough to take up lance and shield, and to place a red cross upon the shoulder. Those who desire to fight the battle of the Lord must cleanse their hearts, and go forth in the spirit of pilgrims rather than knights. I mean, not that they should trust wholly to spiritual weapons—for in truth the infidel is a foe not to be despised—but I mean, that they should lay aside all thoughts of worldly glory, and rivalry one against another."[224]

As the crusaders prepare to embark on their long journey, Henty cautions us about their motives: "It must not be supposed that the whole

---

223 G.A. Henty, *Winning His Spurs: A Tale of the Crusades*, Pennsylvania: Preston Speed Publications, 1997 [First published 1882], pp. 38-39.
224 *Ibid.*, p. 43.

of those present were animated by any strong religious feeling. No doubt there existed a desire, which was carefully fanned by the preaching of the priests and monks, to rescue the holy sepulchre from the hands of the Saracens; but a far stronger feeling was to be found in the warlike nature of the people in those days. Knights, men-at-arms, and indeed men of all ranks, were full of a combative spirit. Life in the castle and hut was alike dull and monotonous, and the excitement of war and adventure was greatly looked for, both as a means of obtaining glory and booty, and for the change they afforded to the dreary monotony of life."[225]

Richard the Lionheart is described as "haughty of his dignity,"[226] though free from personal pride. "He was impatient of contradiction, eager to carry out whatever he had determined upon; and nothing enraged him so much as hesitation or procrastination." And Henty is critical of Richard's execution of Muslim prisoners after the siege of Acre, "[Richard] sullied his reputation by causing all the defenders of Acre to be put to death, their ransom not having arrived at the stipulated time."[227]

When our young hero is captured and brought before Saladin, Saladin gives him a lecture on the bad manners of the Crusaders: "You are brave warriors, and I hear that before you were taken you slaughtered numbers of my people. They did wrong to capture you and bring you here to be killed. Your cruel king gives no mercy to those who fall into his hands. You must not expect it here, you who without pretence of right invade my country, slaughter my people, and defeat my armies. The murder of the prisoners of Acre has closed my heart to all mercy. There, your king put 10,000 prisoners to death in cold blood, a month after the capture of the place, because the money at which he had placed their ransom had not arrived...."[228] This passage at least is a witness to Henty's imaginative power to hold the "other's" or the enemy's point of view.

Saladin is described as "brave in the extreme, and exposed his life as fearlessly as did his Christian rival, and the two valiant leaders recognized the great qualities of each other."[229]

Another British imperialist, H. Rider Haggard also wrote a historical novel of the crusades, *The Brethren* (1904), in which he denounces the folly of the Crusades, and praises Saladin and the Saracens as noble, courageous, and chivalrous.

---

225 *Ibid.*, p. 53.

226 *Ibid.*, p. 59.

227 *Ibid.*, p. 128.

228 *Ibid.*, pp. 145-146.

229 *Ibid.*, p. 190.

In his essay already cited, Robert Irwin argues that Sir Steven Runciman was influenced by American historian Marshall Baldwin's *Raymond III of Tripolis and the Fall of Jerusalem (1140-1187)* which first appeared in 1936. Irwin further observes that Runciman used novelistic techniques to tell a story, "It is not difficult to read Runciman's artfully structured and stylish historical trilogy as a novel."

In an interview, Runciman confessed that his literary style was influenced by Beatrix Potter, author of *Peter Rabbit*, etc., while Beatrix Potter cited Sir Walter Scott as her model.[230] Walter Scott? Isn't that where we came in?

CONCLUSIONS: CRUSADES NOT BARBARIC

Often when criticizing Islam, I am interrupted by the remark that of course Christianity was also once equally culpable of similar crimes. The fact that Christianity certainly was once intolerant does not mean that my criticisms of Islam's intolerance are any less valid. If a Christian makes a specific criticism X of Islam, and Christianity was once also guilty of X, it does not follow that the criticism X is invalid.

Two wrongs do not make a right. Second, Islamic intolerance is presently a far more immediate danger to all, whereas Christian intolerance is a thing of the past, and is no longer a threat to civilization. Christendom's crimes have been recorded by Christians themselves, but, in the present climate of political correctness, many are reluctant to voice any criticism of Islam.

Of course, there is a sense in which one could well agree with criticisms of Islam's intolerance, but go on to insist that Christianity was also once intolerant in order to, perhaps, point out the possibility of Islam evolving in a similar fashion towards tolerance. One could also point out similar shortcomings of Christendom in order to relativize the atrocious behaviour of Islamic civilization, in order not to demonise Islam alone. However, this principle should work both ways; we should equally not demonise Christendom, and be prepared to point to similar shortcomings of Islam. In a recent (December, 2008) television programme, Boris Johnson, the Mayor of London, presented a rather biased programme on the Crusades, but biased against the Christians, laying the blame of the Crusades entirely on the Christians, who are always depicted as barbarians. He

---

230 D. Plante, "Profiles" in *The New Yorker*, Nov.: 77, 1986 (Interview with Runciman); H. Carpenter and M. Prichard, *The Oxford Companion to Children's Literature,* Oxford, 1984., s.v. Potter, Beatrix.

pointed out at that Christians in Spain after the expulsions of the Moors converted a mosque into a church, and called this act "vandalism." However, he failed to point out that the Crusades were a reaction against over three hundred years of *jihad* when the Eastern Christians were persecuted, and hundreds of churches destroyed. He also failed to mention the conversion of the magnificent Byzantine Hagia Sophia into a mosque, (though admittedly this took place after the Fall of Constantinople in 1453—it was a mosque from 29 May 1453 until 1931. But my point is that Islamic *jihad* did not end with the defeat of the Crusaders. On the contrary, in Islamic doctrine all the later Islamic conquests were seen as a part of the religious duty of carrying out *jihad* until the entire the world submits to Islam.)

The Muslim persecution of Christians, or for that matter, all non-Muslims, varied from country to country, ruler to ruler, or century to century. The treatment of non-Muslims, and its scriptural source and justification will be discussed below. Here I can only adumbrate the situation in the Holy Land a hundred years before Pope Urban II's call in 1095 for a crusade to liberate Palestine. The cruelties of Caliph al-Hakim have been recorded by Christian and Muslim historians. In 1003, al-Hakim began the persecution of Jews and Christians in earnest. Historian Ibn al-Dawadari tells us that the first move in a series of acts was the destruction of the church of St. Mark. Al-Musabbihi, a contemporary, recounts that the Christians built this church without a permit—the building of new churches was not permitted. The Al-Rashida mosque was built in its place, eventually extending over, and desecrating Jewish and Christian cemeteries; surely an act of vandalism. The height of al-Hakim's cruelties was the destruction of the Church of the Holy Sepulchre, also known as the Church of the Resurrection, possibly the most revered shrine in Christendom, since it is considered by Christians as Golgotha, (the Hill of Calvary), where the New Testament says that Jesus was crucified, and even the place where Jesus was buried, and hence, of course, the site of the Resurrection. He ordered dismantled "the Church of the Resurrection to its very foundations, apart from what could not be destroyed or pulled up, and they also destroyed the Golgotha and the Church of St. Constantine and all that they contained, as well as all the sacred grave-stones. They even tried to dig up the graves and wipe out all traces of their existence. Indeed they broke up and uprooted most of them. They also laid waste to a convent in the neighbourhood....The authorities took all the other property belonging to the Church of the Holy Sepulchre and its pious foundations, and all its furnishings and treasures."[231] According to Muslim sources the destruction began in September, 1007 C.E. "Most of the Muslim sources view the destruction as a reaction to its magnificence and the fact that it was a world centre for Christian pilgrims, among them many Christians from Egypt; to the splendid processions that were held in the streets of Jerusalem, and to the 'Paschal fire'...."[232]

THE HISTORIOGRAPHY OF THE CRUSADES

In the first period of the historiography of the Crusades—that is to say between 1095 and the end of the sixteenth century—the Crusades were seen as defensive, and a response to the Islamic threats to Christian holy places. The Crusaders were motivated by a fervour to recover lands from the hand of infidels, and to liberate Christians from under the Muslim yoke. But the internal threats of heretics and schismatics were also emphasized.[233]

The second period of crusading historiography was marked by the publication of more scientific histories, with full attention accorded to primary sources. For instance, there appeared in 1611 "the important collection of primary sources on the crusades edited by Jacques Bongars under the title *Gesta Dei per Francos sive orientalium expeditionum et regni Francorum Hierosolimitani historia* and in 1639 of Thomas Fuller's *Historie of the Holy Warre,* which has been called, in spite of its prejudices, the first serious general history of the crusades to treat them as fully in the past and to raise the question of their legitimacy."[234] While Fuller, a Protestant minister, wrote from an anti-Catholic perspective, Louis Maimbourg wrote his pro-Catholic *Histoire des croisades* [1685], dedicated to Louis XIV, with "self-confidence, religiosity, and 'a trace of modern good sense,'" but he veered between enthusiasm and skepticism.

The early eighteenth century judgments can be found in Mosheim. As Rodney Stark put it,

---

231 Moshe Gil, *A History of Palestine: 634-1099*, Cambridge: Cambridge University Press, 1992, p. 373.

232 *Ibid.*, p. 374.

233 Giles Constable, "The Historiography of the Crusades" in *The Crusades from the Perspective of Byzantium and the Muslim World*, edited by Angeliki E. Laiou and Roy Parviz Mottahedeh, 2001, Dumbarton Oaks Trustees for Harvard University, Washington, D.C., published by Dumbarton Oaks Research Library and Collection Washington, D.C.

234 *Ibid.*

However, the notion that the crusaders were early Western imperialists who used a religious excuse to seek land and loot probably was originated by the German Lutheran church historian Johann Lorenz von Mosheim (1693–1755), who wrote:

> The Roman pontiffs and the European princes were engaged at first in these crusades by a principle of superstition only, but when in the process of time they learnt by experience that these holy wars contributed much to increase their opulence and to extend their authority ... [then] ambition and avarice seconded and enforced the dictates of fanaticism and superstition.[235]

As Von Sybel in his very useful survey of *The History and Literature of the Crusades*[236] wrote, "[T]he spirit of the eighteenth century was decidedly opposed to implicit faith, and restlessly active in remodelling science and art. A series of works were written, in greater or less details, which threw light upon the Crusades, and which, taking different views of the facts, subjected the products of the eleventh century to a searching criticism. Voltaire is the foremost of these writers; the part in his "Essai sur les Moeurs" touching on the Crusades is very weak in point of research, for he does not even name any other authorities than William of Tyre, Anna Comnena and Elmacin,[237] and those he scarcely used." Volatire wrote that the Crusades were, "an epidemic of fury which lasted for two hundred years and which was always marked by every cruelty, every perfidy, every debauchery, and every folly of which human nature is capable."[238] The Crusaders left, further argued Voltaire, Europe for Asia only to get rich, and on the way they gave into their vices, which went unpunished; the crimes of the latter and the fanaticism of the others, and the bizarre mixture of religion and chivalry were no longer acceptable in a more enlightened century. For the Encyclopedist, Diderot, the Crusades were, "a time of the deepest darkness and of the greatest folly . . . to drag a significant part of the world into an

---

235 Quoted in Rodney Stark, *God's Battalions: The Case for the Crusades*, New York: Harper One, 2009, p. 6.

236 Heinrich Von Sybel, *The History and Literature of the Crusades*, translated and edited by Lady Duff Gordon, London: Chapman and Hall, 1861, p. 334ff.

237 That is, George Elmacin (or Girgis Al-Makin) (1205–1273), also known as Ibn al-'Amid, a Coptic historian.

238 Voltaire, *Oeuvres Complètes, Vol. 28, Mélanges: Quelques Petites Hardiesses de M.Clair*, Paris: Granier Frères, 1879, p. 560.

unhappy little country in order to cut the inhabitants' throats and seize a rocky peak which was not worth one drop of blood."[239] For David Hume, the Crusades were the "most durable monument of human folly that has yet appeared in any age or nation."[240]

Though he found much to praise in individual Crusaders, Gibbon found the whole enterprise a shameful waste, and an example of clerical led fanaticism, "The principle of the crusades was a savage fanaticism; and the most important effects were analogous to the cause. Each pilgrim was ambitious to return with his sacred spoils, the relics of Greece and Palestine; and each relic was preceded and followed by a train of miracles and visions. The belief of the Catholics was corrupted by new legends, their practice by new superstitions; and the establishment of the inquisition, the mendicant orders of monks and friars, the last abuse of indulgences, and the final progress of idolatry, flowed from the baneful fountain of the holy war. The active spirit of the Latins preyed on the vitals of their reason and religion; and if the ninth and tenth centuries were the times of darkness, the thirteenth and fourteenth were the age of absurdity and fable."[241]

Furthermore, the crusades were misdirected energy, "Great was the increase, and rapid the progress, during the two hundred years of the crusades; and some philosophers have applauded the propitious influence of these holy wars, which appear to me to have checked rather than forwarded the maturity of Europe. The lives and labours of millions, which were buried in the East, would have been more profitably employed in the improvement of their native country: the accumulated stock of industry and wealth would have overflowed in navigation and trade; and the Latins would have been enriched and enlightened by a pure and friendly correspondence with the climates of the East."[242]

However, what is often missed, it seems to me, is Gibbon's compliment to the Crusades tacked onto the end of his famous section, praising the Holy War for, at least, liberating one part of humanity. "The larger portion of the inhabitants of Europe was chained to the soil, without freedom, or property, or knowledge; and the two orders of ecclesiastics and nobles,

---

239 Denis Diderot, *Œuvres Complètes, Tome XIV: Dictionnaire Encyclopédique, Tome II.* Paris: Chez J.L.J. Brière, 1821, s.v. « Croisades », p. 497.

240 David Hume, *A History of England. From the Invasion of Julius Caesar to the Revolution in 1688,* New York: Worthington Co., 1889, [Ist Published 1754-1762] Vol. I, p. 243.

241 Edward Gibbon, *The Decline and Fall of the Roman Empire,* Chapter LXI, London: Penguin Classics, Vol.III, [1788] 1994, p.,727.

242 *Ibid.,* p. 728.

whose numbers were comparatively small, alone deserved the name of citizens and men. This oppressive system was supported by the arts of the—clergy and the swords of the barons. The authority of the priests operated in the darker ages as a salutary antidote: they prevented the total extinction of letters, mitigated the fierceness of the times, sheltered the poor and defenceless, and preserved or revived the peace and order of civil society. But the independence, rapine, and discord, of the feudal lords were unmixed with any semblance of good; and every hope of industry and improvement was crushed by the iron weight of the martial aristocracy. Among the causes that undermined that Gothic edifice, a conspicuous place must be allowed to the crusades. The estates of the barons were dissipated, and their race was often extinguished, in these costly and perilous expeditions. Their poverty extorted from their pride those charters of freedom which unlocked the fetters of the slave, secured the farm of the peasant and the shop of the artificer, and gradually restored a substance and a soul to the most numerous and useful part of the community. The conflagration which destroyed the tall and barren trees of the forest, gave air and scope to the vegetation of the smaller and nutritive plants of the soil."[243]

In fact. I believe Gibbon's position on the Crusades was far more subtle than hitherto acknowledged. Many historians writing one-volume accounts of the Crusades, in their conclusions, tend only to quote Gibbon's comments from Chapter LXI of his *Decline and Fall*. But we need to go back to Chapter XIX to have a fuller picture. Here are some of Gibbon's views from Ch. XIX.[244]

Man, according to Gibbon, is naturally violent, and we are ready to grant the slightest provocation as sufficient cause for war. But we cannot be so indulgent when it comes to holy war—we cannot believe that Jesus would allow fighting unless the motive were pure. We must be sure of the justice of our enterprise. Gibbon does allow that there was some justification for the Crusades, though he believes that the Koran preaches, and the Muslims, in fact, practice, tolerance. And yet, at the same time, Gibbon acknowledges that the Christians were under an "iron yoke," and the Turks posed a serious threat to Christendom:

In the age of the crusades, the Christians, both of the East and

---

243 *Ibid.*

244 Gibbon's views of the Crusades are conveniently gathered together in: *The Life and Letters of Edward Gibbon With His History of the Crusades,* London & New York: Frederick Warne and Company, 1889. All the following quotes are taken from this collection, pp. 368-373.

West, were persuaded of their lawfulness and merit; their arguments are clouded by the perpetual abuse of Scripture and rhetoric; but they seem to insist on the right of natural and religious defence, their peculiar title to the Holy Land, and the impiety of their Pagan and Mahometan foes. The right of a just defence may fairly include our civil and spiritual allies: it depends on the existence of danger; and that danger must be estimated by the twofold consideration of the malice, and the power, of our enemies. A pernicious tenet has been imputed to the Mahometans, the duty of extirpating all other religions by the sword. This charge of ignorance and bigotry is refuted by the Koran, by the history of the Mussulman conquerors, and by their public and legal toleration of the Christian worship. But it cannot be denied, that the Oriental churches are depressed under their iron yoke; that, in peace and war, they asserted a divine and indefensible claim of universal empire; and that, in their orthodox creed, the unbelieving nations are continually threatened with the loss of religion or liberty. In the eleventh century, the victorious arms of the Turks presented a real and urgent apprehension of these losses. They had subdued in less than thirty years the kingdoms of Asia, as far as Jerusalem and the Hellespont ; and the Greek empire tottered on the verge of destruction. Besides an honest sympathy for their brethren, the Latins had a right and interest in the support of Constantinople, the most important barrier of the West; and the privilege of defence must reach to prevent, as well as to repel, an impending assault.

But this just purpose could have been accomplished with less waste, and without sacrificing moral precepts:

But this salutary purpose might have been accomplished by a moderate succour; and our calmer reason might disclaim the innumerable hosts and remote operations, which overwhelmed Asia and depopulated Europe. Palestine could add nothing to the strength or safety of the Latins; and fanaticism alone could pretend to justify the conquest of that distant and narrow province. The Christians affirmed that their inalienable title to the promised land had been sealed by the blood of their divine Saviour: it was their right and duty to rescue their inheritance from the unjust possessors, who profaned his sepulchre, and oppressed the pilgrimage of his disciples. Vainly would it be alleged that the pre-eminence of Jerusalem, and the sanctity of Palestine have been abolished with the Mosaic law; that the God of the Christians is not a local deity, and that the recovery of Bethlem or Calvary, his cradle or his tomb, will not atone for the violation of the moral precepts of the gospel. Such arguments glance aside from the leaden shield of superstition; and the religious mind will not easily relinquish its hold on the sacred ground of mystery and miracle. But the holy wars which have been waged in every climate of the globe, from Egypt to Livonia, and from Peru to Hindostan, require the support of some more general and flexible tenet. It has been often supposed, and sometimes affirmed, that a difference of religion is a worthy cause of hostility; that obstinate unbelievers may be slain or subdued by the champions of the cross; and that grace is the sole fountain of dominion as well as of mercy. Above four hundred years before the first crusade, the eastern and western provinces of the Roman empire had been acquired about the same time, and in the same manner, by the Barbarians of Germany and Arabia. Time and treaties had legitimated the conquests of the Christian Franks; but in the eyes of their subjects and neighbours, the Mahometan princes were still tyrants and usurpers, who, by the arms of war or rebellion, might be lawfully driven from their unlawful possession.

Gibbon is well aware of the importance of the absolutions of their sins in the motivation of many common crusaders:

The merit of military service against the Saracens of Africa and Spain, had been allowed by the predecessors of Urban the second. In the council of Clermont, that pope proclaimed a plenary indulgence to those who should enlist under the banner of the cross; the absolution of all their sins, and a full receipt for all that might be due of canonical penance. The cold philosophy of modern times is incapable of feeling the impression that was made on a sinful and fanatic world. At the voice of their pastor, the robber, the incendiary, the homicide, arose by thousands to redeem their souls, by repeating on the infidels the same deeds which they had exercised against their Christian brethren; and the terms of atonement were eagerly embraced by offenders of every rank and denomination. None were pure; none were exempt from the guilt and penalty of sin; and those who were the least amenable to the justice of God and the church, were the best entitled to the temporal and eternal recompence of their pious courage. If they fell, the spirit of the Latin clergy did not hesitate to adorn their tomb with the crown of martyrdom; and should they survive, they could expect without impatience the delay and increase of their heavenly reward. They offered their blood to the Son of God, who had laid down his life for their salvation: they took up the cross, and entered with confidence into the way of the Lord. His providence would watch over their safety; perhaps his visible and miraculous power would smooth the difficulties of their holy enterprise. The cloud and pillar of Jehovah had marched before the Israelites into the promised land. Might not the Christians more reasonably hope that the rivers would open for their passage; that the walls of the strongest cities would fall at the sound of their trumpets; and that the sun would be arrested in his mid-career, to allow them time for the destruction of the infidels?

Gibbon also acknowledges that that many crusaders had mixed motives, that it was not a simple matter—not all were moved by pure thoughts. It was much easier for the religious authorities to goad the masses into action by promises of absolution of their sins by fighting, not their brethren in Europe, but infidels in foreign lands, with possiblities of achieving immortality as Christian heroes:

Of the chiefs and soldiers who marched to the holy sepulchre, I will dare to affirm, that all were prompted by the spirit of enthusiasm; the belief of merit, the hope of reward, and the assurance of divine aid. But I am equally persuaded, that in many it was not the sole, that in some it was not the leading, principle of action. The use and abuse of religion are feeble to stem, they are strong and irresistible to impel the stream of national manners. Against the private wars of the Barbarians, their bloody tournaments, licentious loves, and judicial duels, the popes and synods might ineffectually thunder. It is a more easy task to provoke the metaphysical disputes of the Greeks, to drive into the cloister the victims of anarchy or despotism, to sanctify the patience of slaves and cowards, or to assume the merit of the humanity and benevolence of modern Christians. War and exercise were the reigning passions of the Franks or Latins; they were enjoined, as a penance, to gratify those passions, to visit distant lands, and to draw their swords against the nations of the East. Their victory, or even their attempt, would immortalize the names of the intrepid heroes of the cross; and the purest piety could not be insensible to the most splendid prospect of military glory.

The vulgar masses were undoubtedly taken with visions of worldly gain, and they believed they would acquire wine, women, and land, and at the same time escape their own state of servitude in Europe:

They could march with alacrity against the distant and hostile nations who were devoted to their arms: their fancy already grasped the golden sceptres of Asia; and the conquest of Apulia and Sicily by the Normans might exalt to royalty the hopes of the most private adventurer. Christendom, in her rudest state, must have yielded to the climate and cultivation of the Mahometan countries; and their natural and artificial wealth had been magnified by the tales of pilgrims, and the gifts of an imperfect commerce. The vulgar, both the great and small, were taught to believe every wonder, of lands flowing with milk and honey, of mines and treasures, of gold and diamonds, of palaces of marble and jasper, and of odoriferous groves of cinnamon and frankincense. In this earthly paradise, each warrior depended on his sword to carve a plenteous and honourable establishment, which he measured only by the extent of his wishes. Their vassals and soldiers trusted their fortunes to God and their master: the spoils of a Turkish emir might enrich the meanest follower of the camp; and the flavour of the wines, the beauty of the Grecian women, were temptations more adapted to the nature, than to the profession, of the champions of the cross. The love of freedom was a powerful incitement to the multitudes who were oppressed by feudal or ecclesiastical tyranny. Under this holy sign the peasants and burghers, who were attached to the servitude of the glebe, might escape from an haughty lord, and transplant themselves and their families to a land of liberty. The monk might release himself from the discipline of his convent: the debtor might suspend the accumulation of usury, and the pursuit of his creditors; and outlaws and malefactors of every cast might continue to brave the laws and elude the punishment of their crimes.

These motives were potent and numerous: when we have singly computed their weight on the mind of each individual, we must add the infinite series, the multiplying powers of example and fashion. The first proselytes became the warmest and most effectual missionaries of the cross: among their friends and countrymen they preached the duty, the merit, and the recompense, of their holy vow; and the most reluctant hearers were insensibly drawn within the whirlpool of persuasion and authority. The martial youths were fired by the reproach or suspicion of cowardice; the opportunity of visiting with an army the sepulchre of Christ, was embraced by the old and infirm, by women and children, who consulted rather their zeal than their strength; and those who in the evening had derided the folly of their companions, were the most eager, the ensuing day, to tread in their footsteps. The ignorance which magnified the hopes, diminished the perils, of the enterprise. Since the Turkish conquest, the paths of pilgrimage were obliterated, the chiefs themselves had an imperfect notion of the length of their way and the state of their enemies; and such was the stupidity of the people, that, at the sight of the first city or castle beyond the limits of their knowledge, they were ready to ask whether that was not the Jerusalem, the term and object of their labours. Yet the more prudent of the crusaders, who were not sure that they should be fed from heaven with a shower of quails or manna, provided themselves with those precious metals, which, in every country, are the representatives of every commodity. To defray, according to their rank, the expenses of the road, princes alienated their provinces, nobles their lands and cattle, peasants their castles and the instruments of husbandry. The value of property was depreciated by the eager competition of multitudes; while the price of arms and horses was raised to an exorbitant height by the wants and impatience of the buyers. Those who remained at home, with sense and money, were enriched by the epidemical disease: the sovereigns acquired at a cheap rate the domains of their vassals; and the ecclesiastical purchasers completed the payment by the assurance of their prayers. The cross, which was commonly sewn on the garment, in cloth or silk, was inscribed by some zealots on their skin: an hot iron, or indelible liquor, was applied to perpetuate the mark; and a crafty monk, who showed the miraculous impression on his breast, was repaid with the popular veneration and the richest benefices of Palestine.

The Romantic reaction to the Enlightenment view of the Crusades was led by Chateaubriand [1768-1848], who wrote: "The writers of the eighteenth century have taken pains to represent the Crusades in an odious light. I was one of the first to protest against this ignorance or injustice. The Crusades were not mad expeditions, as some writers have affected to call them either in their principle or in their results. The Christians were not the aggressors. If the subjects of Omar, setting out from Jerusalem, and making the circuit of Africa, invaded Sicily, Spain, nay, even France, where they were exterminated by Charles Martel, why should not the subjects of Philip I quitting France, make the circuit to Asia, to take vengeance on the descendants of Omar in Jerusalem itself?... Those who perceive in the crusades nothing but a mob of armed pilgrims running to rescue a tomb in Palestine, must take a very limited view of history. The point in question was not merely the deliverance of that sacred tomb, but likewise to decide which of the two should predominate in the world, a religion hostile to civlization, systematically favourable to ignorance, despotism, and slavery, or a religion which has revived among the moderns the spirit of learned antiquity and abolished servitude. Whoever reads the address of Pope Urban II, to the council of Clermont, must be convinced that the leaders in these military enterprises had not the petty views which have been ascribed to them, and that they aspired to save the world from a new inundation of barbarians. The spirit of Islamism is persecution and conquest; the gospel, on the contary, inculcates only toleration and peace. Accordingly the Christians endured for seven hundred and sixty-four years all the oppressions which the fanaticism of the Saracens impelled them to exercise. They merely endeavored to interest Charlemagne in their favour; for neither the conquest of Spain, the invasion of France, the pillage of Greece and the two Sicilies, nor the entire subjugation of Africa, could for near eight centuries rouse the Christians to arms, If at last the shrieks of numberless victims slaughtered in the East; if the progress of the barbarians, who had already reached the gates of Constantinople, awakened Christendom, and impelled it to rise in its own defence, who can say that the cause of the holy wars was unjust? Contemplate Greece, if you would know the fate of a people subjected to the Muslim yoke. Would those, who at this day so loudly exult in the progress of knowledge, wish to live under a religion which burned the Alexandrian library, and which makes a merit of trampling mankind under foot, and holding literature and the arts in sovereign contempt.

"The Crusades, by weakening the Muslim hordes in the very center of Asia, prevented our falling prey to the Turks and Arabs: they did more, they saved us from our own revolutions; they suspended, by the peace of God, our internecine wars; and opened an outlet to that excess of population, which sooner or later occasion the ruin of states.

"With regard to the other results of the Crusades, people begin to admit that these military enterprises were favourable to the progress of science and civilization. Robertson has admirably discussed this subject in his *Historical Disquisition concerning the Knowledge which the Ancients had of India*. I shall add, that in this estimate we must not omit the renown gained by the European arms in these distant expeditions. The time of these expeditions is the heroic period of our history, the period which gave birth to the epic poetry. Whatever diffuses a tinge of the marvellous over a nation, ought not to be despised by that very nation. In vain should we attempt to deny that there is something implanted in our hearts which excites in us a love of glory: man is not absolutely made of positive calculations of profit and loss; it would be debasing him too much to suppose so. It was by impressing upon the Romans the eternity of their city, that their chiefs led them on to the conquest of the world, and spurred them forward to achievements which have gained them everlasting renown."[245]

Rodney Stark admirably sums up some of the modern wrong-headed interpretations of the Crusades: "During the twentieth century, this self-interest thesis [of Gibbon and Mosheim] was developed into an elaborate 'materialist'account of why the Crusades took place. The prolific Geoffrey Barraclough (1908–1984) wrote: '[O]ur verdict on the Crusades [is that it amounted to] colonial exploitation.' Or, as Karen Armstrong confided, these 'were our first colonies.' A more extensive and sophisticated material explanation of why the knights went east was formulated by Hans Eberhard Mayer, who proposed that the Crusades alleviated a severe financial squeeze on Europe's 'knightly class.' According to Mayer and others who

---

245 F.A. de Chateaubriand, *Travels in Greece, Palestine, Egypt, and Barbary During the Years 1806 and 1807,* Trans, by F. Shoberl, New York: Van Winkle and Wiley, 1814, pp. 315-316; French edn.: Chateaubriand, *Itinéraire de Paris à Jérusalem*, ed. Jean-Claude Berchet, Paris: Folio Classique, 2005 [1st published 1811] p. 371-373.

share his views, at this time there was a substantial and rapidly growing number of 'surplus' sons, members of noble families who would not inherit and whom the heirs found it increasingly difficult to provide with even modest incomes. Hence, as Mayer put it, 'the Crusade acted as a kind of safety valve for the knightly class . . . a class which looked upon the Crusade as a way of solving its material problems.' Indeed, a group of American economists recently proposed that the crusaders hoped to get rich from the flow of pilgrims (comparing the shrines in Jerusalem with modern amusement parks) and that the pope sent the crusaders east in pursuit of 'new markets' for the church, presumably to be gained by converting people away from Islam. It is thus no surprise that a leading college textbook on Western civilization informs students: 'From the perspective of the pope and European monarchs, the crusades offered a way to rid Europe of contentious young nobles . . . [who] saw an opportunity to gain territory, riches, status, possibly a title, and even salvation.'"[246]

Sir Steven Runciman's elegantly written three volume history held the field for many decades from 1950s onwards, and his summing up of the Crusades was very influential:[247]

Seen in the perspective of history the whole Crusading movement was a vast fiasco....[T]he tenuous kingdom of Jerusalem and its sister principalities were a puny outcome from so much energy and enthusiasm....One of Pope Urban's expressed aims in preaching the Crusades was to find some useful work for the turbulent and bellicose barons who otherwise spent their energy on civil wars at home; ...[T]he chief benefit obtained by Western Christendom from the Crusades was negative.... Even more harmful was the effect of the Holy War on the spirit of Islam. Any religion that is based on an exclusive Revelation is bound to show some contempt for the unbeliever. But Islam was not intolerant in its early days. Mahomet himself considered that Jews and Christians had received a partial revelation and were therefore not to be persecuted. ...The Holy War begun by the Franks ruined [the] good relations [between Christians and Muslims]. The savage intolerance shown by the Crusaders was answered by growing intolerance amongst the

---

246 Rodney Stark, *God's Battalions: The Case for the Crusades*, New York: Harper One, 2009, p. 8.

247 Steven Runciman, *A History Of the Crusades, Vol.III The Kingdom of Acre and the Later Crusades*, Cambridge: Cambridge University Press, 1951, pp. 469-480.

Moslems. The broad humanity of Saladin and his family was soon to be rare amongst their fellow-believers. By the time of the Mameluks, the Moslems were as narrow as the Franks....The harm done by the Crusades to Islam was small in comparison with that done by them to Eastern Christendom....[T]he destruction of Byzantium [by the Crusaders] was the result of deliberate malice. [The] greed and [the]clumsiness [of the Crusaders] led them to indulge in irreparable destruction....It was the Crusaders themselves who wilfully broke down the defence of Christendom and this allowed the infidel to cross the Straits and penetrate into the heart of Europe...The chief motive that impelled the Christian armies eastward was faith...This genuine faith was often combined with unashamed greed....There was so much courage and so little honour, so much devotion and so little understanding. High ideals were besmirched by cruelty and greed, enterprise and endurance by a blind and narrow self-righteousness; and the Holy War itself was nothing more than a long act of intolerance in the name of God, which is a sin against the Holy Ghost."

Rodney Stark distils the prevailing wisdom: "during the Crusades, an expansionist, imperialistic Christendom brutalized, looted, and colonized a tolerant and peaceful Islam." Stark then argues that this was "Not so. As will be seen, the Crusades were precipitated by Islamic provocations: by centuries of bloody attempts to colonize the West and by sudden new attacks on Christian pilgrims and holy places. Although the Crusades were initiated by a plea from the pope, this had nothing to do with hopes of converting Islam. Nor were the Crusades organized and led by surplus sons, but by the heads of great families who were fully aware that the costs of crusading would far exceed the very modest material rewards that could be expected; most went at immense personal cost, some of them knowingly bankrupting themselves to go. Moreover, the crusader kingdoms that they established in the Holy Land, and that stood for nearly two centuries, were not colonies sustained by local exactions; rather, they required immense subsidies from Europe. In addition, it is utterly unreasonable to impose modern notions about proper military conduct on medieval warfare; both Christians and Muslims observed quite different rules of war. Unfortunately, even many of the most sympathetic and otherwise sensible historians of the Crusades are unable to accept that fact and are given to agonizing over the very idea that war can ever be 'just.' revealing the pacifism that has become so widespread among academics. Finally, claims that Muslims have been harboring bitter resentments about the Crusades for a millennium are nonsense: Muslim antagonism about the Crusades did not appear until about 1900, in reaction against the decline of the Ottoman Empire and the onset of actual European colonialism in the Middle East. And anti-crusader feelings did not become intense until after the founding of the state of Israel."[248]

A new generation of Western scholars of the Middle Ages have been trying to put right the misconceptions that have grown up about the Crusades. As Jonathan Riley-Smith has argued "modern Western public opinion, Arab nationalism, and Pan-Islamism all share perceptions of crusading that have more to do with nineteenth-century European imperialism than with actuality."[249] Muslims in particular have developed "mythistories" concerning the putative injuries they have received at the hands of the Crusaders. The first point that needs to be emphasized is that the Crusades "were proclaimed not only against Muslims, but also against pagan Wends, Balts and Lithuanians, shamanist Mongols, Orthodox Russians and Greeks, Cathar and Hussite heretics, and those Catholics whom the Church deemed to be its enemies."[250]

Second, the Crusades were not "thoughtless explosions of barbarism," rather their underlying rationale was relatively sophisticated, elaborated theologically by Christian nations that were threatened by Muslim invaders who had managed to reach into the heart of Europe, in central France in the eighth century and Vienna in the sixteenth and seventeenth centuries. They were a response to the desecration of the Christian shrines in the Holy Land, the destruction of churches, and the general persecution of Christians in the Near East. A Crusade to be considered legitimate had to fulfill strict criteria. "First, it must not be entered into lightly or for aggrandizement, but only for a legally sound reason, which has to be a reactive one." It was, in other words, waged for purposes of repelling violence or injury and the imposition of justice on wrongdoers. A Crusade was never a war of conversion, rather a rightful attempt to recover Christian territory which had been injuriously seized in the past. "Second, it must be formally declared by an authority recognized as having the power to make such a declaration. Third, it must be waged justly."[251]

---

248 Stark, *op.cit.*, pp. 6-9.

249 Jonathan Rilety-Smith, *The Crusades, Christianity, and Islam*, New York: Columbia University Press 2008, p. 79.

250 *Ibid.*, p. 9.

251 *Ibid.*, pp. 11-12.

The Crusaders were not colonialists, and the Crusades were not engaged in for economic reasons, as many Western Liberals and Liberal economists assumed; most crusaders would have laughed at the prospect of material gain. In fact, crusading became a financial burden as the expenses associated with warfare increased. They were far more concerned with saving not only Christendom from Islam, but also their souls. The role of penance has often been overlooked in crusading thought and practice; many crusaders believed that by taking part in a crusade they were able to repay the debt their sinfulness had incurred.

Nineteenth, and even early twentieth century Europeans unashamedly used crusader rhetoric and a tendentious reading of crusader history to justify their imperial dreams of conquest. For example, after the First World War, "The French Mandate in Syria generated a wave of French historical literature, one theme of which was that the achievements of the crusaders provided the first chapter in a history that had culminated in modern imperialism."[252] As we shall see, the newly emerging Arab nationalists took nineteenth-century rhetoric seriously. A second strand in false, modern interpretations of crusader history was furnished by European romanticism, as for example, manifested in the novels of Sir Walter Scott. As Riley-Smith summarized, "The novels [of Scott] painted a picture of crusaders who were brave and glamorous, but also vainglorious, avaricious, childish and boorish. Few of them were genuinely moved by religion or the crusade ideal; most had taken the cross out of pride, greed, or ambition. The worst of them were the brothers of the military orders, who may have been courageous and disciplined but were also arrogant, privileged, corrupt, voluptuous and unprincipled. An additional theme, the cultural superiority of the Muslims, which was only hinted at in the other novels, pervaded the *The Talisman* [1825]."[253]

Many believe that modern Muslims have inherited from their medieval ancestors memories of crusader violence and destruction. But as Riley-Smith says, nothing could be further from the truth.[254] By the fourteenth century, in the Islamic world the Crusades had almost passed out of mind. Muslims had lost interest, and, in any case, they "looked back on the Crusades with indifference and complacency. In their eyes they had been the outright winners. They had driven the crusaders from the lands they had settled in the Levant and had been triumphant in the Balkans, occupying far more territory in Europe than the Western settlers had ever

---

252 *Ibid.*, p. 60.

253 *Ibid.*, p. 65.

254 *Ibid.*, p. 68.

held in Syria and Palestine."[255]

The Muslim world only began to take an interest in the Crusades again in the 1890s but seen through the prism of Western imperialist rhetoric and European romantic fantasies concocted by Walter Scott. The latter encouraged the myth of the culturally inferior crusaders faced with civilized, liberal, and modern-looking Muslims, and from the former the Muslims derived the equally false idea of a continuing Western assault. Many Arab Nationalists believed "their struggle for independence to be a predominantly Arab riposte to a crusade that was being waged against them. Since the 1970s, however, they have been challenged by a renewed and militant Pan-Islamism, the adherents of which have globalized the Nationalist interpretation of crusade history...."[256]

Thus we now have the spectacle of the modern Islamists very often invoking the Crusades. As Bin Laden wrote, "For the first time the Crusaders have managed to achieve their historic ambitions and dreams against our Islamic umma, gaining control over the Islamic holy places and the Holy Sanctuaries, and hegemony over the wealth and riches of our umma.,"[257] and, "Ever since God made the Arabian Peninsula flat, created desert in it and surrounded it with seas, it has never suffered such a calamity as these Crusader hordes, that have spread in it like locusts, consuming its wealth and destroying its fertility."[258] The battle, according to Bin Laden, is between Muslims—people of Islam—and the Global Crusaders.[259]

As Riley-Smith concludes, "It is this vision of a continuing crusade and of resistance to it that has suddenly and spectacularly forced itself on the world outside. The language employed is often feverish, but a Muslim does not have to be an extreme Islamist to hold the view that the West is still engaged in crusading....Having less to do with historical reality than with reactions to imperialism, the Nationalist and Islamist interpretations of crusade history help many people, moderates as well as extremists, to place the exploitation they believe they have suffered in a historical context and to satisfy their feelings of both superiority and humiliation."[260]

---

255 *Ibid.*, p. 71.

256 *Ibid.*, p. 73.

257 Osama bin Muhammad bin Laden, *Messages to the World*, ed. Bruce Lawrence, trans. James Howarth, London and New York, 2005, p. 16, quoted in Riley-Smith, p. 75.

258 *Ibid.*, p. 59, quoted in Riley-Smith, p. 75.

259 *Ibid.*, quoted in Riley-Smith, p. 75.

260 Riley-Smith, *op.cit.*, p. 76.

3

Jews and the Crusades

PART I

ISLAMIC ANTISEMITISM BEFORE 1096

S ir Steven Runciman in the conclusion to his highly influential, elegantly written *The History of the Crusades*,[1] seems to imply that it was the Christian Crusaders who alone were responsible not only for the "growing intolerance amongst the Moslems," but somehow also for the fading away of Muslim intellectual life, and the subsequent stagnation of Islamic culture: "…an intolerant faith is incapable of progress." Runciman's analysis is no different from so many others that write of Islamic history and culture: what are seen as positive aspects of Islamic Civilization are ecstatically praised, even exaggerated, and all the negative aspects are imputed to the arrival of pestililential Westerners, and where the Arabs, Persians and Muslims in general are seen as passive victims; they are certainly not allowed any autonomy.

But, *pace* Runciman, this will not do as history. Even a cursory glance at the plight of Jews under Muslims *before* the Crusades would be enough to refute Sir Steven's rosy picture of an earlier interfaith utopia. All the persecutions of both Christians and Jews stem directly from the precepts and principles enshrined in the canonical texts of Islam: the Koran; the *Sira*, that is, Ibn Ishaq's biography of Muhammad; the *Hadith*, that is, the Traditions, the record of the deeds and sayings of Muhammad and his companions; and the classical Muslim Koranic commentaries. In other

1 Steven Runciman, *A History of the Crusades, Vol. III, The Kingdom of Acre and the Later Crusades*, Cambridge: Cambridge University Press, 1951, p. 474.

words, "Muslim Jew hatred... dates back to the origins of Islam."[2] It is there in the Koran:

V.51: O you who believe! Take not the Jews and the Christians for friends. They are friends one to another. He among you who takes them for friends is one of them. (V.51)

VIII.67: It is not for any Prophet to have captives until he has made slaughter in the land.

II.61: Wretchedness and baseness were stamped upon them (that is, the Jews), and they were visited with wrath from Allah. That was because they disbelieved in Allah's revelations and slew the prophets wrongfully. That was for their disobedience and transgression.

IV.44-46: Have you not seen those who have received a portion of the Scripture? They purchase error, and they want you to go astray from the path. But Allah knows best who your enemies are, and it is sufficient to have Allah as a friend. It is sufficient to have Allah as a helper. Some of the Jews pervert words from their meanings, and say, "We hear and we disobey," and "Hear without hearing," and "Heed us!" twisting with their tongues and slandering religion. If they had said, "We have heard and obey," or "Hear and observe us" it would have been better for them and more upright. But Allah had cursed them for their disbelief, so they believe not, except for a few.

IV.160-61: And for the evildoing of the Jews, We have forbidden them some good things that were previously permitted them, and because of their barring many from Allah's way. And for their taking usury which was prohibited for them, and because of their consuming people's wealth under false pretense. We have prepared for the unbelievers among them a painful punishment.

IX.29–31: Fight against such of those who have been given the Scripture [Jews and Christians] as believe not in Allah nor the Last Day, and forbid not that which Allah has forbidden by His Messenger, and follow not the religion of truth, until they pay the tribute [poll tax] readily, and are utterly subdued. The Jews say, "Ezra is the son of Allah," and the

---

2 Andrew Bostom, *The Legacy of Islamic Anti-Semitism*, Amherst: Prometheus Books, 2008, p. 33.

Christians say, "The Messiah is the son of Allah." Those are the words of their mouths, conforming to the words of the unbelievers before them. Allah attack them! How perverse they are! They have taken their rabbis and their monks as lords besides Allah, and so too the Messiah son of Mary, though they were commanded to serve but one God. There is no God but He. Allah is exalted above that which they deify beside Him.

IX.34: O you who believe! Lo! many of the (Jewish) rabbis and the (Christian) monks devour the wealth of mankind wantonly and debar (men) from the way of Allah. They who hoard up gold and silver and spend it not in the way of Allah, unto them give tidings of a painful doom.

V.63–64: Why do not the rabbis and the priests forbid their evil-speaking and devouring of illicit gain? Verily evil is their handiwork. The Jews say, "Allah's hands are fettered." Their hands are fettered, and they are cursed for what they have said! On the contrary, His hands are spread open. He bestows as He wills. That which has been revealed to you from your Lord will surely increase the arrogance and unbelief of many among them. We have cast enmity and hatred among them until the Day of Resurrection. Every time they light the fire of war, Allah extinguishes it. They hasten to spread corruption throughout the earth, but Allah does not love corrupters!

V.70–71: We made a covenant with the Israelites and sent forth apostles among them. But whenever an apostle came to them with a message that did not suit their fancies, some they accused of lying and others they put to death. They thought no harm would follow: they were blind and deaf. God is ever watching their actions.

V.82: Indeed, you will surely find that the most vehement of men in enmity to those who believe are the Jews and the polytheists.

V.51: O you who believe! Take not the Jews and the Christians for friends. They are friends one to another. He among you who takes them for friends is one of them.

V.57: O you who believe! Choose not for friends such of those who received the Scripture [Jews and Christians] before you, and of the disbelievers, as make jest and sport of your religion. But keep your duty to Allah of you are true believers.

V.59: Say: O, People of the Scripture [Jews and Christians]! Do you blame us for aught else than that we believe in Allah and that which is revealed unto us and that which was revealed aforetime, and because most of you are evil-doers?

V.66: Among them [Jews and Christians] there are people who are moderate, but many of them are of evil conduct.

XXXIII.26: He brought down from their strongholds those who had supported them from among the People of the Book [Jews of Bani Qurayza] and cast terror into their hearts, so that some you killed and others you took captive.

V.60: Say: "Shall I tell you who will receive a worse reward from God? Those whom [i.e., Jews] God has cursed and with whom He has been angry, transforming them into apes and swine, and those who serve the devil. Worse is the plight of these, and they have strayed farther from the right path."

It is there in the *Sira*[3]:

"Kill any Jews that falls into your power," said the Prophet. (p. 369).

The killing of Ibn Sunayna, and its admiration leading someone to convert to Islam (*Ibid.*).

The killing of Sallam ibn Abu'l-Huqayq (pp. 482-483).

The assassination of Ka'b b. al-Ashraf, who wrote verses against Muhammad (pp. 364–69).

The raid against the Jewish tribe of the Banu'l-Nadir and their banishment (437–45).

The extermination of the Banu Qurayza, between six hundred and eight hundred men (pp. 461–69).

The killing of al-Yusayr (pp. 665–66).

---

3 Ibn Ishaq, *The Life of Muhammad*, trans. Alfred Guillaume 1955: reprint, Oxford: Oxford University Press, 1987.

It is there in the other Muslim historians[4]:

"Then occurred the sariyyah (raid) of Salim Ibn Umayr al-Amri against Abu Afak, the Jew, in (the month of) Shawwal in the beginning of the twentieth month from the hijrah (immigration from Mecca to Medina in 622 C.E.) of the Apostle of Allah. Abu Afak, was from Banu Amr Ibn Awf, and was an old man who had attained the age of 120. He was a Jew, and used to instigate the people against the Apostle of Allah, and composed (satirical) verses (about Muhammad). Salim Ibn Umayr, who was one of the great weepers and who had participated in Badr, said, "I take a vow that I shall either kill Abu Afak or die before him." He waited for an opportunity until a hot night came, and Abu Afak slept in an open place. Salim Ibn Umayr knew it, so he placed the sword on his liver and pressed it till it reached his bed. The enemy of Allah screamed and the people who were his followers, rushed to him, took him to his house and interred him."

It is there in the *Hadith*[5]:

"Bani An-Nadir and Bani Quraiza fought, so the Prophet (Muhammad) exiled Bani An-Nadir and allowed Bani Quraiza to remain at their places. He then killed their men and distributed their women, children and property among the Muslims, but some of them came to the Prophet and he granted them safety, and they embraced Islam. He exiled all the Jews from Medina. They were the Jews of Bani Qainuqa, the tribe of Abdullah bin Salam and the Jews of Bani Haritha and all the other Jews of Medina."

BEFORE 1096

Since Sir Steven argues that Islamic intolerance began after the Crusasdes, here are examples of the persecution of Jews in Islamic lands before 1096: the massacre of more than 6,000 Jews in Fez (Morocco) in 1033; of the hundreds of Jews killed between 1010 and 1013 near Cordoba, and other parts of Muslim Spain; of the massacre of the entire Jewish community of roughly 4,000 in Granada during the Muslim riots of 1066. Referring to the latter massacre, Robert Wistrich writes: "This was a disaster, as

---

4 Sa'd, *Kitab al-Tabaqât al Kabir*, trans. S. M. Haq, New Delhi: Kitab Bhavan, 1972, vol. 1, p. 32.
5 al-Bukhāri, *The Book of al-Maghazi* (Raids), trans. M. Muhsin Khan, vol. 5, book 59 of *Sahih*, New Delhi: Kitab Bhavan, 1987, *Hadith* no. 362, p. 241.

serious as that which overtook the Rhineland Jews thirty years later during the First Crusade, yet it has rarely received much scholarly attention." Wistrich continues: "In Kairouan [Tunisia] the Jews were persecuted and forced to leave in 1016, returning later only to be expelled again."[6]

What of the putative "culture of conviviencia," that is, the Golden Age of Tolerance in Spain before, it is claimed, it was destroyed by the intolerance of the Almohads. Unfortunately, "The Golden Age" also turns out to be a myth, invented, ironically, by the Jews themselves. The myth may well have originated as early as the twelfth century, when Abraham Ibn Daud in his *Sefer ha-Qabbalah* contrasted an idealised period of tolerance of the salons of Toledo in contrast to the contemporary barbarism of the Berber dynasty. But the myth took a firm grip on the imagination of the Jews in the nineteenth century thanks to the bibliographer Moritz Steinschneider and historian Heinrich Graetz, and perhaps the influence of Benjamin Disraeli's novel *Coningsby*, published in 1844. Here is a passage from the latter novel giving a romantic picture of Muslim Spain, "..that fair and unrivaled civilization in which the children of Ishmael rewarded the children of Israel with equal rights and privileges with themselves. During these halcyon centuries, it is difficult to distinguish the followers of Moses from the votary of Mohammed. Both alike built palaces, gardens and fountains; filled equally the highest offices of state, competed in an extensive and enlightened commerce, rivaled each other in renowned universities."[7] Against a background of a rise in the pseudo-scientific racism of the nineteenth century, Jane Gerber has observed that Jewish historians looked to Islam "... for support, seeking real or imagined allies and models of tolerance in the East. The cult of a powerful, dazzling and brilliant Andalusia in the midst of an ignorant and intolerant Europe formed an important component in these contemporary intellectual currents."[8] But Gerber concludes her sober assessment of the Golden Age Myth with these reflections, "The aristocratic bearing of a select class of courtiers and poets, however, should not blind us to the reality that this tightly knit circle of leaders and aspirants to power was neither the whole of Spanish Jewish history nor of Spanish Jewish society. Their gilded mo-

---

6 Robert Wistrich, *Antisemitism-The Longest Hatred*, Schocken Books, New York, 1991, p. 196.

7 Benjamin Disraeli, *Coningsby*, Book IV, Ch. X, quoted in Bernard Lewis, *Islam in History*, New York, 1973, p. 317 n.15.

8 Jane Gerber, "Towards an Understanding of the Term: 'The Golden Age' as an Historical Reality" in ed. Aviva Doron, *The Heritage of the Jews of Spain*, Tel Aviv: Levinsky College of Education Publishing House, 1994, p. 16.

ments of the tenth and eleventh century are but a brief chapter in a longer saga. No doubt, Ibn Daud's polemic provided consolation and inspiration to a crisis-ridden twelfth century elite, just as the golden age imagery could comfort dejected exiles after 1492. It suited the needs of nineteenth century advocates of Jewish emancipation in Europe or the twentieth century contestants in the ongoing debate over Palestine....The history of the Jews in Muslim lands, especially Muslim Spain, needs to be studied on its own terms, without myth or countermyth."[9]

Some scholars, such as the great historian Shlomo Dov Goitein (d. 1985), taking into account the discoveries of the Cairo Geniza, revised their ideas about the situation of Jews in Islamic lands.[10] Another example of a scholar who changed his mind was Léon Poliakov, author of the monumental work *The History of Antisemitism*, which appeared in four volumes in French between 1955 and 1978. In Volume Two,[11] Poliakov paints, on the whole, a very favorable picture of the treatment of the Jews under Islam. He finds Muhammad, a man of genius, "simple, humane, and wise" and Islam, "a religion of tolerance above all." Astonishingly, Poliakov devotes a meagre two lines to the persecution of the Jews. Two lines in which he downplays all the acts of intolerance such as the massacre of Banu Qurayza, or the expulsion of the Banu Qaynuqa and Banu Nadir, while the political assassinations or torture of Jewish leaders and writers are not mentioned at all! Poliakov goes out of his way to contrast what he believes is the essentially benign attitude of the Muslims to the intolerance of the Christians who were, according to him, far more "inclined to plunge… into bloodbaths." He really seems to have convinced himself that the Jews and Christians lived, on the whole, "peacefully and prosperously in all parts of the Islamic Empire until our time." However, when he was in his eighties, he came into contact with the work of Bat Ye'or on the *dhimmis*, or the plight, persecution and periodic massacres of non-Muslims under Islam, and changed his mind completely.[12] Just a few weeks before his death in 1997, Poliakov agreed to write a preface[13] to the French edition

---

9 *Ibid.*, pp. 21-22.

10 Shlomo Dov Goitein, "Evidence on the Muslim Poll Tax from Non-Muslim Sources: A Geniza Study," *Journal of the Economic and Social History of the Orient* (JESHO) 6 (1963): 278-95, reptined in Andrew Bostom, *The Legacy of Islamic Anti-Semitism*, Amherst: Prometheus Books, 2008, pp. 481-488.

11 Léon Poliakov, *The History of Antisemitism, Vol. II: From Mohammed to the Marranos*, Trans. by Natalie Gerardi [Original French Edn., Paris: Calmann-Lévy, 1961] Philadelphia: University of Pennsylvania Press, pp. 19-81.

12 Personal communication from Bat Ye'or.

13 Personal communication from Léon Poliakov.

of my book, *Why I am Not a Muslim*, [*Pourquoi je ne suis pas musulman*]. Unfortunately, before he had finished his preface, Poliakov tripped on the stairs when coming down from his library, banged his head severely, and later died in hospital at the age of 87.

PART II

THE MASSACRES OF 1096

2.1. THE SOURCES

Our knowledge of the events of 1096 is derived from both Christian and Hebrew sources. However the Christian material on the persecution of the Jews is slight. "The only crusade chroniclers who mention the bands that devastated a number of northern European Jewish communities were Ekkehard of Aura and Albert of Aix."[14] Ekkehard gives a brief description of the attacks of 1096, Albert gives a little more detail, and they corroborate to some extent the Jewish sources, but in all their accounts do not add up to much.

The Jewish sources, three in all, describe more fully the assaults on Jews and their responses. Robert Chazan,[15] a Professor of Hebrew and Judaic Studies at New York University who has devoted some twenty years to this subject conveniently refers to them, in his *European Jewry and the First Crusade*, as L, the lengthy narrative, often attributed to Solomon bar Samson, and S, the shortest of the three, sometimes called the Mainz Anonymous. The third text, P, perhaps the least interesting, contains original elegiac poetry with the name-acrostic Eliezer bar Nathan and is ascribed to that twelfth-century Mainz rabbinic authority. However, there is considerable debate as to the reliablity of the *Hebrew Chronicles* of the First Crusade. While Robert Chazan is convinced of their reliability, Ivan Marcus,[16] Professor at Yale University, heeding the advice of Salo Baron, thinks far more basic work needs to be done before one can decide. Marcus writes, "Many scholars have dealt with the subjects treated here. The texts, are very problematic, and Chazan has not heeded Salo Baron's call over thirty

---

14 Robert Chazan, *European Jewry and the First Crusade*, Berkeley: University of California Press, 1987, p. 39.

15 *Ibid.*, pp. 38-50.

16 Ivan G. Marcus, "Review of *European Jewry and the First Crusade* by Robert Chazan" in *Speculum*, Vol. 64, No. 3 (Jul., 1989), pp. 685-688.

years ago: 'a renewed scrutiny of all the available sources might justify a new truly critical edition of these chronicles' (*A Social and Religious History of the Jews*, 2nd rev. ed., 4 [1957], 286). It is still a desideratum. Although they are relatively short—L is only twelve and a half folio pages—they are complex. Parallel passages are sometimes found in two or more of the texts, and some contain blank spaces due to omissions or erasures. Ultraviolet inspection might recover some of these, but that requires examining the manuscripts, not just the microfilms. Not only should the erasures be examined but several scholars' corrections and emendations must also be systematically evaluated. Thus, M. Brann published a detailed review of the Neubauer and Stern edition (*Monatsschrift für Geschichte und Wissenschaft des Judentums* 37 [1893], 285-88), in which he noted several errors of transcription and unnecessary emendations. Dozens of additional corrections are in Nathan Porges's lengthy articles (*Revue des études juives* 25 [1892], 181-201; 26 [1893], 183-97). The corrections in these studies have been ignored here. Another scholar, also not mentioned, studied the way the three texts are related. Isaiah Sonne (*Revue des études juives* 96 [1933], 123-24) concluded that the editor of L made use of P and S. He observed that when the blocks of text common to L and P refer to Christianity, the term tsahan ("stench") is used; when blocks common to L and S appear, the term tinnuf ("filth") is found, and when blocks parallel to all three texts occur, both terms appear. Chazan's contrary view that P is derived from L and that S and L are older does not account for Sonne's evidence, which is not discussed. And since P is just as important as L and S, a translation of it should have been included in a book basing itself on these three short texts…. Before a reasonably accurate translation can be made, we first need a new critical edition of the Hebrew texts that is based on a thorough consideration of the manuscripts themselves, all previous scholarly literature on them, and a careful appreciation for the characteristic features of Ashkenazic Hebrew. The Latin sources should also be translated and appended."

There are further problems that are not addressed by Chazan. These so-called chronicles are not documentary records that can be taken at face value, rather "[t]hey are highly edited, rhetorically colored, and liturgically motivated literary reworkings of circular letters and oral reports, written for definite purposes. The narrators were concerned with praising and exonerating local pious Jews who felt compelled to kill their own families and then commit suicide. To make their case, they insisted on using a Temple typology: Jews are pictured as pure sacrifices who may not be touched by polluting, impure Christians. The martyrs acted justifiably as both Temple priests and as holy sacrifices. The narrators quantified only the martyrs and ignored or downplayed the Jews who did convert, as Baron noted. That these sources are literary texts, even though of a special type, is also clear from their obvious differences of style. In L, lengthy prayers frame the accounts of attacks on several towns, their Jews' defensive political reactions, and subsequent acts of martyrdom. In P, very brief descriptions of a limited number of episodes introduce liturgical poems. And in S, an attention to the Christian townsmen and other human factors also serves to interpret the events portrayed."[17]

2.2 EXPLANATIONS OF THE MASSACRES OF 1096

Nonetheless, even if we discount the details to be found in these chronicles, "general corroboration exists in the contemporary Latin and later Hebrew sources that riots occurred and that some Jews killed their families and themselves."[18]

The Jews were the first people to suffer as the first band of crusaders wound their way to the East through the Rhineland, which was the center of intellectual life of Ashkenazic, that is, Northern European Jewry, with its two great, vibrant communities of Mainz and Worms. In general, the Jewish communities in Northern Europe had seen great growth during the tenth and eleventh century but Jews were never considered the equals of Christians, and were constantly reminded of the official dogma of the Roman Catholic Church that they were in error though they had once "possessed the truth of revelation, misread it, and thereby forfeited their covenantal relationship with the Deity."[19] And of course, the Jews were held responsible for the Crucifixion of Christ, the Savior they should have accepted. These negative attitudes were embodied in the central rituals of the Church, and were passed onto large parts of the Christian populace. The Church did call for the toleration of Jews in their midst, where they were allowed to practice their religion, as long the Christians authorities assessed and ruled that the Jews were not a threat to Christians and Christianity.

There seem to also have been political, social and economic reasons for the persecution of the Jews in Europe. However, reading historians' accounts of the "reasons" for, and "causes" of, Christian antisemitism leaves one with an uneasy feeling that somehow Christians were being excused

---

17 Ivan Marcus, *op.cit.*, p. 686.

18 *Idem.*

19 Robert Chazan, *op.cit.*, p. 28.

since there were "good reasons" for their antipathies towards Jews, and that the Jews somehow "had it coming to them." Though I should emphasize that no respectable Western historian ever explicitly states anything like this, and has never used terms like "had it coming to them," or that there were "good reasons" for the Christians' hatred. However, all rationalizing explanations of antisemitism engender such misgivings. Here are two rationalizing explanations of the rise of Christian antisemitism at the time of the First Crusade. Sir Steven Runciman wrote, "The prohibition of usury in western Christian countries and its strict control in Byzantium left them [the Jews] an open field for the establishment of money-lending houses throughout Christendom. Their technical skill and long traditions made them pre-eminent also in the practice of medicine. Except long ago in Visigothic Spain they had never undergone serious persecution in the West. They had no civic rights; but both lay and ecclesiastical authorities were pleased to give special protection to such useful members of the community. The kings of France and Germany had always befriended them; and they were shown particular favour by the archbishops of the great cities of the Rhineland. But the peasants and poorer townsmen increasingly in need of money as a cash economy replaced the older economy of services, fell more and more into their debt and in consequence felt more and more resentment against them; while the Jews, lacking legal security, charged high rates of interest and extracted exorbitant profits wherever the benevolence of the local ruler supported them.

"Their unpopularity grew throughout the eleventh century, as more classes of the community began to borrow money from them; and the beginnings of the Crusading movement added to it. It was expensive for a knight to equip himself for a Crusade; if he had no land and no possessions to pledge, he must borrow money from the Jews. But was it right that in order to go and fight for Christendom he must fall into the clutches of members of the race that crucified Christ? The poorer Crusader was often already in debt to the Jews. Was it right that he should be hampered in his Christian duty by obligations to one of the impious race? The evangelical preaching of the Crusade laid stress on Jerusalem, the scene of the Crucifixion. It inevitably drew attention to the people at whose hands Christ had suffered. The Moslems were the present enemy; they were persecuting Christ's followers. But the Jews were surely worse; they had persecuted Christ Himself."[20]

---

20 Steven Runciman, *A History of the Crusades, Vol. I, The First Crusade and the Foundation of the Kingdom of Jerusalem*, Cambridge: Cambridge University Press, 1951, pp., 134-35.

Jean Richard, Emeritus Professor at the University of Dijon, France, gives a similar rationalizing account, "The motives for these outbursts [of violence] may, of course, be connected to the envy aroused by the wealth of the Jews, and the resentment provoked by their practice of usury. The widespread recourse to credit which began during the course of the eleventh century, and the seemingly brazen prosperity of Jewish moneylenders, no doubt encouraged such explosions, which were not confined to the Christian West; the first great wave of hatred of which the Jews were victims in the eleventh century took place around 1066 in Muslim Spain, at Grenada."[21]

Antisemitism is clearly, in part, a result of social and economic tensions, but it is only half the truth. Maurice Samuel in his *The Great Hatred*[22] [1940] pointed out the inadequacy of the materialist interpretation of antisemitism. Three years later Joshua Trachtenberg, in his classic study, *The Devil and the Jews*,[23] brought the discussions back to the real source of antisemitism, rumour, superstition, crass credulity, and fanaticism, in other words, human irrationality in all its forms: "Hatred of the Jew is not the result of a rational process....No, hatred of the Jew rests upon no rational base. When everything possible has been said about the psychological xenophobia that rejects 'difference' and resents minority cultures, about economic and social frictions that exacerbate social relations, about the astute and persuasive propaganda techniques of anarchical demagogues, about the need for a "scapegoat" for release of social tension, about the imperfections of the Jews themselves, and their abnormal economic status—and all these are potent immediate stimuli of active Jew hatred—the ultimate source, buried deep in the mass subconscious, is still untouched. Underneath the present stimuli, and contributing to them their explosive potentiality, lies the powder keg of emotional predisposition, of a conception of the Jew which has nothing to do with facts or logic."[24]

Ironically, while Sir Steven argues that Christianity was responsible for Islamic intolerance, Trachtenberg suggests that one of the contributing factors to the rise of Christian antisemitism in the later Middle Ages was

---

21 Jean Richard, *The Crusades c.1071-c.1291*, Cambridge: Cambridge University Press, 1999, p. 39.

22 Maurice Samuel [died 1972], *The Great Hatred*, New York: Alfred A.Knopf, 1940.

23 Joshua Trachtenberg, [died 1959], *The Devil and the Jews: The Medieval Conception of the Jew and Its Relation to Modern Antisemitism* [Original Edn. 1943, Yale University Press], NewYork: Harper Torchbook, 1966.

24 Joshua Trachtenberg, *op.cit.*, pp. 2-3.

"the rising menace of Islam."[25] Christian antisemitism reached its apogee in the post-Crusade period, but it was the result of centuries of demonisation of the Jew as devil, sorcerer, and ritual murderer.

2.3 NARRATIVE OF THE MASSACRES OF 1096

We now need to get to the narrative of the actual massacres. After the preaching of the First Cruasade in 1095, various bands of undisciplined cruasaders descended on the towns of the Rhineland, led by individuals about whom, for the most part, we know little. One leader was Duke Emich von Leiringen, a petty lord of the Rhineland, who was well aware of the possibilities of exploiting the religious fervor of the masses for his own profit. "He persuaded his followers to begin their Crusade on 3 May with an attack on the Jewish community at Spier [Speyer], close to his home. It was not a very impressive attack. The Bishop of Spier, whose sympathies were won by a handsome present, placed the Jews under his protection. Only twelve were taken by the Crusaders and slain after their refusal to embrace Christianity; and one Jewess committed suicide to preserve her virtue. The bishop saved the rest and even managed to capture several of the murderers, whose hands were cut off in punishment."[26]

Emich and his troops arrived in Worms on 18 May. A rumour went round that the Jews had captured and drowned a Christian and then had used the water where his corpse was kept to poison the city wells. Emich and his men attacked the Jewish quarter and killed every Jew they captured. The bishop opened his palace to the fleeing Jews but Emich's men broke in and slaughtered, on May 20, all the Jews, about five hundred. Our primary source, the *Hebrew Chronicle* of Solomon bar Simson, which dates from about 1140, calculates eight hundred as the total number slain over the two days. Here is Solomon bar Simson's vivid, but horrific account[27]: "On the twenty-third of Iyar[28] they attacked the community of Worms.

---

25 *Ibid.*, p. 11.

26 Steven Runciman , *op.cit.*, p. 139.

27 Shlomo Eidelberg (editor and translator), *The Jews and the Crusades. The Hebrew Chronicles of the First and Second Crusades*, New Jersey: KTAV Publishing house, Inc., 1996, p. 23.

28 Iyar (from Akkadian ayyaru, meaning "Rosette; blossom") is the eighth month of the civil year (which starts on 1 Tishrei) and the second month of the ecclesiastical year (which starts on 1 Nisan) on the Hebrew calendar. The name is Babylonian in origin. It is a spring month of 29 days. Iyar usually falls in April–June on the Gregorian calendar. [*Encyclopaedia Judaica*, ed., Fred Skolnik, New York: Thomson Gale: Macmillan Reference, 2007, 2nd Edn. s.v. "Iyyar".]

The community was then divided into two groups; some remained in their homes and others fled to the local bishop seeking refuge. Those who remained in their homes were set upon by the steppe-wolves who pillaged men, women, and infants, children and old people. They pulled down the stairways and destroyed the houses, looting and plundering; and they took the Torah Scroll, trampled it in the mud, and tore and burned it. The enemy devoured the children of Israel with open maw.

"Seven days later, on the New Moon of Sivan—the very day on which the Children of Israel arrived at Mount Sinai to receive the Torah-those Jews who were still in the court of the bishop were subjected to great anguish. The enemy dealt them the same cruelty as the first group and put them to the sword. The Jews, inspired by the valor of their brethren, similarly chose to be slain in order to sanctify the Name before the eyes of all, and exposed their throats for their heads to be severed for the glory of the Creator. There were also those who took their own lives, thus fulfilling the verse: 'The mother was dashed in pieces with her children.'[Hosea 10:14] Fathers fell upon their sons, being slaughtered upon one another, and they slew one another—each man his kin, his wife and children; bridegrooms slew their betrothed and merciful women their only children. They all accepted the divine decree wholeheartedly and, as they yielded up their souls to the Creator, cried out: 'Hear, O Israel, the Lord is our God, the Lord is One.' The enemy stripped them naked, dragged them along, and then cast them off, sparing only a small number whom they forcibly baptized in their profane waters. The number of those slain during the two days was approximately eight hundred—and they were all buried naked. It is of these that the Prophet Jeremiah lamented: 'They that were brought up in scarlet embrace dunghills.' [Lamentations 4:5] ....May God remember them for good."

On May 25, Emich and his men entered the city of Mainz. Despite the efforts of Archbishop Rothard to save the Jews, once again Emich's men broke in and began two days of pillaging and murdering of Jews. Some Jews accepted conversion to Christianity and were spared, but they later regretted their moment of weakness and committed suicide. About a thousand Jews were killed in Mainz. Here we can cite a Christian primary source, Albert of Aix,[29] who gives an account strikingly similar to the *Hebrew Chronicle*: "But Emico and the rest of his band held a council and,

---

29 "Albert of Aix (or Aachen) wrote a history of the Crusades down to c. 1120. He is the most important source for the history of the popular crusade. He wrote in the mid twelfth century and never visited the East. His History is based on eyewitness accounts and written sources." http://www.fordham.edu/halsall/source/albert-cde.asp

after sunrise, attacked the Jews in the hall with arrows and lances. Breaking the bolts and doors, they killed the Jews, about seven hundred in number, who in vain resisted the force and attack of so many thousands. They killed the women, also, and with their swords pierced tender children of whatever age and sex. The Jews, seeing that their Christian enemies were attacking them and their children, and that they were sparing no age, likewise fell upon one another, brother, children, wives, and sisters, and thus they perished at each other's hands. Horrible to say, mothers cut the throats of nursing children with knives and stabbed others, preferring them to perish thus by their own hands rather than to be killed by the weapons of the uncircumcised. From this cruel slaughter of the Jews a few escaped; and a few because of fear, rather than because of love of the Christian faith, were baptized."[30]

Emich and his men now headed for Cologne, but the Jews, having heard of the massacre in Mainz, hid among their Christian friends and acquaintances in the neighbouring villages. The synagogue was burnt and a Jew and a Jewess who refused to apostasize were killed. The archbishop was able to prevent further excesses.

After Cologne, Emich decided his work in the Rhineland had been successfully accomplished, and now headed for Hungary. But some of his unruly followers wanted to rid the entire Moselle valley of all Jews, and therefore broke off from the main party and made for Trier. Again the Archbishop was able to shelter the Jews in his palace. However, some Jews were very nervous and began fighting among themselves, while others jumped into the Moselle and drowned. The Crusaders "moved onto Metz, where twenty-two Jews perished."[31] This roving band of Crusaders then returned to Cologne where they discovered that Emich had left, and so "proceeded down the Rhine, spending from 24 to 27 June in massacring the Jews at Neuss, Wevelinghofen, Eller and Xanten. They they dispersed, some returning home, others probably merging with the army of Godfrey of Bouillon."[32]

A certain Volkmar, about whom we know very little, also set out for the Rhineland with a band of over ten thousand men to join Peter the Hermit, in April 1096. They arrived in Prague at the end of May, and on June 30 began massacring the Jews in the city despite the protests of Bish-

---

30 August. C. Krey, *The First Crusade: The Accounts of Eyewitnesses and Participants*, Princeton: 1921, pp. 54-56.

31 Runciman, *op.cit.*, p. 139.

32 *Ibid.*, p. 140.

op Cosmas. The victims numbered several thousand.[33] They proceeded to Hungary but the Hungarians did not approve of their behaviour and attacked Volkmar and his men, many of whom were killed. We have no knowledge of what happened to Volkmar himself.[34]

The third of the murderous triumvirate, Gottschalk, left with a large company of crusaders for the Rhineland and Bavaria soon after Volkmar's departure in April. On the way they paused at Ratisbon to massacre the Jews there. But on Gottschalk and his men's arrival in Hungary the tables were turned as the Hungarians did not appreciate the Crusaders' pillaging and looting. King Coloman of Hungary did not trust them, and eventually had his army massacre them to a man. The Hungarians dealt in similar fashion with Emich and his army which was utterly routed in a fierce battle at Wiesselburg.

It is worth remarking at this point that several noblemen and bishops tried to protect the Jews, occasionally risking their own lives, though many may have been bribed, and others were hoping to save the Jews so as to see them eventually baptised. The common people also showed, on occasion, some compassion and pity for the plight of the Jews and gave them shelter as in Cologne. Some Christian chroniclers condemned the massacres in no uncertain terms, as for example this anonymous Saxon writer,[35] "...the enemy of mankind lost no time sowing tares among the wheat, raising up false prophets, mingling untrue brothers and licentious women with the army of Christ. By their hypocrisy, by their lies, by their impious corruptions, they caused dissension in the army of the Lord....They decided to avenge Christ upon the pagans and the Jews. This is why they killed 900 Jews in the city of Mainz without sparing the women and children.... Indeed, it was pitiful to see the great and many heaps of bodies that were carried out of the city of Mainz on carts..."

But then again we find many Christian accounts of the massacres that clearly approve of what befell "the impious Jews" who were "truly enemies of the Church," as in those written by the monk Bernhold and the chronicler Fruitolf.[36]

---

33 Léon Poliakov, *The History of Anti-Semitism, Vol. I, From the Time of Christ to the Court Jews*, trans. Richard Howard. Philadelphia: University of Pennsylvania Press, 2003 [Original Edn. in French Calmann-Lévy, Paris, 1955], p. 45.

34 Runciman, *op.cit.*, p. 140.

35 *Monumenta Germaniae Historica, Scriptores*, [MGH, SS.] edd. G.H.Pertz, T.Mommsen et al, (Hanover: Reichsinstitut für ältere deutsche Geschichtskunde, 1826-) Vol. 6, Annales sax. p. 729.

36 See MGH, SS Vol. 5, p. 464; Vol. 6, p. 208; quoted in Léon Poliakov, *The History of Anti-Semitism, Vol. I, From the Time of Christ to the Court Jews*, trans. Richard

2.4 FURTHER CRUSADES

Pope Eugenius III and St. Bernard of Clairvaux preached a new crusade in 1146, and its preaching was again followed by the pillaging, looting and killing of the Jews. As Poliakov says, "And what had been only a popular and spontaneous outbreak fifty years before was this time doctrinally exploited by fiery monk-preachers. Thus Abbé Pierre of Cluny in France: 'What is the good of going to the end of the world, at great loss of men and money, to fight the Saracens, when we permit among us other infidels who are a thousand times more guilty toward Christ than the Mohammedans?'[37] Thus the monk Rudolf in Germany: '…First avenge the Crucified upon His enemies living here among us, and then go off to fight the Turks!'"[38]

There were incidents and massacres in Cologne, Speyer, Mainz, and Würzburg in Germany, and in Carentan, Ramerupt, and Sully in France; the number of victims reaching several hundred. Poliakov claims that what was even more significant was the emergence for the first time of "the accusation of ritual murder, followed by the accusation of the profanation of the Host."[39] However, perhaps he meant "re-emergence" since the accusation of ritual murder goes back to Classical Antiquity; it is to be found in the writings of Apion [died c. 45-48 CE], Posidonius [died c. 51 BCE], Apollonius Molon [1st Century BCE], and Socrates Scholasticus [died c. 450 CE].

Léon Poliakov summarizes the fate of the Jews each time a crusade was embarked upon: "Thus, each time medieval Europe was swept by a great movement of faith, each time the Christians set out to face the unknown in the name of the love of God, hatred of the Jews was fanned into flame virtually everywhere. And the more the pious impulses of the heart sought satisfaction in action, the worse became the Jews' lot.

"Virtually every time a Crusade was preached, the same consequences could be anticipated. In 1183 (The Third Crusade), there were great massacres in England—in London, York, Norwich, Stamford, and Lynn;

Howard. Philadelphia: University of Pennsylvania Press, 2003 [Original Edn. in French Calmann-Lévy, Paris, 1955], p. 51.

37 Dom Martin Bouquet, *Recueil des historiens des Gaules et de la France*, Paris 1752, [also 1865] Vol. 14, p. 642, quoted by Poliakov, *op.cit.*, p. 48.

38 Account of Rabbi Ephraim bar Jacob of Bonn in Adolf Neubauer and Moritz Stern, *Hebräische Berichte über die Judenverfolgungen während der Kreuzzüge*, Berlin, 1892, p. 188, quoted by Poliakov, *op,cit.*, p. 48.

39 Poliakov, Vol. I, p. 49.

twenty years later, at the time of the Albigensian Crusade, there were persecutions in the Midi. When a Crusade was ineffectually preached in 1236, massacres also occurred in western France, in England, and in Spain...."[40]

The Crusades showed the vulnerability of the Jews, who in these moments of crises were forced to turn to noblemen and kings for protection. These secular powers protected the Jews since they derived some benefit from them. The Crusades generally, in the words of the Encyclopaedia Judaica, "were firmly imprinted on the historic consciousness of the Jews. This period became singled out in the popular mind as the start of and explanation for the misfortunes of the Jews, although in fact the excesses were only symptomatic of a process which had already been set in motion earlier." But henceforth the history of the Jews that unfolded was a tragic one since "there now began a period of intermittently recurring massacre and persecution which colored European Jewish experience for centuries to come."[41]

---

40 *Ibid.*
41 Article, "Crusades", in *Encyclopaedia Judaica*, 2nd Edn, 2008.

4
The Plight of Jews in North West Africa Under Islam Between 1148-1912

Paul B. Fenton & David G. Littman, *L'Exil au Maghreb: La condition Juive sous l'Islam 1148-1912*, PUPS [Presses de L'Université Paris-Sorbonne], Paris, 2010. 792pp. Illustrated [Black and White Photos and Color Plates], Maps, List of Illustrations, Bibliography, Glossary [of Hebrew and Arabic Terms], Index of Names, Index of Places, Analytical Table of Contents, [In French].

Abraham Ibn Ezra, Hebrew scholar and polymath, left Andalusia in 1140 C.E. just before the invasion of the Almohads, a particularly violent and bigotted Islamic dynasty of North Africa and Spain [reigned 1130-1269] which destroyed so many Jewish communities, and towns. He wrote a lament on this destruction of North African and Hispanic settlements:

> I weep like an ostrich for Lucena [cf. Lam.4:3 and Mic. 1:8].
> Her remnant dwelt innocent and secure...
> Alas, the city of Cordoba is forsaken, her ruin as vast as the sea!
> Her sages and learned men perished from hunger and thirst.
> Not a single Jew was left in Jaen or Almeria;
> Majorca and Málaga struggle to survive...
> I cry out like a woman in labor for the congregation of Sjilmasa—
> A city where genius and wisdom flourished; their brilliance obscured the darkness....

Woe, the congregation of Fez is no more; this day they are
given to the plunderer;
Where is the protection for the congregation of Tlemsan?
Its glory is melted away.
A bitter voice I raise over the fate of Ceuta and Meknes;
I rend my garments for Dar'ī already vanquished...[1]

Ibn Ezra's elegy serves as a sad but fitting motto to Paul Fenton and
David Littman's scholarly and indispensable survey of the plight of Jews in
North West Africa [Maghreb] under Islam between 1148-1912. No two
scholars could be better qualified than Fenton and Littman for such an immense task. Paul Fenton is Assistant Director of the Department of Arabic
and Hebrew Studies at the University of Paris-Sorbonne, where he is also
Professor of Hebrew Language and Literature. He is a world authority on
Jewish Civilization under Islam, and author of *Moïse ibn Ezra, philosophe et
poète andalou du XIIeme siècle* (1997); and *Juda ibn Malka: La Consolation
de l'expatrié spirituel.*

David Littman, with a B.A. and an M.A. degree in Modern History
and Political Science from Trinity College, Dublin, began his research on
this subject in 1970, first in the archives of the Ministry of Foreign Affairs
(*Ministère des Affaires Étrangères Français*), more informally known as *le
Quai d'Orsay*, and secondly, in the extraordinary archives of The Alliance
Israélite Universelle [AIU: a Paris-based international Jewish organization
created in 1860 by the French statesman Adolphe Crémieux to defend the
human rights of Jews around the world; it promotes the ideals of Jewish
self-defense and self-sufficiency. The motto of the organization is *Kol yis-
rael arevim zeh bazeh*,—"All Jews bear responsibility for one another." The
AIU wished to advance the Jews of the Middle East through education
and culture, and to that end established schools so that by 1900 it was
running 100 schools with a combined student population of 26,000. The
bulk of the schools were in Morocco, Tunisia and Turkey]. Nor did David
Littman forget the archives of the Foreign Office in London, U.K. Littman
has published numerous articles on the Jews of North West Africa and the
Orient. Of particular relevance is Littman's pioneering monograph on Sir
Moses Montefiore's mission to Morocco between 1863-1864 which appeared in 1985 in a volume commemorating the centenary of Sir Moses.
Since 1986, he has dedicated himself to defending Human Rights at the

---

1 Abraham Ibn Ezra: *Twilight of a Golden Age: Selected Poems of Abraham Ibn Ezra,*
edited and translated by Leon J. Weinberger, Tuscaloosa (Alabama): University of
Alabama Press, 1997, pp. 3-4.

United Nations in Geneva in his capacity as representative of several non-governmental organisations.

The book is dedicated to the memory of Hayyim Zeev Hirschberg [1903-1976], the eminent historian of North West African Judaism. Littman began a collaboration with Hirschberg in the 1970s which was unfortunately cut short by the latter's premature death in 1976. Nonetheless, Hirschberg instilled in Littman the importance of the archives of the AIU which were to provide irrefutable proof of the abject condition of the Jews in the Maghreb in the nineteenth century, destroying along the way a number of myths that were current up to that time.

This work will surely become the definitive source book on its subject—supplemented perhaps with some details, but unlikely ever to be completely superseded. All further research on North African Jewry surely must begin here. It is organized along principles established by such scholars as Jacob Landau in his *Jews in Nineteenth-Century Egypt* [1969], and Bat Ye'or in her *Le Dhimmi: Profil de l'opprimé en Orient et en Afrique du Nord* [1980]; that is to say, each work begins with an historical introduction that summarises and surveys the entire period in question. It is then followed by the original documents from the various archives. While Jacob Landau is content to provide the documents in their original languages (Hebrew, Arabic, Italian, and French), Fenton and Littman and for that matter Bat Ye'or have translated all the documents into French, have carefully noted and annotated each source. In a series of scholarly footnotes each contributor—traveller, historian, diplomat, poet—is identified and his biographical details, which are quite substantial in some cases, are given. Obscure terms, and characters that flit through the extracts are explained, and brought to light. The book is a pleasure to handle physically—a feast for the intellect as well as the eyes, and other senses since it is printed on glossy paper (accounting for the book's weight of over three pounds). It is illustrated with ten colour plates of paintings by Delacroix, Alfred Dehodencq, Du Nouÿ, and others, and sixty three black and white pictures of places, events, and copies of documents.

The source material is divided geographically, (North West Africa generally, then Algeria and Morocco) and into two parts, First, we have the historical and literary sources [part A, of which there are 135 extracts], and then the truly archival material [Part B, of which there are 185 extracts]. The greatest amount of material comes from the nineteenth century though we have startling eyewitness accounts from the twelfth century onwards. Unlike Algeria, we possess much contemporary Jewish accounts of their situation under Islam in Morocco, particularly from the 1850s onwards. It is unfortunately a story of pillage, the torching of synagogues, the burning of Hebrew sacred texts, the rape and abduction of Jewish women and murders.

To give an example, I shall quote from the original eighteenth century English source that is translated into French in Fenton and Littman's book:

> It has been observed in squabbles among them, or when a poor Man falls out with his ass, that the first name is *carran* (*i.e.*) cuckold, then he calls him son of a Jew....[p.45]

> In the middle of the City live the Jews, having a Place to themselves, the Gates of which are locked at Night, which Privilege they also have in most of the Cities of this Emperor's Dominions. They have an Alcayde to guard their Gates, and protect them against the Common-People, who otherwise would plunder them; for they live in great Subjection, it being Death for them to curse, or lift up a Hand against the meanest Moor, so that the Boys kick them about at their Pleasure, against which they have no other Remedy but to run away, away, they are obliged to pull off their Shoes whenever they pass by a Mosque, and to wear black Cloaths and Caps; nor are they allowed the use of Horses; for Ben Hattar himself (tho' he had Power over Life and Death) was always forced to ride a Mule..." [p.185]

The source is John H. Windus, *A Journey to Mequinez, the Residence of the Present Emperor of Fez and Morocco, On the Occasion of Commodore Stewart's Embassy thither for the Redemption of the British Captives in the Year 1721*, London, Jacob Tonson, 1725. Fenton and Littman's footnote explains that Ben Hattar [died 1724] was a Jewish merchant from Meknès, often employed by the Emperor Mawlay Isma'il as financial advisor in his diplomatic negotiations. In 1721, he negotiated notably a commercial treaty with the British Commodore Stewart. A further footnote tells us all that we would wish to know about John H. Windus.

The latter [fl. 1725] was a historian who accompanied Commodore Charles Stewart, who had been sent to negotiate the release of three hundred English captives. Windus gathered much material on the country in the four months he spent there. Windus' account was the second ever published in English on Morocco (after that of Addison). His book went through several editions and generated a great deal of interest, particularly

Windus's recitation of the daily life in the Moroccan countryside.

Even a cursory glance at the analytical table of contents gives a grim picture of the situation of Jews in the Maghreb. Confining ourselves to nineteenth century Morocco, here is a rapid *tour d'horizon*:

SUFFERANCE IN ISOLATION (1800-1860)

A 70: The inequality of Jews in front of the Law, (Fez, c. 1800).
A 71: The Jews of Morocco live in a state of slavery of the most horrible kind, (1803).
A.72: The Sultan exempts a Jewish interpreter from wearing disntinctive clothing, (Marrakech. c. 1806).
A.73: Jews cannot leave Morocco without imperial authorisation, (1808).
A.74: The payment of Jizya described by an American navigator, (Mogador, 1815).
A.75: Constraint imposed on Jews, (c. 1820).
A.76: The sack of the Jewish Quarter of Fez as seen by a Muslim chronicler, (1820),

Now some examples from the archives:

THE RISE IN PERSECUTION OF THE JEWS OF THE MAGHREB, AND THE HUMANITARIAN INTERVENTION OF EUROPEAN JEWS (1863-1864).

B.3 Persecutions at Chechaouan, (1864).
B.4 Persecutions of Jews of Demnate, (1864).
B.5 The presecutions continue despite the protection of France, (1864).
B.6. Disastrous consequences of the events of Safi, (1864).
B.7 In the footsteps of Moses Montefiore.

I hope I have been able to give an idea of the riches of material gathered in this remarkable collection. I trust that eventually an English translation will appear since the contents deserve the widest possible dissemination.

5

George Eliot, Daniel Deronda, & Zionism: Some Observations

George Eliot's *Daniel Deronda* was first published in 1876, and proved to be her last novel. The novel begins in August 1865, and is thus set in, and a searching analysis of, the Victorian society of her day. *Daniel Deronda* is at once a love story, and a novel of ideas—two interwoven strands running through it. One strand concerns the life and moral development of the heroine, Gwendolen Harleth, a selfish but sparkling woman of great charm at home in the fashionable, upper-class world of Victorian England, and the other looks with empathy at the world of Jews and their aspirations, mainly in England but also in the wider European context. Bridging the two worlds is the good, wise, compassionate Daniel Deronda, brought up as an English gentleman, who discovers that his mother was Jewish, and by the end of the novel takes up the cause of restoring the Jewish nation in Palestine.

Henry James, who was not only a distinguished novelist but a considerable literary critic, set the tone of all subsequent criticisms of the novel in his celebrated "*Daniel Deronda*: A Conversation" written in the year of *Daniel Deronda's* publication, 1876,

> Constantius....Little by little I began to feel that I cared less for certain notes than for others. I say it under my breath—I began to feel an occasional temptation to skip. Roughly speaking, all the Jewish burden of the story tended to weary me.

> Theodora....As for the Jewish element in *Deronda*, I think it is a very fine idea; it's a noble subject. Wilkie Collins and Miss

Braddon would not have thought of it, but that does not condemn it. It shows a large conception of what one may do in a novel.

Pulcheria….You cannot persuade me that *Deronda* is not a very ponderous and ill-made story. It has nothing that one might call a subject. A silly young girl and a solemn, sapient young man who doesn't fall in love with her! That is the *donnée* of eight monthly volumes.

F. R. Leavis in *The Great Tradition*[1] voiced his desire to see the "bad half" represented "by Deronda himself, and what may be called in general the Zionist inspiration" unshackled from the novel altogether and the good half preserved independently under the title Gwendolen Harleth. Barbara Tuchman calls the novel "peculiarly schizoid," and unrealistic since it never contends with the real problems besetting any Jews contemplating resettling in Palestine, "Like all the productions of non-Jewish enthusiasts for the Return, *Deronda* never hesitates a moment over the problems that so harassed actual Jews—assimilation, anti-semitism, Judaism as religion or as nationality, living dog or dead lion. The problem of reviving the desire for nationality never occurs to them, any more than the economics of the business—the actual physical process of getting to Palestine, of acquiring land, of making a living. They skip over all that to plunge at one stride into Palestine, where a revived Israel will emerge full grown like Athena."

Pace F. R. Leavis, the Deronda half is closely interwoven with the moral development of Gwendolen Harleth, and is essential for the contrast of Daniel's high moral seriousness, and his eventual discovery of a purposeful life, to, for example, the utter brutality, the callousness, and the lack of any ethical urgency of the life of Gwendolen's husband, Grandcourt, and all those in the latter's orbit. Thus it is nonsensical to hope to arrive at a new, self-contained novel simply by cutting out the "Deronda half" in such a unnatural manner.

Pace Tuchman, Eliot argues the case for assimilation, broaches the subject of antisemitism, and laments the position of women in Judaism, and so much more, in the fine chapter where Daniel meets his mother for the first time as an adult:

"Then you have become unlike your grandfather in that,"

---

1 F.R. Leavis, *The Great Tradition*, London: Chatto and Windus, 1948.

said the mother, "though you are a young copy of him in your face. He never comprehended me, or if he did, he only thought of fettering me into obedience. I was to be what he called 'the Jewish woman' under pain of his curse. I was to feel everything I did not feel, and believe everything I did not believe. I was to feel awe for the bit of parchment in the mezuza over the door; to dread lest a bit of butter should touch a bit of meat; to think it beautiful that men should bind the tephillin on them, and women not,—to adore the wisdom of such laws, however silly they might seem to me. I was to love the long prayers in the ugly synagogue, and the howling, and the gabbling, and the dreadful fasts, and the tiresome feasts, and my father's endless discoursing about Our People, which was a thunder without meaning in my ears. I was to care for ever about what Israel had been; and I did not care at all. I cared for the wide world, and all that I could represent in it. I hated living under the shadow of my father's strictness. Teaching, teaching for everlasting—'this you must be,' 'that you must not be'—pressed on me like a frame that got tighter and tighter as I grew. I wanted to live a large life, with freedom to do what every one else did, and be carried along in a great current, not obliged to care. Ah!"—here her tone changed to one of a more bitter incisiveness—"you are glad to have been born a Jew: You say so. That is because you have not been brought up as a Jew. That separateness seems sweet to you because I saved you from it.". . . .

"I beseech you to tell me what moved you—when you were young, I mean—to take the course you did," said Deronda, trying by this reference to the past to escape from what to him was the heartrending piteousness of this mingled suffering and defiance. "I gather that my grandfather opposed your bent to be an artist Though my own experience has been quite different, I enter into the painfulness of your struggle. I can imagine the hardship of an enforced renunciation."

"No," said the Princess, shaking her head, and folding her arms with an air of decision. "You are not a woman. You may try—but you can never imagine what it is to have a man's force of genius in you, and yet to suffer the slavery of being a girl. To have a pattern cut out—'this is the Jewish woman; this is what you must be; this is what you are wanted for; a woman's heart must be of such a size and no larger, else it must be pressed small, like Chinese feet; her happiness is to be made as cakes are, by a fixed receipt.' That was what my father wanted. He wished I had been a son; he cared for me as a makeshift link. His heart was set on his Judaism. He hated that Jewish women should be thought of by the Christian world as a sort of ware to make public singers and actresses of. As if we were not the more enviable for that! That is a chance of escaping from bondage."

"Was my grandfather a learned man?" said Deronda, eager to know particulars that he feared his mother might not think of.

She answered impatiently, putting up her hand, "Oh yes,—and a clever physician—and good: I don't deny that he was good. A man to be admired in a play—grand, with an iron will. Like the old Foscari before he pardons. But such men turn their wives and daughters into slaves. They would rule the world if they could; but not ruling the world, they throw all the weight of their will on the necks and souls of women. But nature sometimes thwarts them. My father had no other child than his daughter, and she was like himself."

George Eliot herself said that she had written *Daniel Deronda* "to ennoble Judaism," and to requite a moral debt owed to the Jews, as she explains to Harriet Beecher Stowe in the following letter:

As to the Jewish element in 'Deronda,' I expected from first to last, in writing it, that it would create much stronger resistance, and even repulsion, than it has actually met with. But precisely because I felt that the usual attitude of Christians towards Jews is — I hardly know whether to say more impious or more stupid, when viewed in the light of their professed principles, I therefore felt urged to treat Jews with such sympathy and understanding as my nature and knowledge could attain to. Moreover, not only towards the Jews, but towards all Oriental peoples with whom we English come in contact, a spirit of arrogance and contemptuous dictatorialness is observable which has become a national disgrace to us. There is nothing I should care more to do, if it were possible, than to rouse the imagination of men and women to a vision of human claims in those races of their fellow-men who most differ from them in customs and beliefs. But towards the Hebrews we western people, who have been reared in Christianity, have a peculiar debt, and, whether we acknowledge it or not, a peculiar thoroughness of fellowship in religious and moral sentiment. Can anything be more disgusting than to hear people called "educated" making small jokes about eating ham, and showing themselves empty of any real knowledge as to the relation of their social and religious life to the history of the people they think themselves witty in insulting? They hardly know that Christ was a Jew. And I find men, educated, supposing that Christ spoke Greek. To my feeling, this deadness to the history which has prepared half our world for us, this inability to find interest in any form of life that is not clad in the same coat-tails and flounces as our own, lies very close to the worst kind of irreligion. The best that can be said of it is that it is a sign of the intellectual narrowness — in plain English, the stupidity — which is still the average mark of our culture.

Yes, I expected more aversion than I have found. But I was happily independent in material things, and felt no temptation to accommodate my writing to any standard except that of trying to do my best in what seemed to me most needful to be done; and I sum up with the writer of the Book of Maccabees, — "If I have done well, and as befits the subject, it is what I desired; and if I have done ill, it is what I could attain unto."[2]

Throughout the novel, George Eliot makes clear that her empathy for the Jews was but a part of a greater enterprise of widening our sympathies in general. "Art's greatest benefit to men," wrote George Eliot, "is to widen their sympathies."[3]

Daniel Deronda embodies all her ideals, the man who exemplifies the widest sympathies for others and other ways of being. Eliot tells us in Chapter 16, "There had sprung up in him a meditative yearning after wide knowledge.... Daniel had the stamp of rarity in a subdued fervour of sympathy, an activity of imagination on behalf of others, which did not show itself effusively, but was continually seen in acts of considerateness that stuck his companions as moral eccentricity." Deronda also displayed a

2 *George Eliot's Life as Related in Her Letters and Journals,* Vol. III, Boston, 1895, pp. 241-242.

3 George Eliot, "The Natural History of German Life," *Westminster Review,* July 1856, p. 54.

"boyish love of universal history, which made him want to be at home in foreign countries, and follow in imagination the travelling students of the middle ages." A little later, Daniel confesses, "I want to be an Englishman, but I want to understand other points of view. And I want to get rid of a merely English attitude in studies."

Daniel always sided with the "objects of prejudice, and in general with those who got the worst of it....". In Chapter 36, Daniel with unusual severity tells Gwendolen to acquire more knowledge so that "life would be worth more to you: some real knowledge would give you an interest in the world beyond the small drama of personal desires. It is the curse of your life—forgive me—of so many lives, that all passion is spent in that narrow round, for want of ideas and sympathies to make a larger home for it. Is there any single occupation of mind that you care about with passionate delight or even independent interest?"

In Chapter 40, Daniel is said to have a nature that "was too large, too ready to conceive regions beyond his own experience...." After his encounter with his mother, Daniel felt an older man, "He had gone through a tragic experience which must forever solemnise his life, and deepen the significance of the acts by which he bound himself to others" (Ch.53). Towards the end of the book [Ch.69], we get a glimpse of Gwendolen's moral awakening, "she was for the first time feeling the pressure of a vast mysterious movement, for the first time being dislodged from her supremacy in her own world, and getting a sense that her horizon was but a dipping onward of an existence with which her own was revolving."

Also towards the end of the novel, Mordecai, the Jewish visionary and brother of Mirah, whom Daniel eventually marries, gives us a mystical vision of the unity of mankind,

> "Seest thou, Mirah," he said once, after a long silence, "the Shemah, wherein we briefly confess the divine Unity, is the chief devotional exercise of the Hebrew; and this made our religion the fundamental religion for the whole world; for the divine Unity embraced as its consequence the ultimate unity of mankind. See, then—the nation which has been scoffed at for its separateness, has given a binding theory to the human race. Now, in complete unity a part possesses the whole as the whole possesses every part: and in this way human life is tending toward the image of the Supreme Unity: for as our life becomes more spiritual by capacity of thought, and joy therein, possession tends to become more universal, being independent of

gross material contact; so that in a brief day the soul of a man may know in fuller volume the good which has been and is, nay, is to come, than all he could possess in a whole life where he had to follow the creeping paths of the senses. In this moment, my sister, I hold the joy of another's future within me: a future which these eyes will not see, and which my spirit may not then recognise as mine. I recognise it now, and love it so, that I can lay down this poor life upon its altar and say: 'Burn, burn indiscernibly into that which shall be, which is my love and not me.' Dost thou understand, Mirah?"

CHRISTOPHER HITCHENS, EDWARD SAID, AND DANIEL DERONDA

Christopher Hitchens defended George Eliot's *Daniel Deronda* from Edward Said and two others, concluding his contribution to the series *Art of Criticism* with the following remark: "This counterpoint—between the rising incense and the dying cadence, the triumphant and the modest, the prophetic and the quotidian—is nowhere more boldly confronted than in the chapters of *Daniel Deronda*, which have already easily outlived the distinctly earthbound, confining objections made to them."[4]

Said complains of "the total absence of any thought about the actual inhabitants of the East, Palestine in particular."[5] Hitchens points out that Said is looking "through a retrospective optic."[6] Said accuses Eliot of being callous: "The few references to the East in Daniel Deronda are always to England's Indian colonies, for whose people—as people having wishes, values, aspirations—Eliot expresses the complete indifference of absolute silence."[7] To this argument from silence, Hitchens had already replied earlier in the lecture by quoting a letter that George Eliot had written to Harriet Beecher Stowe quoted above.

Hitchens denies that Eliot "could not care less about the colonial subjects of the British Crown," by quoting her:

We do not call ourselves a dispersed and a punished people; we are a colonising people and it is we who have punished others.[8]

---

4 Christopher Hitchens, *For the Sake of Argument*, London: Verso, 1994, p. 337.

5 Edward Said, *The Question of Palestine*, New York: Vintage, 1980, p. 65.

6 Christopher Hitchens, *op.cit.*, p. 337.

7 Edward Said, *op.cit.*, p. 65.

8 George Eliot, "The Modern Hep! Hep! Hep!" in Impressions of Theophrastus Such in

Are we to adopt the exclusiveness for which we have punished the Chinese?[9]

He [Mixtus] continues his early habit of regarding the spread of Christianity as a great result of our commercial intercourse with black, brown and yellow populations; but this is an idea not spoken of in the sort of fashionable society that Scintilla collects around her husband's table; and Mixtus now philosophically reflects that the cause must come before the effect, and that the thing to be striven for is the commercial intercourse—not excluding a little war if that also should prove needful as a pioneer of Christianity.[10]

[T]he Irish, also a servile race, who have rejected Protestantism though it has been repeatedly urged on them by fire and sword and penal laws, and whose place in the moral scale may be judged by our advertisements, where the clause "No Irish need apply" parallels the sentence which for many polite persons sums up the question of Judaism—"I never did like the Jews."[11]

This, as Hitchens notes, "scarcely supports a finding of indifference towards the colonized."[12]

Though Eliot in her generosity sees the establishment of a new nation in the East as "a halting-place of enmities," a reconciliation of the East with the West, Said refuses to acknowledge that Jews are Easterners or Orientals at all. That would spoil his vision of the establishment of Israel as a Western conspiracy, his Manichaean view of the world as a battle between the East and the West. Said is silent about Jews of Arab lands, even though there were Jewish communities at the time of the Romans in Egypt, North Africa, Morocco, the eastern Mediterranean, and Persia, long before the Arab conquests of the seventh century. For George Eliot, the purpose of the novel was to extend our moral sympathies; Edward Said remained un-

---

Theophrastus Such, Jubal, and Other Poems and The Spanish Gypsy, Chicago: Donohue, Henneberry, 1900, p. 136.

9 *Ibid.*, p. 148.

10 George Eliot, "A Half-Breed" in Impressions of Theophrastus Such in *Theophrastus Such, Jubal, and Other Poems and The Spanish Gypsy*, Chicago: Donohue, Henneberry, 1900, p. 76.

11 George Eliot, "The Modern Hep! Hep! Hep!" p. 144.

12 Christopher Hitchens, *For the Sake of Argument*, p. 338.

willing to extend his sympathies to Eastern Jews.

BRITISH ZIONISM

George Eliot's advocacy of Palestine as a homeland for the Jews must, of course, be seen against the background of nineteenth century Britain's "Restorationism" as Zionism was then termed, as well as the nineteenth century German and Italian national liberation movements. Eliot's novel is set during the period when the Kingdom of Prussia defeated the Austrian Empire at the Battle of Königgrätz, sometimes referred to as the Battle of Sadowa in Bohemia, on July 3, 1866—a battle often listed as one of the twenty decisive battles of the world. We could also take a much longer view, and place Eliot's ideas in the context of Britain's entire historical rapport with Palestine.

Barbara Tuchman takes the story of Britain's attachment to Palestine to the early Middle Ages. Britain had been developing such an attachment for various religious, spiritual and cultural reasons for a very long time, and the principal one among these was, of course, the English Bible and its prophecies. The Bible came to be adopted, in the words of Thomas Huxley, as "the national epic of Britain." Even the origins of the British Church were sought in Palestine, and they were found in the person of Joseph of Arimathea, the rich Jew and secret disciple of Jesus, and a member of the Sanhedrin. He is said to have founded the Abbey of Glastonbury in 63 C.E. More certainly, Britons showed a decided propensity to go on pilgrimage to the Holy Land beginning within two generations of the conversion of Constantine. And by the time of St. Willibald of Wessex, who arrived in Palestine in 721 C.E. the custom was well-established, though we do not know the names of the British pilgrims. One of the later known pilgrims was Saewulf, who wended his way to Jerusalem in 1102. In the *Canterbury Tales* of Chaucer [died 1400], the Wife of Bath boasts that she has been on pilgrimage to Jerusalem three times.

Rather strangely, the Crusades did not really penetrate into English consciousness as one might have expected. King Richard the Lionheart, who hardly spent any time in England, did inspire some legends and folklore about his adventures in Palestine, as did the valorous deeds of Robert Curthose [died 1134] in the First Crusade. The exploits of Curthose, the eldest son of William the Conqueror, were celebrated much later by Thomas Heywood, the Elizabethan playwright, in about the year 1600 when the latter's play *Four Prentices of London* was staged to enthusiastic crowds.

Enter Robert and Tancred, Godfrey [of bouillon] and Charles,
with their shields and scutcheons, drum and soldiers:
Godfrey's shield, having a maidenhead with a crown
in it; Charles's shield the Haberdasher's Arms.

Robert: Behold the high walls of Jerusalem,
Which Titus and Vespasian once brake down:
From off these turrets have the ancient Jews
Seen worlds of people mustering on these plains.
Oh, princes, which of all your eyes are dry,
To look upon this temple, now destroy'd?
Yonder did stand the great Jehovah's house,
In midst of all his people, there he dwelt:
Vessels of gold did serve his sacrifice,
And with him for the people spake the priests.
There was the ark, the shewbread, Aaron's rod,
Sanctum sanctorum, and the Cherubins.
Now in that holy place, where God himself
Was personally present, Pagans dwell,
False gods are rear'd, each temple idols bears.
Oh, who can see this, and abstain from tears?

Godfrey: This way, this sacred path our Saviour trod,
When he came riding to Jerusalem,
Whilst the religious people spread his way
With flowers and garments, and Hosanna cry'd.
Yonder did stand the great church, where he taught,
Confuting all the Scribes and Pharisees.
This place did witness all his miracles:
Within this place did stand the judgment seat,
Where Pontius Pilate with the elders sate,
Where they condemn'd him to be whipp'd and crown'd,
To be derided, mock'd, and crucified,
His hands bor'd through with nails, his side with spears.
Oh, who can see this place, and keep his tears?

But the Crusades were not entirely without consequence for our
story, as Barbara Tuchman conjectures, "[i]t may be that the Bible would
never have been able in later time to take such deep root in the English
body had not English blood been shed in the land of the Bible over so

many years."[13]

By the time of Queen Elizabeth, the English had become familiar with Jerusalem and its environs thanks largely to the availability of the Bible in English, to which we now turn. In the thirteenth century, "the first question ever asked by an Inquisitor of a 'heretic' was whether he knew any part of the Bible in his own tongue."[14] The story of the Bible in English is the story of the brave individuals who defied the Inquisitor, and who were determined to make the Bible available in the vernacular so that everyone from the ploughman to the baker had direct access, without the intermediation of a priest, to the words and deeds of Jesus and all those patriarchs and prophets inspired by God.

The story of the Bible in English picks up really with the work of John Wycliffe [alternative spellings Wyclif, Wycliff, Wiclef, Wicliffe, or Wickliffe], born circa 1328 – died 31 December 1384]. However, it would be churlish to pass by the efforts of earlier sages who quoted from the Bible in Latin, or who rendered the Bible into Anglo-Saxon. Saint Gildas, who probably died in the year 570 C.E. wrote a sermon in three parts, *De Excidio et Conquestu Britanniae* or *On the Ruin and Conquest of Britain*, recounting the conquest of his land by Saxons, Jutes, and Danes. "After every battle he cites an Old Testament analogy and on every page quotes from the Pentateuch, the Prophets, or the Psalms."[15] The learned and Venerable Bede [born 672 or 673; died 735] translated The Gospel according to John into Anglo-Saxon; King Alfred, ever solicitous of the education of his people, translated the Psalms and the Ten Commandments. Bible stories were also done into Old English; the Scriptures were written in parallel columns beside the Latin.[16]

Caedmon [died between 679- 684] is said by Bede to have devoted himself to religious poetry, and to translations from the Old and New Testaments into Old English, the language of his only surviving lines, the opening of his poem known as *Caedmon's Hymn*. *The Heliand* is an epic poem in Old Saxon composed in the first half of the ninth century recounting the life of Jesus, and is based on pseudo-Tatian's *Gospel Harmony*. The author of the *Heliand* is also thought to have written a poem on Genesis, based largely on the Bible account.

---

13 Barbara Tuchman, *Bible and Sword: England and Palestine from the Bronze Age to Balfour*, New York: Ballantine Books, [1956] Reprinted 1984, p. 53.

14 Benson Bobrick, *Wide as the Waters: The Story of the English Bible and the Revolution It Inspired*, New York: Penguin Books, [2001 1st Edn.], 2002, p. 11.

15 Barbara Tuchman, *op.cit.*, p. 3.

16 *Ibid.*, p. 87.

Aelfric of Eynsham [c. 955– c. 1010], also Alfric, and known as Aelfric the Grammarian, was an English abbot, and a writer in Old English of hagiography, homilies, biblical commentaries, and other genres. He wrote *Judith*, a homily in 452 verses around the year 1000. It is written in Old English alliterative prose, and paraphrases the Biblical original. Aelfric also wrote a paraphrase of parts of the Old Testament, known as the *West Saxon Gospels*, rather reluctantly fearing that its wider dissemination would lead common people to believe that the practices of the Ancient Israelites were still acceptable for Christians. His homily on Judith is not to be confused with the *Judith* an anonymous Old English paraphrase of the Biblical story of Holofernes in the Book of Judith. The exact date of the latter is disputed, some suggest the early tenth century for its composition, others would date it even later. Richard Rolle [1290–1349],[17] an English mystic, translated several parts of the Bible including the Psalms into a Northern English dialect; later copies were adapted into Southern English dialects.

These old and Middle English verses, paraphrases, and translations had no influence on the translations into English of the Old and New Testament that began in earnest only with John Wycliffe. As I hope to devote an entire article in several parts to the Bible in English, I shall only adumbrate the story of translations leading up to the magnificent Authorised Version of King James of 1611.

John Wycliffe [c.1328-1384] defended the right of every man, whether cleric or layman, to examine the Bible for himself. Only the Bible could be the standard by which Church doctrine must be tried; the opinions of popes, cardinals and friars were worthless except in so far as they were founded on Scripture itself. The only way to free Christian minds of the corrupt tyrannies of papal rule was to make the Bible available to them directly so that they could judge for themselves.[18] A full literal translation of the Bible into English was the only way make it accessible to everyman and woman, the partial translations into Old English or Anglo-Saxon of the Middle Ages were inadequate since the latter languages were no longer comprehensible to the majority of Englishmen.

By Wycliffe's day, against a background of English patriotism and the birth of English literature with the works of William Langland [c.1332 – c 1386], John Gower [c. 1330 – 1408], and his friend, Geoffrey Chaucer [c. 1343 –1400], the call for a complete translation became more and more

---

17 Alec Gilmore, *A Dictionary of the English Bible and its Origins*, Sheffield (U.K.): Sheffield Academic Press, 2000, p. 145.

18 Bobrick Benson, *op.cit.*, p. 50.

frequent and adamant, and had taken a nationalistic cast.[19] The Wycliffe Bible of 1380 was in fact a translation of the Latin Vulgate by two of Wycliffe's friends, John Purvey and Nicholas of Hereford, and was the first complete English Bible. A second version, far less literal, came out after Wycliffe's death in 1384, and contains far more native English idiom, and became the accepted one.[20]

William Tyndale [1494-1536], often called the Father of the English Bible, studied at Oxford and Cambridge, and became proficent in Greek. Like Wycliffe, Tyndale wanted to have the New Testament in a language that the ordinary man or woman could understand. His translation of the NT came out in 1525, and was the first to be printed, and the first to be translated from the original Greek. He also began to translate the OT from the Hebrew, but never completed his task.

Miles Coverdale [1488-1569], educated at Cambridge was an Augustinian Friar, and eventually a bishop. Coverdale worked as Tyndale's assistant, and helped him with the Pentateuch. Coverdale's Bible came out in 1535, and was the first complete printed edition of the Bible in English. As he had no pretence to any profound knowledge of either Greek or Hebrew, Coverdale made generous use of Tyndale's translation, and also relied on the Vulgate, Luther's German Bible, Zwingli and Pagninus. However, he did provide the translation of the Psalms for the Book of Common Prayer, the revised version of which appeared in 1662.

The Authorised Version of 1611, also known as the King James Version [KJV], was the work of 54 scholars, and prepared in Shakespeare's England, containing some of the most sublime English prose and poetry, poetry and prose that has influenced the English language and the course of English literature. Strictly speaking it was not an original translation, even though many of the scholars had some knowledge of Hebrew, Aramaic, and Greek, but more of an inspired redaction relying upon previously published work, such as the Bible translations of Tyndale, Coverdale, and others. It has been calculated that 80 per cent of the words for the NT come from Tyndale, for example.

T. H. Huxley reminds us, writing in the nineteenth century, the importance of the Bible to England and English culture,

And then consider the great historical fact that for three centuries, this Book has been woven into the life of all that is best and noblest in English history; that it has become the national

---

19 *Ibid.*, p. 52.
20 Alec Gilmore, *op.cit.*, p. 186.

epic of Britain, and is familiar to noble and simple, from John-o 'Groat's Mouse to Land's End, as Dante and Tasso once were to the Italians; that it is written in the noblest and purest English, and abounds in exquisite beauties of mere literary form; and, finally, that it forbids the veriest hind who never left his village to be ignorant of the existence of other countries and other civilizations, and of a great past, stretching back to the further limits of the oldest nations in the world. By the study of what other book could children be so much humanized and made to feel that each figure in the vast historical procession fills, like themselves, but a momentary space in the interval between two Eternities; and earns the blessings or the curses of all time, according to the effort to do good and hate evil?[21]

Barbara Tuchman summarises the significance of these English translations as well, "With the translation of the Bible into English and its adoption as the highest authority for an autonomous English Church, the history, traditions, and moral law of the Hebrew nation became part of the English culture; became for a period of three centuries the most powerful single influence on that culture. It linked, to repeat Matthew Arnold's phrase, 'the genius and history of us English, and our American descendants across the Atlantic, to the genius and history of the Hebrew people.'[22] This is far from saying that it made England a Judaeophile nation, but without the background of the English Bible it is doubtful that the Balfour Declaration would ever have been issued in the name of the British government or the Mandate for Palestine undertaken, even given the strategic factors that later came into play."[23]

In the Age of Discovery, especially in the sixteenth century, commerce, not salvation, was the chief attraction of the East. And yet, there were always travellers to the East, moved by curiosity and the Renaissance spirit of inquiry, who left journals and diaries that kept alive acquaintance with the Holy Land.

On January 5, 1648, the following petition was addressed,

To the Right Honourable Thomas Lord Fairfax, His Excellen-

21 T.H. Huxley, *Science and Education: Essays*, New York: D. Appleton and Company, 1896, p. 398.

22 Matthew Arnold, *Culture and Anarchy*, New York: The Macmillan Company, [1869, Ist Edn.] 1920, p. 101.

23 Barbara Tuchman, *op.cit.*,p. 80.

cy, England's General, and the Honourable Council of Warre, convened for God's Glory, Israel's Freedom, Peace, and Safety,

The humble Petition of Johanna Cartwright, Widow, and Ebenezer Cartwright, her Son, free-bom of England, and now Inhabitants of the City of Amsterdam,

Humbly sheweth,

That your Petitioners, being conversant in that city with and amongst some of Israel's race, called Jews, and growing sensible of their heavy outcryes and clamours against the intolerable cruelty of this our English nation, exercised against them by that (and other) inhumane exceeding great massacre of them, in the reign of Richard the Second, King of this land, and their banishment ever since, with the penalty of death to be inflicted upon any if 'they return into this land; that by discourse with them, and serious perusal of their Prophets, both they and we find, that the time of the recall draweth nigh; whereby they together with us shall come to know the Emanuel, the Lord of life, light, and glory, even as we are now known of him; and that this nation of England, with the inhabitants of the Netherlands, shall be the first and readiest to transport Israel's sons and daughters, in their ships, to the land promised to their forefathers, Abraham, Israel, and Jacob, for an everlasting inheritance.

For the glorious manifestation whereof, and pyous means thereunto, your Petitioners humbly pray, that the inhumane cruel statute of banishment, made against them, may be repealed, and they, under the Christian banner of charity and brotherly love, may again be received and permitted to trade and dwell amongst you in this land, as now they do in the Netherlands. By which act of mercy, your Petitioners are assured of, the wrath of God will be much appeased towards you for their innocent bloodshed; and they thereby daily enlightened in the saving knowledge of him, for whom they look daily, and expect, as their King of Eternal Glory, and both their and our Lord God of Salvation (Christ Jesus). For the glorious accomplishing whereof, your Petitioners do and shall ever address themselves to the true peace, and pray, &c.[24]

The petition of the Cartwrights, two English Puritans living in the Netherlands, reflects the extent to which attitudes in seventeenth century England had changed, a change wrought by the English Bible working through the Puritan movement. In earlier centuries, Palestine had been seen as a land of largely Christian Associations. "Now it came to be remembered as the homeland of the Jews, the land carrying the Scriptural promise of Israel's return."[25] It is at the beginning of the seventeenth century that the movement among the English for the return of the Jews to Palestine began, but it was not a movement for the sake of the Jews, but for the sake of the promise made to them.[26]

> According to Scripture the kingdom of Israel for all mankind would come when the people of Israel were restored to Zion. Only then would the world see the advent of the Messiah or, in Christian terms, the Second Advent. The return was visioned, of course, only in terms of a Jewish nation converted to Christianity, for this was to be the signal for the working out of the promise.[27]

As early as 1621, Sir Henry Finch, a British Member of Parliament and Puritan common lawyer, had exhorted, in "The World's Great Restauration [Restoration], or The Calling of the Jews and with them of all Nations and Kingdoms of the Earth to the Faith of Christ," the Jews to reclaim the Holy Land, "Out of all the places of thy dispersion, East, West, North and South, His purpose is to bring thee home again and to marry thee to Himself by faith for evermore."[28]

It is from the middle of the seventeenth century that we find the second of the two motives that compelled the British to take an interest in Palestine. We have already emphasized the religious motive, but from now on we shall encounter the profit motive, whether commercial, military, or imperial.

---

24 Stephen C. Manganiello, *The Concise Encyclopedia of the Revolutions and Wars of England, Scotland, and Ireland, 1639-1660*, Lanham [MD]: Scarecrow Press, Inc. 2004, p. 285. [Tuchman gives 1649 as the date of the petition.]

25 Barbara Tuchman, *op.cit.*, p. 122.

26 *Ibid.*

27 *Ibid.*

28 British Zionism at: http://www.mideastweb.org/britzion.htm, accessed 3 Jan. 2010.

By the nineteenth century, an evangelical version of Protestantism also believed that the conversion of the Jews could not come about until the restoration of the Jews to Palestine. Among the early advocates of Restorationism were Lord Lindsay, Lord Shaftesbury, Lord Palmerston, Disraeli, Lord Manchester, Holman Hunt, Sir Charles Warren, Hall Caine, Charles Henry Churchill, and of course, George Eliot. For example, Lord Lindsay wrote: "[The soil of] Palestine still enjoys her sabbaths, and only waits for the return of her banished children, and the application of industry, commensurate with her agricultural capabilities, to burst once more into universal luxuriance, and be all that she ever was in the days of Solomon."[29]

While Charles Henry Churchill, a British resident of Damascus, wrote in 1841 a letter to the Jewish philanthropist Moses Montefiore stating, "...I consider the object to be perfectly obtainable. But, two things are indispensably necessary. Firstly, that the Jews will themselves take up the matter unanimously. Secondly, that the European powers will aid them in their views..."[30]

Anthony Ashley Cooper, Earl of Shaftesbury, an Evangelical Christian, was also a fervent restorationist, and perhaps the greatest influence on the views of George Eliot. He wrote, "The inherent vitality of the Hebrew race reasserts itself with amazing persistence. Its genius, to tell the truth, adapts itself more or less to all the currents of civilization all over the world, nevertheless always emerging with distinctive features and a gallant recovery of vigor." Shaftesbury had confessed to his biographer, Edwin Hodder, in his belief in the Second Advent, which "has always been a moving principle in my life, for I see everything going on in the world subordinate to this great event."[31] And since the restoration of the Jews was required for the Second Advent, Shaftesbury "never had a shadow of a doubt that the Jews were to return to their own land...It was his daily prayer, his daily hope. 'Oh pray for the peace of Jerusalem!' were the words engraven on the ring he always wore on his right hand."[32]

Lord Shaftesbury undoubtedly influenced Prime Minister Palmerston and his successors in the government, whom he also urged to protect the Jews already living in Palestine. A report in *The Times* in 1840 hinted

---

29 Crawford, A.W.C. (Lord Lindsay), *Letters on Egypt, Edom and the Holy Land*, London: H. Colburn, 1847, V II, p. 71.

30 Quoted in Barbara Tuchman, *op.cit.*, chapter xi, p. 209.

31 Edwin Hodder, *The Life and Work of the Seventh Earl of Shaftesbury*, K.G. London: Cassell &Co. Ltd.,1887, Ch.xxiii, p. 524.

32 Barbara Tuchman, *op.cit.*, p. 178.

that Lord Shaftesbury had tried to ascertain the views of the Jews on the proposed restoration, and whether and when they were ready to live in Palestine and invest their capital in agriculture, whether they would pay for their own passage, whether they would be willing to live under Turkish rule, protected by Britain, France, Russia, Prussia and Austro-Hungary. Shaftesbury had convinced Palmerston to write to the British Ambassador in Constantinople:

> There exists at the present time among the Jews dispersed over Europe, a strong notion that the time is approaching for their nation to return to Palestine...It would be of manifest importance to the Sultan to encourage the Jews to return and to settle in Palestine because the wealth which they would bring with them would increase the resources of the Sultan's dominions; and the Jewish people, if returning under the sanction and protection and at the invitation of the Sultan, would be a check on any future evil designs of Mehmet Ali or his successors... I have to instruct Your Excellency strongly to recommend to hold out every just encouragement to the Jews of Europe to return to Palestine.[33]

CHARLOTTE ELIZABETH AND THE RESTORATION OF THE JEWS

George Eliot is usually considered the first novelist to have discussed "Zionism," that is the restoration of the Jews to Palestine, in *Daniel Deronda*, which was published in 1876. Perhaps we should now change that to "the first distinguished novelist," after considering the work of one Charlotte Elizabeth Tonna, who wrote under the name, "Charlotte Elizabeth." Her "Zionist novel," *Judah's Lion* was published in 1843. Hugh Fitzgerald,[34] a regular contributor to the *New English Review*, advised me to have a look at her works before assigning priority. I confess I had never heard of her.

Charlotte Elizabeth Tonna ("Charlotte Elizabeth") [1790 – 1846] wrote prolifically under her baptismal name, Charlotte Elizabeth. She was born in Norwich, Norfolk, the daughter of Reverend Michael Browne, an Anglican priest and a canon at Norwich Cathedral. Charlotte was brought

---

33 Barbara Tuchman, *op.cit.*, p. 175.

34 Hugh Fitzgerald is incidentally one of the great prose writers in English of the last fifty years, comparable to Roger Scruton, Christopher Hitchens, and Bernard Lewis.

up in a Tory, royalist, Church-of-England family. Early in her life, Charlotte Elizabeth acquired her passions: first, the plight of English factory workers, second, evangelical religion, and finally gardening. On the death of her father [1812], she moved to London with her mother. There she met Cpt. George Phelan whom she married six months later. After two years in Canada, where her husband was stationed in the British army, they moved to Ireland where they lived from 1819 to 1824. During this time, she converted to Evangelical Protestantism, became anti-catholic, and began her literary career, writing for the Dublin Tract Society in the early 1820's. Legally separating from her husband who was posted abroad once more, Charlotte Elizabeth eventually returned to England where she took residence in Clifton near Bristol. There, she met Hannah More who also wrote religious tracts and homilies.

In her *Personal Recollections* written at the end of 1840,[35] Charlotte Elizabeth explains her interest in Jews and Palestine, or as her husband put it, "her long-cherished hopes, the incipient restoration of Israel."[36]

One of the most interesting and delightful subjects opened to me by my study of the Scriptures during this happy period was that of the Jews. I had always felt deeply interested for them, and looked forward to their conversion, individually, to Christ; but nationally I was still in the dark about them. Now I plainly saw the nature and extent of God's covenanted pledge to Abraham, and became fully convinced that their national restoration was a revealed truth, and that the church would never attain to any triumph on earth in which the Jews, as Jews, did not bear a very prominent part. Happily untaught in the spiritualizing process by which the divine promises to Israel are wrested from their evident, literal sense, I took all that I read as primarily applicable to those who were distinctly addressed by name, though plainly seeing that there was an allowable adaptation of them to the Gentile church. Many a time have I knelt down, with the ninth chapter of Daniel spread before me, fervently and with tears pleading in his words for his people. It was not until long afterwards that, on urging upon a pious clergyman the duty of combining in some great effort for the conversion of the Jews, I learnt to my surprise and delight of

35 L.H.J. Tonna, "Memoir of Charlotte Elizabeth" in *The Works of Charlotte Elizabeth*, New York: M.W. Dodd, 1848, Vol. 1, p. 115.
36 *Ibid.*, p. 126.

the existence of such a society. I need not tell you that the impression made on my mind by the Bible when I had no other teacher, has been continually deepened for twenty years; and that nothing which man could say or write ever for a moment shook my conviction on the subject. I laid hold on the word of promise, and urged it on all within my reach, from my very first intercourse with Christians; and I have watched with joy the rapid unfolding of God's purposes towards the Jews, both in disposing the hearts of Gentiles towards their course, and in evidently preparing the way for their speedy restoration."[37]

Some critics and historians see Tonna as a "Zionist"—though strictly speaking the term[38] itself did not come into use until 1896—and her novel *Judah's Lion* as a Zionist novel.[39] Elizabeth's novel recounts the story of an English Jew, Alick Cohen, and his voyage to the Holy Land where moved by his experiences he converts to Christianity, retaining, however, his Jewish identity. The title of the novel is itself a subtle reminder of the theme of the inextricable and intertwined destinies of two nations, England and Jewish Palestine. The character Gunner Gordon reflects on this theme; his sense of gratitude to Judaism recalls George Eliot's remark in her letter to Harriet Beecher Stowe that "… towards the Hebrews we western people, who have been reared in Christianity, have a peculiar debt, and whether we acknowledge it or not, a peculiar thoroughness of fellowship in religion and moral sentiment…[the English reveal] themselves empty of any real knowledge as to the relations of their own social and religious life to the history of the people they think themselves witty in insulting. They hardly know that Christ was a Jew… "[40]

---

37 *The Works of Charlotte Elizabeth*, New York: M.W. Dodd, 1848, Vol. 1, p. 45.

38 "Zionism" was coined by an Austrian Jew, Nathan Birnbum, in 1890; Birnbaum worked with Theodore Herzl on the first Zionist Congress in Basle in 1897. According to the *Oxford English Dictionary*, "zionism" first appears in print in England in the *Jewish Chronicle*, May 1896.

39 Elizabeth Kowaleski, "'The Heroine of Some Strange Romance': The Personal Recollections of Charlotte Elizabeth Tonna," *Tulsa Studies in Women's Literature*, Vol. 1, No. 2 (Fall 1982): 141–153 (n. 6, 152); Linda H. Peterson, *Traditions of Victorian Women's Autobiography*, Charlottesville and London: University Press of Virginia, 1999, pp. 44–46; Monica Correa Fryckstedt, "Charlotte Elizabeth Tonna and The Christian Lady's Magazine," in *Victorian Periodicals Review*, 14:2 (Summer 1981) pp. 43-51.

40 *The George Eliot Letters*, ed. Gordon S. Haight, New Haven, 1954-5, 1977-8, Vol. VI, Oct. 29, 1876, pp. 301-302 Oct. 29, 1876,

As Alick gazes at the flag of England with its three lions, Gordon remarks, "Ay, Mr. Cohen, there floats the Lion of Judah."

"The Lion of England, I suppose you mean," said an officer somewhat sharply, who had caught the remark as he passed.

"The Lions of England, Sir, and the Lion of Judah also, I believe," answered the Gunner, touching his cap, "I have heard it so remarked, and by one well read in heraldry."

"Holloa, Sharp!" cried the other, "come, here's this fellow Gordon making Jews of us all!"

"Pardon me, gentlemen," said the Gunner, as several gathered round at this summons, "I believe you will find on examination, that the arms of England contained only two lions, until our Richard the First added a third, after his conquest in Palestine, and that third lion he probably adopted as the well-known standard of the country where his greatest exploits were performed, and a chief type of Him, 'the Lion of the tribe of Judah,' whose cause he professed to uphold against the infidel Saracens." ....

"Judah's Lion!" thought [Alick]; "what a strange idea that is; and yet I don't see but it may be perfectly correct. Richard bore the title of Coeur-de-lion, and might, in consideration of that distinction, clap a third lion upon his shield. He might, to be sure; but on the other hand, how very natural it would be that he, who became by his conquests lord of Palestine, should incorporate that trophy with his own. Judah's lion!" he again repeated, chuckling as the thought arose, "if so, why England fights under our banner—she may point to the standard of the despised Jew, and say, '*in hoc signo vinces.*' [Under this sign/banner, you shall conquer.] I'll go this very night to the Gunner's cabin, and get some further information from him. 'Twill be better at any rate than turning into bed at such an unreasonable hour." ...

"May I sit with you a little while, Mr. Gordon? May I ask you a few questions about the Lion?"

The Gunner sprang from his seat, bolted the door, and said in a voice that faltered with suppressed emotion, "As long as you please you shall sit here, and nobody shall interrupt us while we talk, as by God's blessing we will talk"—and he clasped his hands together as he leaned them on the Bible—

"on the most stirring, the most glorious of all subjects—'the Lion of the tribe of Judah!'"

"You are very fond of our people, Mr. Gordon," said Alick, smiling.

"Sir, I owe to your people more than my life: I owe to them this book, the writings of Moses and the prophets, who were all Jews; the writings of the Evangelists and Apostles, who were all likewise Jews: and through them the knowledge of my Lord and Saviour, the King of the Jews, God over all, blessed for ever!"[41]

Despite her evident sense of gratitude to the Jews for all that has given her life any kind of meaning, Charlotte Elizabeth does not, unlike George Eliot, see the Jews and their aspirations as ends in themselves, but as a means to the fulfillment of an Evangelical Christian prophecy. *Daniel Deronda* is also taken to be a Zionist novel, at least in the sense of being a "prophetic inspirer of Zionism and of the state of Israel." But as Gertrude Himmelfarb in her masterpiece, *The Jewish Odyssey of George Eliot*, argues "[t]here is some warrant for those claims. *Daniel Deronda* appeared twenty-one years before the first meeting of the Zionist Congress in Basle and seventy-two years before the establishment of the state of Israel. But Eliot was a Zionist with a difference. When Deronda emigrated to Palestine, he did so not out of the fear of pogroms, or as a response to a Holocaust, or even to escape the barbs and slights of the English mode of polite anti-Semitism, but rather to fulfill a proud and unique heritage. His mentor, Mordecai, was a learned as well as a passionate Jew who felt in his soul, as he said, the faith and the history of his people—his 'nation'. It was this sense of nationality that inspired his vision of Judaism and that he transmitted to his disciple Deronda. And it was this theme that Eliot returned to in her last essay, when she likened Jewish nationality to the admirable sentiment that had inspired her own countrymen in their evolution as a nation."[42]

Eliot's "vision of Judaism and a Jewish state was all the more remarkable precisely because it was *disinterested*, because, unlike Deronda..., she was not Jewish and had no personal stake in it."[43]

---

41 Charlotte Elizabeth, *Judah's Lion*, New York: Charles Scribner, [1843] 1852, pp. 29-35.

42 Gertrude Himmelfarb, *The Jewish Odyssey of George Eliot*, New York: Encounter Books, 2009, pp. 10-11.

43 *Ibid.*, p. 153. Emphasis added by Ibn Warraq.

EDWARD SAID AND THE QUESTION OF PALESTINE

I. *"A Land without a People for a People without a Land."*

Not only does Edward Said incorrectly attribute the first use of the phrase to Israel Zangwill, a British writer, he also misquotes it, as "a land without people [sic], for a people without land [sic]."[44] As Adam M. Garfinkle has noted, "the absence of the indirect article 'a' before the word 'people' substantially changes the meaning of the phrase from the political to the demographic and literal. The omission obscures the phrase's proper nineteenth-century intellectual context and substitutes a literal and obviously false remark suitable for marketing the real and imagined Zionist insensitivities of the past for current uses."[45] In the political sense, the Palestinian people were not constituted politically as a nation before 1920; as Zeine N. Zeine writing in 1973 noted, "The world in which the Arabs and Turks lived together was, before the end of the nineteenth century, politically a non-national world. The vast majority of the Muslim Arabs did not show any nationalist or separatist tendencies except when the Turkish leaders themselves, after 1908, asserted their own nationalism...."[46]

We have already encountered Lord Shaftesbury as the Evangelical Christian who wished to see the Restoration of the Jews to Palestine. His wish was rekindled at the height of the Crimean War over what the eventual disintegration of the Ottoman Empire might portend. Speaking of Greater Syria, a large indeterminate area of the Ottoman Empire, Shaftesbury wrote in July 1853 that it was "a country without a nation," and needed to be matched to "a nation without a country." He asked, "Is there such a thing? To be sure there is, The ancient and rightful lords of the soil, the Jews!"[47]

John Lawson Stoddard [1850-1931], an American lecturer who illustrated his talks with slides (stereographs) of the many exotic countries that he visited. In his lectures that were published in 1897, Stoddard revealed his own Christian Zionism and wrote, "At present Palestine supports only six hundred thousand people, but with proper cultivation it can easily maintain two and half millions. You [the Jews] are a people without a country; there is a country without a people. Be united. Fulfil

---

44 Edward Said, *The Question of Palestine*, New York: Vintage Books, [1979] 1980, p. 9.

45 Adam M. Garfinkle, "On the Origin, Meaning, Use and Abuse of a Phrase," in *Middle Eastern Studies* (Oct. 1991), p. 541.

46 Quoted by Adam M. Garfinkle, *op.cit.*, p. 541.

47 *Ibid.*, p. 543.

the dreams of your old poets and patriarchs. Go back,—go back to the land of Abraham."[48]

Though published in 1897 these remarks were in fact written in 1891. Stoddard clearly does not believe that Palestine was uninhabited since he a gives a census figure (600,000), and thus "without a people" was meant in the political sense, and that is how it was transmitted to and taken by Zionists such as Herzl.

II. DANIEL DERONDA AND ZIONISM

I have already discussed Christopher Hitchens' defense of *Daniel Deronda*. Here I should like to return to an analysis of Edward Said's contemptuous dismissal of George Eliot.[49] Said quotes a long passage from the novel, placing phrases in italics, [ironically given his casual way with the indefinite article in his quote on "land without people," instead of "land without a people," Said puts in one which is not in the original novel, "there is a store of wisdom" when in fact Eliot wrote "there is store of wisdom..."]:

> They [the Jews] have wealth enough *to redeem the soil from debauched and paupered conquerors*; they have the skill of the statesman to devise, the tongue of the orator to persuade. And is there no prophet or poet among us to make the ears of Christian Europe tingle with shame at the hideous obloquy of Christian strife *which the Turk gazes at as at the fighting of beasts to which he has lent an arena*? There is a store of wisdom among us to found *a new Jewish polity, grand, simple, just, like the old*— a republic where there is equality of protection, an equality which shone like a star on the forehead of our ancient community, *and gave it more than the brightness of Western freedom amid the despotisms of the East.* Then our race shall have an organic centre, a heart and brain to watch and guide and execute; *the outraged Jew shall have a defence in the court of nations*, as the outraged Englishman or American. And the world will gain as Israel gains. For there will be a community in the van of the

---

48 *Ibid.*, p. 544.

49 I have drawn freely on Irfan Khawaja's penetrating analysis of Said on Eliot which appeared on-line in the comments section of the *New English Review*. But the views expressed in this section are entirely my responsibility; Dr. Khawaja may well not accept my interpretations.

East which carries the culture and the sympathies of every great nation in its bosom; *there will be a land set for a halting-place of enmities, a neutral ground for the East as Belgium is for the West.* Difficulties? I know there are difficulties. But let the spirit of sublime achievement move in the great among our people, and the work will begin." [Said's emphases]

As we saw with his treatment of *The Talisman*, where he automatically takes the Christian knight's views as Scott's, Said assumes, without providing us with any evidence, that Mordecai's views are Eliot's. In fact, a close reading of Eliot's novel provides enough evidence to the contrary. As Kenneth M. Newton argues that by looking at the speech by Mordecai, in the Hand and Banner tavern scene in Chapter Forty-Two of *Daniel Deronda*, urging the creation of an organic centre for the Jews in Palestine "in the light of the Jewish-maiden-and-Gentile-king episode at the end of Chapter Sixty-One, which reveals that Mordecai's idealism omits inconvenient aspects of reality, gives one a different, more critical perpsective on the speech. It is political rhetoric directed at a susceptible Deronda…not at the other members of the group, all of whom are familiar with Mordecai's ideas and disagree with them, and is meant to be seen as such."[50]

The narrator of the novel always keeps a distance, and does not lay any claim to second-sight: "'Second sight' is a flag over a disputed ground"[51]—and while, at first, seeming to present Mordecai as a true visionary, steps back and introduces the possibility that Mordecai may not be the genuine article after all: "No doubt there are abject specimens of the visionary, as there is a minim mammal which you might imprison in the finger of your glove. That small relative of the elephant has no harm in him; but what great mental or social type is free from specimens whose insignificance is both ugly and noxious? One is afraid to think of all that the genus 'patriot' embraces…." Here, it is not at all clear whether Mordecai will remain a 'minim mammal' or mature into 'a great mental or social type,' that is a visionary elephant. As Newton reiterates, Eliot's "treatment of Mordecai is more distanced than most critics have admitted."[52]

And can Mordecai be taken to stand for Zionism, since he is, after all, a character in a novel? Said's main complaint seems to be that Morde-

---

50 Kenneth M. Newton, "Second Sight: Is Edward Said right about *Daniel Deronda*?" in *The Times Literary Supplement* [London, May 9, 2008] p. 14.

51 G. Eliot, *Daniel Deronda*, Book Five, Chapter 38, Harmondsworth: Penguin Classics, 1987 [1876], p. 527.

52 Kenneth M. Newton. *op. cit.*, p. 15.

cai, and therefore, by Said's logic, Eliot, do not acknowledge the existence, and therefore do not recognize the rights, of "the actual inhabitants of the East, Palestine in particular."[53]

However, before addressing the question of the implications of Zionism for the actual inhabitants of Palestine, let us take the first batch of words italicized by Said in the Eliot quote above: "*to redeem the soil from debauched and paupered conquerors.*" It is not clear if Eliot means the original Arab conquerors of Jerusalem, or the *de jure* rulers, that is the Turks. Said is well aware that Palestine was in fact under the Turkish Imperial yoke but dare not draw any conclusions from that fact; only the West and Jews are seen as the "imperialists." But, of course, nineteenth century Zionism has no affinities—neither intellectual nor historical—with Western imperialism, even though it was denounced by the Soviet Union as an instrument of British imperialism and of international capitalism.[54] First, Jews had lived there for millennia before being expelled by various conquerors, or gone into voluntary exile to escape intolerable conditions.[55] Second, in the late nineteenth century, when *Daniel Deronda* was written (1876), there were still Jews living in Palestine; we have accounts of their presence in Jerusalem, for example, from countless Western travellers to

---

53 Edward Said, *The Question of Palestine*, New York: Vintage Books, 1980 [Ist edn. 1979], p. 65.

54 Samuel Katz, *Battleground: Fact and Fantasy in Palestine*, New York: Taylor Productions Ltd. 2002 [Ist published 1973] p. 83.

55 There have been a number of attempts to delegitimize Israel's claims, and have been done so by claiming that the "Jews" in Israel—and indeed elsewhere—are not Jews at all, have nothing to genetically connect them to the original Jews of Judea. One such attempt is Shlomo Sand's *The Invention of the Jewish People* (London: Verso, 2009). It has won all sorts of prizes in Europe but is, in fact, a very shoddy piece of scholarship, well replied to by Anita Shapira, "Review Essay: Jewish-people deniers," in *The Journal of Israeli History* Vol. 28, No. 1, March 2009, 63–72; and Martin Goodman, *The Times Literary Supplement* (*TLS*), 26 February 2010; Shlomo Sand responds, *TLS*, Letters to the Editor, 10 March 2010; Martin Goodman responds, *TLS*, Letters to the Editor, 24 March 2010. And of course Sand was definitively refuted by scientific studies published in two prestigious science journals. Doron M. Behar *et al*, "The Genome-wide structure of the Jewish people" in *Nature*, 8 July, 2010, Vol. 466, pp. 238-242; and Gil Atzmon *et al.*, "Abraham's Children in the Genome Era: Major Jewish Diaspora Populations Comprise Distinct Genetic Clusters with Shared Middle Eastern Ancestry" in *The American Journal of Human Genetics*, Volume 86, Issue 6, 850-859, 03 June 2010. The studies showed that "Jewish communities in Europe and the Middle East share many genes inherited from the ancestral Jewish population that lived in the Middle East some 3,000 years ago, even though each community also carries genes from other sources—usually the country in which it lives," Nicolas Wade, *New York Times*, 9 June 2010, p. A14.

the Holy Land. Thus, the principle motivation behind Zionism was a sense of nationality, of a people who felt their faith and their history in their very being, attached to and deeply rooted in a particular place. As Samuel Katz expressed it, "the central fact of 3500 years of Jewish history [was] the passion of the Jewish people for the land of Israel."[56] The impetus behind European imperialism can perhaps justifiably be characterised as economic exploitation, "but in the land of Israel, or as the Romans renamed it, Palestine, there were no resources to exploit, and no native population that might be set to work. Indeed, the only people who tilled the soil were the Zionist pioneers, and the only riches the pitiful sums brought by the pioneers themselves."[57] For Said, Zionism is, in Cameron S. Brown's phrase "the Jewish daughter of European imperialism,"[58] though, as Brown goes on to point out, when Said wrote his book, the majority of Israelis were actually of Oriental, that is, of Middle Eastern and North African descent.

Jews had lived in what were to become Muslims lands at least two millennia before Muhammad's supposed birth in 570 CE. Starting with Palestine itself: the earliest nonbiblical reference to ancient Israel appears in a short poem on a victory stela which was erected in 1209 BCE in the funerary temple, in Thebes, of Egyptian pharaoh Merneptah (reigned 1213-1203 BCE): "Israel is laid waste and his seed is not." It is clear "that Israel was a political-ethnic entity of sufficient importance to the Egyptians to warrant mention alongside the three Canaanite city-states."[59] Hard archaeological evidence, while it may cast doubt on some central narratives in the Tanakh or the Old Testament, relegating them to the realms of mythology, surprisingly reveals a continuous Israelite presence in the Land of Israel since the Bronze Age, that is since 3,500 BCE. As archaeologist Israel Finkelstein and historian Neil Asher Silberman put it, in their scientifically rigorous work *The Bible Unearthed*,[60] "Most of the people who formed early Israel were local people—the same people whom we see in the highlands throughout the Bronze and Iron Ages."[61] Further archaeo-

---

56 Samuel Katz, *op. cit.*, p. 85.

57 Hugh Fitzgerald, personal communication, July, 2013.

58 Cameron S. Brown, "Answering Edward Said's *The Question of Palestine*", in *Israel Affairs*, Vol. 13, No. 1, January, 2007, pp. 55-79; p. 60.

59 Lawrence E. Stager, "Forging an Identity: The Emergence of Ancient Israel" in Coogan, Michael D., ed. *The Oxford History of the Biblical World*, Oxford: Oxford University Press, 1998, p. 91.

60 Israel Finkelstein & Neil Asher Silberman, *The Bible Unearthed: Archaeology's New Vision of Ancient Israel and the Origin of its Sacred Texts*, New York: Simon and Schuster, 2002 [Ist pub. 2001], p. 118.

61 Bronze Age: 3,500 BCE—1150 BCE; Iron Age: 1150 BCE—586 BCE.

logical artifacts uncovered at Tel Dan, northern Israel talk of the House of David, and "there is hardly a question that it tells the story of the assault of Hazael, king of Damascus, on the northern kingdom of Israel around 835 BCE."[62]

Here is a quick gallop through the history of Jewish communities in the other lands. The earliest epigraphic evidence on the presence of Jews in Morocco comes from the second century CE.[63] The presence of Jews in Algeria since the first centuries of the common era is attested by epitaphs.[64] We have reliable evidence of Jewish presence in Libya in the time of Ptolemy Lagos (ruled Egypt 323–282 BCE); he settled Jews "in the Cyrenean Pentapolis to strengthen his regime there, probably in 312 B.C.E."[65] Egyptian Jews trace their history back to the time of Jeremiah, but it was probably not until the conquest of Alexander the Great in 332 BCE that there was a second great wave of Jewish emigration to Egypt. "Alexander's successors in Egypt, the Ptolemid dynasty, attracted many Jews early in their reign to settle in Egypt as tradesmen, farmers, mercenaries, and government officials. During their reign Egyptian Jewry enjoyed both tolerance and prosperity. They became significant in culture and literature, and by the first century C.E., accounted for an eighth of the population of Egypt."[66] The first firm evidence of Jewish life in Yemen is the tombs of Himyarī Jews in Beth She'arim, dated to the beginning of the third century CE, thus, by the second half of the second century CE, there were Jewish settlements in Yemen.[67] "The Diaspora of Iraq was one of the most ancient of the Jewish people. The Jews came to Babylon after the destruction of the First Temple (586 B.C.E.), or even 10 years earlier, with the exile of Jehoiachin. They integrated into their land of captivity and took part in its economic and cultural development."[68] "Dating back to biblical times, the Jewish community in Syria developed due to the proximity of the Jewish center in Palestine. Thus, according to Josephus, Ezra was commanded by the Persian Xerxes to appoint judges among the Jews 'to hold court in all of Syria and Phoenicia' (Ant. 11:129). During the Second Temple period, the Jewish community apparently thrived, and

---

62 Israel Finkelstein & Neil Asher Silberman, *op.cit.*, p. 129.

63 *Encyclopaedia Judaica*, ed., Fred Skolnik, New York: Thomson Gale: Macmillan Reference, 2007, 2nd Edn, s.v. "Morocco."

64 *Ibid.*, s.v. "Algeria."

65 *Ibid.*, s.v. "Libya."

66 *Ibid.*, s.v. "Egypt."

67 *Ibid.*, s.v. "Yemen."

68 *Ibid.*, s.v. "Iraq."

even Roman governors of Syria were known to fall under the influence of the Jewish multitudes (cf. Philo, *Legatio ad Gaium 355–367*). Similarly, Josephus, in describing the tribulations of the Jews of Antioch, begins by stressing that 'the Jewish race, densely interspersed among the native populations of every portion of the world, is particularly numerous in Syria, where intermingling is due to the proximity of the two countries. It was at Antioch that they especially congregated, possibly owing to the greatness of that city, but mainly because the successors of King Antiochus [Epiphanes, 175–164 B.C.E.] had enabled them to live there in security' (Wars 7:43). These Jews therefore flourished and were in a position to send costly offerings to the Temple at Jerusalem. The community was granted citizen rights equal to those of the Greeks (*ibid.*; cf. Apion 2:39, where these rights were granted by the founder of the city, Seleucus I Nicator)."[69]

Thus Jews are indeed Oriental, but the latter term does not convey the diversity of the non-European origins of the Jews of Israel. The Mizrahi (Eastern) Jews are the descendants of Jews from Babylon—modern Iraq, Iran, Central Asia (Uzbekistan), Azerbaijan, Georgia, Syria, Kurdistan, Bahrain, Afghanistan, Pakistan, India, and the Yemen. The Sephardim, after their expulsion from Spain in 1492 and Portugal in 1497, lived in the Near East (in various parts of the Ottoman Empire), while the Maghrebim lived for centuries in North Africa.

As Sir Martin Gilbert reminds us, "In the four years between 1948 and 1951 a total of 687,739 Jewish refugees reached Israel. Of these about one quarter—some 100,000—arrived from Europe. About 500,000— more than three quarters—arrived from Arab and Muslim lands."[70] Gilbert gives more precise figures for Jewish emigration from Arab and Persian lands to Israel between 1947 and 1957, in what he calls the Second Exodus: Morocco 260,000; Algeria 14,000; Libya 35,000; Egypt 29,525; Yemen and Aden 50,552; Iraq 129,290; Syria 4,500; Iran 31,000; Lebanon 6,000. Thus a total of 559,867 Oriental Jews had arrived in Israel by 1957. But these cold figures hide a history of poverty, hunger, persecution, rape, and murder. As Gilbert explained, "Jews who have lived under Muslim rule, wherever they live today, are determined to make the international community aware of their sufferings in the aftermath of the 1948-49 Arab-Israeli War."[71] In an interview on 27 July 2000, President Bill Clinton brought up the issue often forgotten, that is, compensation

---

69 *Ibid.*, s.v. "Syria."

70 Martin Gilbert, *In Ishmael's House: A History of Jews in Muslim Lands*, New Haven: Yale University Press, 2010, p. 310.

71 *Ibid.*, p.325.

for the dispossessed Jews: "[A fund ought to be set up that] should compensate the Israelis who were made refugees by the war, which occurred after the birth of the State of Israel. [Israel] is full of people, Jewish people, who lived in predominantly Arab countries who came to Israel because they were made refugees in their own land."[72] The expelled Jews bore their burden with dignity without becoming professional victims; nor did they seek revenge by turning into suicide bombers. Said, in *The Question of Palestine*, claims that he is "horrified by the terror in Palestinian men and women who were *driven to do such things*,"[73] thus exonerating the Palestinians of any moral responsibility. But how is it that these persecuted Jews brutally expelled from lands they had been living in centuries before the arrivals of the Muslims were not driven to acts of terrorism. These Jews had exercised moral restraint.

The Land of Israel itself also saw anti-Jewish riots incited by the extremist Mufti of Jerusalem, Amin el-Husseini. They started in Jerusalem on 23 August 1929, soon spread to agricultural settlements, and later to Tel Aviv and Haifa. In Hebron, more than sixty Jews were slaughtered, including old people, women and children. The total number of Jewish victims was over 130.[74]

Lacking space, I shall pick the situation of Libyan Jews as emblematic of the fate of all Jews in Muslim lands in the years just before and just after the creation of Israel in 1948, though, of course, one must always bear in mind that the fate of all Jews living under Islam at all times as *dhimmis* was precarious. After the creation of the Arab league in Cairo, in March, 1945, there were four days of anti-Jewish riots in Tripoli and other Libyan towns, starting on November 4. The violence was intensified by false rumours of the murder of the Grand Cadi and the Mufti of Tripoli. Ten synagogues were burnt and looted. Jewish homes were besieged—men, women and children were attacked with knives, and clubs, knocked down and then finished off with daggers. In Zanzur forty of the 120 Jews were murdered. A total of 129 Libyan Jews were killed during four days of rioting; in Tripoli alone 150 Jews were seriously injured, and 4,200 Jewish traders lost all their belongings and homes; many women and girls were raped, and more than four thousand Jews fled and took refuge in camps set up by the British Military Administration [BMA]. And despite fine

---

72 Quoted in Martin Gilbert, *op.cit.*, p. 327.

73 Edward Said, *The Question of Palestine*, New York: Viking Books, 1980 [Ist. Published, 1979], Introduction, p. xii.

74 H.H. Ben-Sasson, ed., *A History of the Jewish People*, Cambridge: Harvard University Press, 1976 [Ist pub. in Hebrew, 1969], p. 1007.

words from various Muslim leaders asking for calm, peace, and reconciliation, the BMA reported, "Leading Arab personalities severely censured this shameful aggression. But no general, deep-felt sense of guilt seems to animate the Arab community at large: nor has it been too active in offering help to the victims."[75]

Let us now look at the *"debauched and paupered conquerors"* of Palestine.

Travellers[76] to the Holy Land throughout the ages testify to the desolation of the land, and the lack of population to work the rich, fertile land. Here is one description from the eighteenth century, by Thomas Shaw [1694-1751], Fellow of Queen's College, Oxford, and a Fellow of the Royal Society, who worked as a chaplain in Algiers between 1720 and 1733, and subsequently published an account of his travels in Barbary and the Levant in 1738. Shaw observed, "The Holy land, were it as well inhabited and cultivated as formerly, would still be more fruitful than the very best part of the coast of Syria or Phoenice [sic]. For the soil itself is generally much richer; and, all things considered, yields a more preferable crop. … The barrenness, or scarcity, which some authors may either ignorantly or maliciously complain of, does not proceed from the incapacity, or natural unfruitfulness of the country, but from the want of inhabitants, and from the great aversion likewise there is to labor and industry, in those few who posses it. There are besides, such perpetual discord and depredations among the petty princes, who share this fine country, that, allowing it was better peoples, yet there would be small encouragement to sow, when it was uncertain, who should gather in the harvest."[77]

Travellers to Palestine in the nineteenth century observed what they considered to be the degraded condition of its inhabitants, Christian, Jews, and Muslims alike. Even if we take into account their personal prejudices

---

75 Quoted in Martin Gilbert, *op.cit.*, p. 205.

76 There are so many testimonies that I have not had the space to quote, but interested readers should consult, among others, the travel writings of: Hasselquist, Fredrick, and Carl von Linné, *Voyages and Travels in the Levant: In the Years 1749, 50, 51, 52; Containing Observations in Natural History*, London: Printed for L. Davis and C. Reymers, 1766; Buckingham, James Silk, *Travels in Palestine: Through the Countries of Bashan and Gilead, East of the River Jordan, Including a Visit to the Cities of Geraza and Gamala in the Decapolis*, London: Longman, Hurst, Rees, Orme, and Brown, 1822; Robinson, Edward, and Eli Smith, *Biblical Researches in Palestine, and in the Adjacent Regions. A Journal of Travels in the Year 1838*, Boston: Crocker and Brewster; [etc.], 1856.

77 Thomas Shaw, *Travels, or Observations relating to several parts of Barbary and the Levant*, Oxford: Printed at the Theatre, [Ist published 1738] 1757, Tome Two, Part II, Chapter 1, pp. 336-337.

and perspectives, do not their observations stand as accurate reports of actual conditions?

At the very moment that the phrase "A land without a people and a people without a land" was coined, in 1844, by the anonymous reviewer[78] of Rev. Alexander Keith's *The Land of Israel*,[79] an American Christian minister began his journey to the Holy Land, and came to a similar conclusion as Keith. John Price Durbin [1800-1876] was a Methodist clergyman, president of Dickinson College, and, from 1831, Chaplain of the Senate. His travels in the Near East in the early 1840s resulted in two volumes of *Observations in the East*.[80] Durbin wrote, "I will assume the generally conceded fact that the Turkish Empire is approaching its fall...When the decayed fabric of the Moslem Empire shall fall to pieces, who shall possess its various parts?"[81]

The Turkish Empire was decaying, and some of the inhabitants were living wretched lives: "We followed the ravine southward to the village of Siloam [Shiloh], a miserable abode of miserable Arabs, in the cliff on the left side. A number of rude huts appear to hang on the face of the rock: behind them are sepulchral chambers, which now form the abodes of many of these wretched beings. The living have cast out the dead, and taken up their residence among the tombs; but, indeed, such wretched specimens of humanity were they, that a miracle like a resurrection would be necessary to raise them to the dignity of man."[82]

Durbin throughout paints a picture of desolation, decay, misery and filth of the people and places that he visited in Egypt, and the Holy Land.[83] He found Palestine sparsely populated. Standing on the mountains of Judea, Durbin observes, "The country is desolate, *without inhabitant*...Then the whole land was green, and yielded abundant harvests for the support of a teeming population; now it was almost as silent as the grave."[84] Here he describes his walk in Hebron, which is thirty kilometres south of Jeru-

---

78 *The United Secession Magazine*, Published by John Wardlaw, Edinburgh, 1844, p. 189.

79 Alexander Keith, *The Land of Israel According to the Covenant with Abraham, with Isaac, and with Jacob*, Edinburgh: William Whyte and Co. 1843, p. 43. Keith wrote, "a people without a country; even as their own land, as subsequently to be shown, is in a great measure a country without a people."

80 John Price Durbin, *Observations in the East, Chiefly in Egypt, Palestine, Syria, and Asia Minor*, New York: Harper and Brothers, 2 vols. 1845.

81 *Ibid.*, Vol. I, p. 343.

82 *Ibid.*, Vol. I, p. 239.

83 *Ibid.*, Vol. I, pp. 17, 19, 22, 30, 91.

84 *Ibid.*, Vol. I pp. 205-206. Emphasis added.

salem, "The streets are narrow, dirty, and dark, and the buildings much dilapidated. Many stalls, and even whole passages in the bazars [sic], were unoccupied. The mutton, grapes, and bread were abundant and good. The population is variously estimated by travellers from 5000 to 10,000; perhaps there may be 7000, of which several hundred are miserably poor Jews, who linger around the home of their great progenitor, and drag out a wretched life, shut up in a dark, pestilential quarter of the town, where they have two small synagogues. We heard not of a single Christian inhabitant. *The appearance of the buildings suggests that population, trade, and wealth are decreasing.* The city has not recovered from the terrible stroke inflicted upon it in 1834 by Ibrahim Pacha, when he took it by storm and gave it up to pillage, simply because the inhabitants resisted the Egyptian conscription, and wished to throw off the galling yoke of Muhammad Ali. As seen from a distance, the town is beautiful. The solid stone edifices, covered with white, flat roofs, each surmounted by a low, white dome, make an agreeable impression, but the illusion is dispelled the moment the traveller enters within the walls."[85]

Durbin describes parts of Jerusalem as "a world of desolation" where "you may see some deep cistern, now dry, or some pool, once furnishing pure water, now a mere sink for filth and rubbish."[86] As for the Jewish Quarter, for Durbin, "No description could give an adequate idea of its squalid filth and wretchedness. The houses are built of stone, but many of then are dilapidated, repairs seem never to be made....[I]ts streets are almost impassable from the collections of filth—the refuse of slaughterhouses, and abominations of all sorts—which block up the way, and fill the atmosphere with noisome odours. The Jewish population is confined to this quarter, and numbers, perhaps, about five thousand. They are supported by the contributions of their brethren in Europe for the purpose of keeping up their ancient worship in the Holy City. Their fidelity is to be praised, though their condition is to be pitied."[87]

Of the Wailing Wall, Durbin writes, "They have puchased of the Turks the privilege of approaching the ancient Temple wall at this spot, which is called their Place of Wailing, to weep over the fallen glory of their race, under the very ruins of their once magnificent sanctuary. ...On Friday they assemble here in considerable numbers, and cry, 'Our inheritance is turned to strangers, our house to aliens.' The Book of the Law is read by aged men, and women walk up and down the small area, occasionally

---

85 *Ibid.*, Vol. I, p. 211. Emphasis added.

86 *Ibid.*, Vol. I, p. 257.

87 *Ibid.*, Vol. I, p. 277.

approaching the wall to kiss it, pouring forth lamentations and prayers.... And here they still linger, with the pertinacity that has always formed one of their strongest characteristics, bewailing the desolation of Judah, and waiting for the time when God shall 'renew their days as of old.'"[88]

Then at the end of volume I, Durbin makes these remarkable observations on 'the present state of Palestine': "The facts to be particularly remarked are the *emptiness of the land with respect to population*, indicating that Providence is making room for the sons of Israel. *The land is comparatively 'desolate without inhabitant'. Every few miles the traveller passes amid the ruins of cities, towns, and villages, whose inhabitants are gone. The population is still decreasing; but it is to be noted that this decrease is altogether among the Mohammedans.* There is a gradual increase of the Christian population, and within a few years a rapid increase of the Jewish. When the sons of Israel shall be permitted to acquire permanent titles to the soil, and be protected in the enjoyment of its products, the whole land will become fruitful as in former days; the stones will be gathered out of the valleys; the hills be terraced; the pools and cistern cleansed and repaired, and filled with the early and the latter rains; the cities and towns be rebuilt; and the land will teem again with its millions of people."[89]

Mark Twain travelled in the Holy Land in 1867, and wrote with humour, irony, skepticism, irreverence, and above all, with honesty of what he observed. Just before reaching the Sea of Galilee, "We traversed some miles of desolate country whose soil is rich enough, but is given over wholly to weeds—a silent mournful expanse, wherein we saw only three persons…"[90]

On the outskirts of Tabor, he remarks, "A desolation is here that not even imagination can grace with the pomp of life and action, We reached Tabor safely, and considerably in advance of that iron-clad swindle of a guard. We never saw a human being on the whole route, much less lawless hordes of Bedouins."[91]

And finally, here is Twain's summing up of the desolation of Palestine:

> Of all the lands there are for dismal scenery, I think Palestine must be the prince. The hills are barren, they are dull of color, they are unpicturesque in shape. The valleys are unsightly

---

88 *Ibid.*, Vol. I, p. 278.

89 *Ibid.*, pp. 347-347. Emphasis added.

90 Mark Twain, *Innocents Abroad / Roughing It*, New York: Literary Classics of the United States, 1984 [*Innocents Abroad*, Ist Published 1869], Chapter XLVII, p. 387.

91 *Ibid.*, Chapter XLIX, p. 414.

deserts fringed with a feeble vegetation that has an expression about it of being sorrowful and despondent. The Dead Sea and the Sea of Galilee sleep in the midst of a vast stretch of hill and plain wherein the eye rests upon no pleasant tint, no striking object, no soft picture dreaming in a purple haze or mottled with the shadows of the clouds. Every outline is harsh, every feature is distinct, there is no perspective—distance works no enchantment here. It is a hopeless, dreary, heart-broken land.

Small shreds and patches of it must be very beautiful in the full flush of spring, however, and all the more beautiful by contrast with the far-reaching desolation that surrounds them on every side. I would like much to see the fringes of the Jordan in spring time, and Shechem, Esdraelon, Ajalon, and the borders of Galilee—but even then these spots would seem mere toy gardens set at wide intervals in the waste of a limitless desolation. Palestine sits in sackcloth and ashes. Over it broods the spell of a curse that has withered its fields and fettered its energies. Where Sodom and Gomorrah reared their domes and towers, that solemn sea now floods the plain, in whose bitter waters no living thing exists—over whose waveless surface the blistering air hangs motionless and dead—about whose borders nothing grows but weeds, and scattering tufts of cane, and that treacherous fruit that promises refreshment to parching lips, but turns to ashes at the touch. Nazareth is forlorn; about that ford of Jordan where the hosts of Israel entered the Promised Land with songs of rejoicing, one finds only a squalid camp of fantastic Bedouins of the desert; Jericho the accursed lies a moldering ruin to-day, even as Joshua's miracle left it more than three thousand years ago; Bethlehem and Bethany, in their poverty and their humiliation, have nothing about them now to remind one that they once knew the high honor of the Saviour's presence; the hallowed spot where the shepherds watched their flocks by night, and where the angels sang Peace on earth, good will to men, is untenanted by any living creature, and unblessed by any feature that is pleasant to the eye. Renowned Jerusalem itself, the stateliest name in history, has lost all its ancient grandeur, and is become a pauper village; the riches of Solomon are no longer there to compel the admiration of visiting Oriental queens; the wonderful temple which was the pride and the glory of Israel is gone, and the Ottoman crescent is lifted above the spot where, on that most memorable day in the annals of the world, they reared the Holy Cross. The noted Sea of Galilee, where Roman fleets once rode at anchor and the disciples of the Saviour sailed in their ships, was long ago deserted by the devotees of war and commerce, and its borders are a silent wilderness; Capernaum is a shapeless ruin; Magdala is the home of beggared Arabs; Bethsaida and Chorazin have vanished from the earth, and the "desert places" round about them where thousands of men once listened to the Saviour's voice and ate the miraculous bread sleep in the hush of a solitude that is inhabited only by birds of prey and skulking foxes.

Palestine is desolate and unlovely. And why should it be otherwise? Can the curse of the Deity beautify a land?

Palestine is no more of this work-day world. It is sacred to poetry and tradition—it is dream-land.[92]

Said, in the passage from *The Question of Palestine*, with which I began this section, also italicizes this phrase: *and gave it more than the brightness of Western freedom amid the despotisms of the East.* Ottoman tyranny has been much written about by even Arab historians, and thus cannot be dismissed as a figment of the Western racist imagination. For example, here is a summary from two Turkish historians, "…[H]atred [of Ottomans] is actually reflected in textbooks. …Saudi Government has been trying to remove the traces of the Ottomans in Mecca and Medina, and the Ottoman state is accused of being colonialist and tyrannical state in all Arab histories."[93]

Comte de Volney[94] [1757-1820], historian, and orientalist, friend of Benjamin Franklin and Thomas Jefferson,[95] was no ordinary traveller to the Holy Land, spitting out ill-informed hasty judgements. He spent seven months in Ottoman Egypt, nearly two years in Greater Syria, which then

---

92 *Ibid.*, Ch. LVI, pp. 485-486.

93 Akgündüz, Ahmed & Öztürk, Said, *Ottoman History - Misperceptions and Truths*, Rotterdam: IUR Press, 2011, p. 358.

94 Constantin François de Chassebœuf. The name Volney is made up of Voltaire, and Ferney, where Voltaire lived.

95 Jefferson was to translate most of Volney's *Les Ruines, ou méditations sur les révolutions des empires* [1791], as *Ruins of Empire*.

included, along with present-day Syria, Lebanon and Israel, and above all, he learnt Arabic. The result is his compelling account of life in Palestine at the end of the eighteenth century, *Voyage en Egypte et en Syrie* [1787], which contains one of the most sustained critiques of the vices and short-comings of the Ottoman system of economics, justice, ethics, and treat-ment of women written in the West before the twentieth century—and blissfully free of that modern disease, political correctness. But it is not only the Ottoman government that is found wanting, all the ills in the Islamic world are attributed to the Koran, Muhammad, and the system he put in place.

Comte de Volney castigates those Western romantics "with a superfi-cial knowledge of the theory of Mahometan jurisprudence" who think it is superior to the system of justice in the West, "Daily experience proves, that there is no country wherein justice is more corrupted than in Egypt, Syria, and no doubt, all the rest of the Turkish empire. Venality is nowhere more open, nor more impudent. The parties may bargain for their cause with the Cadi [judge, magistrate], as they would for any common commodity. ... Corruption is habitual and general; and how is it possible to be otherwise, where integrity is ruinous, and injustice lucrative; where each Cadi, decid-ing without appeal, fears neither a revision of his sentence, nor punish-ment for his partiality; and where, in short, the want of clear and precise laws, afford a thousand ways of avoiding the shame of an evident injustice, by opening the crooked paths of commentaries and interpretations?"[96]

The source of all the vices is the spirit of Islam, "To convince himself of this, the reader has only to examine their revered book. In vain do the Mahometans boast that the Koran contains the seeds and even the perfec-tion of all political and legislative knowledge, and jurisprudence: nothing but the prejudice of education, or the partiality of interest can dictate, or admit such a judgment. Whoever reads the Koran, must be obliged to confess, that it conveys no notion, either of the relative duties of mankind in society, the formation of the body politic, or the principles of the art of governing; nothing, in word, which constitutes a legislative code [It does contain some contradictory laws concerning polygamy, divorce, slavery, succession.] The rest is merely a chaos of unmeaning phrases; and em-phatical declarations on the attributes of God, from which nothing is to be learnt; a collection of puerile tales, and ridiculous fables; and, on the whole, so flat and fastidious composition that no man can read it to the end.... But should any general tendency or semblance of meaning be vis-

---

96 Comte de Volney, *Travels Through Syria and Egypt, in the Years 1783, 1784, and 1785*, London: G.G.J. & J. Robinson, 1788, Second edition. Vol.II, p. 391.

ible through the absurdities of this delirious effusion, it is the inculcation of a fierce and obstinate fanaticism."[97]

Finally, Comte de Volney uses the word that Edward Said italicizes without comment, "despotism": "What is the tendency of this [the teachings of the Koran], but to establish the most absolute despotism in him who commands, and the blindest devotion in him who obeys?, and such was the object of Mahomet."[98]

Volney holds Muhammad and the Koran responsible: "It certainly may be safely asserted, of all the men who have ever dared to give laws to nations, none was more ignorant than Mahomet; of all the absurd compositions ever produced, none is more truly wretched than his book. Of this, the transactions of the last twelve hundred years in Asia are a proof; for were I inclined to pass from particular to general observations, it would be easy to demonstrate, that the convulsions of the government, and the ignorance of the people, in that quarter of the globe, originate more or less immediately in the Koran, and its morality; ..."[99]

I shall return to Comte de Volney, when I discuss the work of a modern historian which amply confirms his conclusions, and frequently cites him.

Moving onto the nineteenth century, here are Mark Twain's reflections on Turkish tyranny: "[The Ottoman government's] Three Graces are Tyranny, Rapacity, Blood...Abdul-Aziz, Sultan of Turkey, Lord of the Ottoman Empire [which was] a blot upon the earth—a degraded, poverty-stricken, miserable, infamous agglomeration of ignorance, crime, and brutality...[T]he feeble Abdul-Aziz, the genius of Ignorance, Bigotry and Indolence..."[100]

Further on, Twain elaborates:

If ever an oppressed race existed, it is this one we see fettered around us under the inhuman tyranny of the Ottoman Empire. I wish Europe would let Russia annihilate Turkey a little—not much, but enough to make it difficult to find the place again without a divining-rod or a diving-bell. The Syrians are very poor, and yet they are ground down by a system of taxation that would drive any other nation frantic. Last year their taxes were heavy enough, in all conscience—but this year they have

---

97 *Ibid.*, p. 394.
98 *Ibid.*, p. 395.
99 *Ibid.*, p. 397.
100 Twain, *op.cit.*, pp. 101-103.

been increased by the addition of taxes that were forgiven them in times of famine in former years. On top of this the Government has levied a tax of one-tenth of the whole proceeds of the land. This is only half the story. The Pacha of a Pachalic does not trouble himself with appointing tax-collectors. He figures up what all these taxes ought to amount to in a certain district. Then he farms the collection out. He calls the rich men together, the highest bidder gets the speculation, pays the Pacha on the spot, and then sells out to smaller fry, who sell in turn to a piratical horde of still smaller fry. These latter compel the peasant to bring his little trifle of grain to the village at his own cost. It must be weighed, the various taxes set apart, and the remainder returned to the producer. But the collector delays this duty day after day, while the producer's family are perishing for bread; at last the poor wretch, who cannot but understand the game, says, "Take a quarter—take half—take two-thirds if you will, and let me go!" It is a most outrageous state of things.

These people are naturally good-hearted and intelligent, and with education and liberty would be a happy and contented race. They often appeal to the stranger to know if the great world will not some day come to their relief and save them. The Sultan has been lavishing money like water in England and Paris, but his subjects are suffering for it now.[101]

The impressions of Comte de Volney, Mark Twain and others in the eighteenth and nineteenth century are confirmed by modern historians in the twentieth, historians such as Thomas A. Indinopulos [1935-2010], who was director of the Jewish Studies Program at Miami University, from 1999 to 2006. Indinopulos wrote,

[What Volney called] "despoiling government" was embodied in the person of the Ottoman sultan, an oriental despot, for whom Palestine, as all of the other twenty imperial provinces, existed to be exploited. The better word is fleeced. Appropriately enough, the non-Muslim Christian and Jewish subjects of the realm were called raya or sheep.

The fleecing of both Muslim and non-Muslim subjects began

---

101 Twain, *op.cit.*, pp. 350-351.

in Istanbul and took the form of a system of taxation that relied on the entire bureaucracy of the empire, beginning with the twenty-six pashas or provincial governors. The Ottoman tax system was a snake whose head was in Istanbul and whose tail touched every town and village of the empire. Sometimes the tail was stronger than the head. Uncertain of the amount of revenue he could collect from each province, the sultan preferred quick returns. Each year he would auction off to the highest-bidding pasha the tax farm for Palestine. The bidding was fierce because the position was lucrative. None bid higher than Pasha Ahmad al-Jazzar, who was governor of western Palestine and the northern Galilee for almost thirty years (1773--1803), and would gain a place in world history by repulsing Bonaparte's invasion.

Auctioning off the taxing rights for the province of Palestine initiated the taxing system. The pasha bought the tax right for one million piastres, let us say. In turn he would lease the tax right to his deputy governor for two million piastres; and the deputy governor would then farm out the tax collection for appropriately high sums to village sheiks and other lesser despots. Not surprisingly, two-thirds of Palestine's agricultural produce went toward the payment of taxes. "Everything is taxed," wrote W. J. Stracey, a contemporary observer, "every fruit tree, so none are planted; every cow or horse ... every vegetable sold out of a private garden. Every eighth egg is not taxed but taken by the government."

The incentive to cultivate crops was destroyed when one knew that any surplus would be taken for taxes or simply confiscated by the pasha's army for its own use. Peasants crippled their farm animals in order to keep them from being seized by the army. Roads to villages were damaged or left unrepaired by peasants who hoped to prevent the entry of soldiers or tax collectors. Food was hoarded and hidden. Hunger was common. Volney observed that villagers "were reduced to a little flat cake of barley ordourra, to onions, lentils, and water." When these were gone, they roasted acorns. As soon as the corn turned yellow it was picked and hidden in mountain caves. During periods of drought there were reports of cannibalism. Hunger and other deprivations had reduced a population of more than a million in previous generations to 300,000 at the start of the nineteenth century. Sometimes a peasant would make a gift of his land to the Muslim religious trust, which could not be taxed, and then he would live off the produce. Occasional tax rebellions that occurred in the towns of Nablus, Gaza, and Damascus were ruthlessly suppressed.[102]

This tyranny culminated in the genocide of the Armenians in the early twentieth century—the number of deaths have been estimated as between 600,000 and 850,000.[103] Turkish historian Taner Akçam, one of the first Turkish academics to acknowledge the Armenian Genocide, gives the background to the various declarations made by the European powers concerning the massacres: "When the news reached Europe that a mass slaughter of the Armenians was taking place, a joint announcement was made: 'In light of these crimes, which Turkey has perpetrated against humanity and civilization, the Entente Powers openly inform the Sublime Porte that they will hold the members of the Ottoman Government and their subordinates who are involved in the massacre personally accountable for this crime'...On December 18, 1916 the Entente, in a reply to the peace memo of US President Woodrow Wilson, declared that one of its main war objectives was to 'save the nations held captive under the bloody oppressions of the Turks'. Similar words were voiced by the French foreign minister on January 10, 1917: '[t]he lofty war aims include the rescue of peoples now living under the murderous tyranny of the Turks and to upsroot and cast out of Europe the Ottoman Empire, which has proven that it is, in extreme measure, foreign to Western Civilization.'"[104]

There is another Genocide that is not so well-known, perhaps, that of the Assyrians. "When the Ottomans captured northern Iran in the early months of 1915, they plundered and killed the Assyrian community there; when they were forced to withdraw several months later they turned on their own Assyrians."[105] David Gaunt estimates the number of deaths as

---

102 Thomas A. Indinopulos, *Weathered by Miracles: A History of Palestine From Bonaparte and Muhammad Ali to Ben-Gurion and the Mufti*, Chicago: Ivan R. Dee, 1999, pp. 3-5.

103 Efraim and Inari Karsh, *Empires of the Sand: The Struggle for Mastery in the Middle East 1789-1923*, Cambridge: Harvard University Press, 1999, p. 157.

104 Taner Akçam, *From Empire to Republic: Turkish Nationalism & the Armenian Genocide*, London: Zed Books, 2004, pp. 184-185.

105 E.& I. Karsh, *op.cit.*, p. 161.

300,000.[106] To which should be added the Greek Genocide, when somewhere between 350,000 and 500,000 Greeks were killed by the Turks.[107]

Italics are no substitute for argument and evidence.

To wish to immigrate to someplace does not necessarily imply that one wants to deprive the inhabitants of that place of their human rights. Far more argument, and evidence, is needed if Said really wishes to show that the Jews want to harm the natives of Palestine in any way; one can settle there without prejudice to the Palestinians. Many Zionists in the early twentieth century felt that it was both undesirable and unnecessary to transfer the Arab population. Moshe Smilansky declared in 1914 that "there is still much space for a great number of new settlers, and the former [i.e. the Palestinians] will in due course become a minority among the numerous newcomers."[108] As Cameron S. Brown pointed out, "Berl Locker not only recognized 'the living right of another people, the Arab people, which has been living in the country for centuries',[109] but also plainly stated that 'this need [for a Jewish national home] can be satisfied in this particular country, without ejecting or displacing or harming anyone'[110] or without 'economically displacing'[111] them either." David Ben-Gurion did not entertain the idea of transfer of Arabs, and wrote "All of our aspirations are built on the assumption—that has been verified by all of our activity in the Land [of Israel]—that there is enough room for us and for the Arabs on this land."[112]

---

106 Gaunt, David; Bet-Şawoce, Jan, *Massacres, resistance, protectors: Muslim-Christian relations in Eastern Anatolia during World War I*, Piscataway, NJ: Gorgias Press, 2006.

107 Hlamides, Nikolaos, "The Greek Relief Committee: America's Response to the Greek Genocide," *Genocide Studies and Prevention*, Volume 3, Issue 3, December 2008, pp. 375–83.

108 Quoted by Yosef Gorny, *Zionism and the Arabs, 1882-1948*, New York, 1987, p. 77; it was in turn quoted by Cameron S. Brown in his truly superb destruction of Said's *The Question of Palestine*, "Answering Edward Said's *The Question of Palestine*", in *Israel Affairs*, Vol.13, No. 1, January, 2007, pp. 55-79; p. 65.

109 Berl Locker, *The Jews and Palestine: Historical Connection and Historic Right*, 4th Edn., (trans. from Yiddish by Joseph Leftwich), London, 1938, p. 23, cited by Cameron S. Brown, *op.cit.*, p. 63.

110 Berl Locker, *op.cit.*, p. 28, cited by Cameron S. Brown, *op.cit.*, p. 65.

111 Berl Locker, *op.cit.*, p. 24, cited by Cameron S. Brown, *op.cit.*, p. 65.

112 Letter from David Ben-Gurion to his son Amos (Hebrew, translated by Cameron S. Brown), 5 October 1937, p. 3. Ben Gurion Archives; cited by Cameron S. Brown, *op.cit.*, p. 66.

The Arabs in 1948—only later would they become, for political reasons, the Palestinian people—were not driven from Palestine but were exhorted to leave by their own leaders, who reassured them "that their departure would help in the war against Israel."[113] Here is how *The Economist* reported the events on October 2, 1948: "Of the 62,000 Arabs who formerly lived in Haifa not more than 5,000 or 6,000 remained. Various factors influenced their decision to seek safety in flight. There is but little doubt that the most potent of the factors were [sic] the announcements made over the air by the Higher Arab Executive, urging the Arabs to quit...It was clearly intimated that those Arabs who remained in Haifa and accepted Jewish protection would be regarded as regarded as renegades."[114] Arab newspapers like the Jordanian *Falastin*, and Arab intellectuals like Edward Atiyah confirmed these facts.[115] And yet, Mahmoud Abbas, president of the Palestinian National Authority, in an op-ed titled "The Long Overdue Palestinian State" published in *The New York Times* on May 16, 2011, claimed that he, and hundreds of other Palestinians, had been expelled from Palestine 63 years earlier, contradicting his own previous accounts in which he admitted that his family had left voluntarily.[116]

We have seen the nature of the land (during the first half of the nineteenth century most of the land of Palestine lay uncultivated), but whose land was it? In 1858, the Ottoman government published a law defining the different categories of land, and the ownership rights to them. Of the five categories established, three were under state control: [1] *miri*—tillable land; [2] *matruka*—public lands, including roads, open pasture, and so on; and [3] *mawat*—ownerless land.

While the the fourth category was *waqf*—lands of the religious trusts, belonging to the religious and charitable foundations. The only one that provided for complete private ownership was *mulk*. As Gudrun Krämer explains, "The greater part of the cultivable area was regarded as state land (*miri*) that, if it was regularly cultivated, could be farmed, mortgaged, and leased either individually or communally. From a legal point, however, it could be transformed into neither private property nor religious endowment. All that could be transmitted and inherited was the claim to revenue over the land and the right to usufructuary possession, or usufruct for short

113 Samuel Katz, *Battleground: Fact and Fantasy in Palestine*, New York: Taylor Productions, Ltd, 2002 [Ist. Published, 1973], p. 13.

114 Quoted in Samuel Katz. *op.cit.*, p. 15.

115 All quoted by Samuel Katz, *op.cit.*, pp. 15-17.

116 Sol Stern, *A Century of Palestinian Rejectionism and Jew Hatred*, New York: Encounter Books, 2011, pp. 1-5.

(*tasaruff*). Only the Sultan and his closest family members were entitled to establish relgious endowments on *miri* land (so-called sultanic *awqaf*)…. Hence, in Palestine as in most parts of the Empire (Egypt was a special case) private property in agricultural land was not legally recognized."[117]

Contrary to anti-Zionist propaganda, which shrilled that the Palestinian farmer was working peacefully on his land when he was driven off by Jewish immigrants, "the Palestinian peasant was indeed dispossessed, but by his fellow-Arabs: the local sheikh and village elders, the Government tax-collector, the merchants and money-lenders; and, when he was a tenant-farmer (as was usually the case), by the absentee-owner. By the time the season's crop had been distributed among the all these, little if anything remained for him and his family, and new debts generally had to be incurred to pay off the old. Then the Bedouin came along and took their 'cut', or drove the hapless fellah of the land altogether."[118]

As for Jewish land purchases, Moshe Aumann points out, "the first enduring Jewish agricultural settlement in modern Palestine was founded not by European refugees, but by a group of old-time families, leaving the overcrowded Jewish Quarter of the Old City of Jerusalem. (According to the Turkish census of 1875, by that time Jews already constituted a majority of the population of Jerusalem and by 1905 comprised two-thirds of its citizens. The Encyclopaedia Britannica of 1910 gives the population figure as 60,000, of whom 40,000 were Jews.)."[119] Further villages were founded in 1878, and 1882, and other farming villages followed in rapid succession.

Much of the subsequent land purchases was from absentee landlords—I provide the statistics below; most of the land purchased had not been cultivated previously because of its swampy, or rocky nature; the price of land rose as a consequence of the high demand; and the Jewish pioneers introduced new farming methods.

Gudrun Krämer gives the details of the land purchases during the Mandate era, "According to the (incomplete) statistics for the years 1878 to 1936, only 9.4 percent of the 681,978 dunams [1 dunam = approx. 1000m², but see footnote[120]] legally acquired in this period by Jews were

---

117 Gudrun Krämer, *A History of Palestine: From the Ottoman Conquest to the Founding of the State of Israel*, Princeton: Princeton University Press, 2008 [Ist published in German, 2002] pp. 47-48.

118 Moshe Aumann, *Land Ownership in Palestine, 1880-1948*, Israel Academic Committee on the Middle East (1976) p. 119.

119 *Ibid.*, p. 120.

120 During the late Ottoman Empire, the dunam was 919 square meters, or 9,892

sold by local farmers. More than two-thirds were sold by great landowners who had acquired the land in the second half of the nineteenth century. Among these great landowners, 52.6 percent were (former) Ottoman citizens who did not reside in Palestine, and were hence considered "foreign" absentee landlords; 24.6 percent were local Arabs, including members of the great urban notable families....The sales were economically motivated and the gains high....Jewish purchasers were as a rule prepared to pay a price above market value and the expected yields."[121]

A. Granott brings the story up to 1947, "The total area of land in Jewish possession at the end of June 1947 amounted to 1,850,000 dunams, of this 181,100 dunams had been obtained through concessions from the Palestinian Government, and about 120,000 dunams had been acquired from Churches, from foreign companies, from the Government otherwise than by concessions, and so forth. It was estimated that 1,000,000 dunams and more, or 57 per cent, had been acquired from large Arab landowners...."[122]

Thus Jews did not illegally dispossess the Palestinian Arab farmer; land was purchased from local Arab farmers, and large Arab landowners, either absentee or local.

As Abdul Razak Kader, the Algerian political writer, now living in exile in Paris, wrote in his article entitled, "Is Israel a Thorn or a Flower in the Near East?" (*Jerusalem Post*, Aug. 1, 1969):

> The Nationalists of the states neighbouring on Israel, whether they are in the government or in business, whether Palestinian, Syrian or Lebanese, or town dwellers of tribal origin, all know that at the beginning of the century and during the British Mandate the marshy plains and stone hills were sold to the Zionists by their fathers or uncles for gold, the very gold which is often the origin of their own political or commercial careers. The nomadic or seminomadic peasants who inhabited the frontier regions know full well what the green plains, the afforested hills and the flowering fields of today's Israel were like before.

---

square feet, or 0.227 acres. Since the 1920s, the dunam in Israel/Palestine, Syria and Jordan and Turkey has been enlarged to 1,000 square meters, or 10763.9 square feet, or 0.25 acres.

121 Gudrun Krämer, *op.cit.*, p. 245.

122 A. Granott, *The Land System in Palestine,* London, 1952, p. 278, quoted by Moshe Aumann, *op.cit.*, pp. 121-122.

The Palestinians who are today refugees in the neighbouring countries and who were adults at the time of their flight know all this, and no anti-Zionist propaganda—pan-Arab or pan-Moslem—can make them forget that their present nationalist exploiters are the worthy sons of their feudal exploiters of yesterday and that the thorns of their life are of Arab, not Jewish, origin.[123]

Eliot is not racist simply because she fails to mention the natives; as we showed above Eliot does indeed express grave concern, elsewhere, about the subjects of the British Empire. For Said, George Eliot's views were representative of "the culture of high liberal capitalism."[124] He gives no arguments as to how Zionism, or even the novel, *Daniel Deronda*, is connected to capitalism. Such a claim is, incidentally, an example of the very essentialism that he accuses Orientalists of.

Said seems not to have understood the motivation of Zionism or the subtext in *Daniel Deronda*, a failing betrayed by his overplaying the importance of the Holocaust and antisemitism in the formation of Zionism.

In Book One, Chapter Three of *Daniel Deronda* we find the following passage:

Pity that Ofiendene was not the home of Miss Harleth's childhood, or endeared to her by family memories! A human life, I think, should be well rooted in some spot of a native land, where it may get the love of tender kinship for the face of earth, for the labors men go forth to, for the sounds and accents that haunt it, for whatever will give that early home a familiar unmistakable difference amidst the future widening of knowledge: a spot where the definiteness of early memories may be inwrought with affection, and kindly acquaintance with all neighbors, even to the dogs and donkeys, may spread not by sentimental effort and reflection, but as a sweet habit of the blood.[125]

Both Gwendolen and Daniel Deronda are in search of roots, which will assure them a secure identity. As Gertrude Himmelfarb wrote, in her

---

123 Quoted by Moshe Aumann, *op.cit.*, p. 127.

124 Edward Said, *The Question of Palestine*, p. 61.

125 G. Eliot, *Daniel Deronda*, Harmondsworh (UK): Penguin Classics, 1987 [Ist Published 1876], Book One, Chapter Three

elegant study on George Eliot, "This is the underlying motif of the novel: the quest for identity, most obviously, of Deronda and Mirah searching for their parents and heritage, but also Gwendolen searching for her true self."[126]

Himmelfarb explains further, "When Deronda emigrated to Palestine, he did so not out of fear of pogroms, or as a response to a Holocaust, or even to escape the barbs and slights of the English mode of polite anti-Semitism, but rather to fulfill a proud and unique heritage. His mentor, Mordecai, was a learned as well as a passionate Jew who felt in his soul, as he said, the faith and the history of his people—his "nation." It was this sense of nationality that inspired his vision of Judaism and that he transmitted to his disciple Deronda."

George Eliot's "Jewish question was not the relation of Jews to the Gentile world," Himmelfarb elaborates, "but the relation of Jews to themselves, to their own people and their own world, the belief and traditions that were their history and their legacy. This Jewish question was predicated upon a robust Judaism, the creed of a nation that could find its fulfillment only in a polity and a state."

The creation of Israel is often seen as response to the Holocaust. But, continues Himmelfarb, "*Daniel Deronda*, long predating both the Holocaust and the founding of Israel (and the pogroms and Dreyfus Affair that motivated the leaders of the Zionist movement), presents a very different view of Jewish history and the Jewish people. It reminds us that Israel is not merely a refuge for desperate people, that the history of Judaism is more than the bitter annals of persecution and catastrophe, and that Jews are not only, certainly not essentially, victims, survivors, martyrs, or even an abused and disaffected minority. For Deronda (as for Eliot), the Jewish identity was not imposed upon them by others. It was not the anti-Semite who 'creates the Jew'. It was Judaism, the religion and the people, that created the Jewish state, the culmination of a proud and enduring faith that defined the Jewish 'nation', uniting Jews even as they were, and, as they remain, physically dispersed."[127]

In *Culture and Imperialism*,[128] Said sings the praise of exile, and rejects the kind of nationalism envisaged by Daniel Deronda, settled and rooted in a particular place, "Yet it is no exaggeration to say that libera-

126 Gertrude Himmelfarb, *The Jewish Odyssey of George Eliot*, New York: Encounter Books. 2009, pp. 77-78.

127 *Ibid.*, pp. 149-150.

128 Edward Said, *Culture and Imperialism*, London: Vintage, 1994 [Ist Published 1993] pp. 401-408.

tion as an intellectual mission, born in the resistance and opposition to the confinements and ravages of imperialism, has now shifted from the settled, established, and domesticated dynamics of culture to its unhoused, decentred, and exilic energies whose incarnation today is the migrant, and whose consciousness is that of the intellectual and artist in exile, the political figure between domains, between forms, between homes, and between languages."[129] He rambles on in a similar vein for a further six or seven pages about the joys of migrancy and exile. He seems oblivious to the contradictory fact that all his intellectual life has been spent in apparently defending just that kind of nationalism rooted in place and home. A nominal, secular Christian, Said loved parading his internationalism, and yet endorsed an Arab nationalism which, in the end, never managed to break free from Islam.

Was his life a fraud from beginning to end?

JOHN STUART MILL AND RACISM

Edward Said wrote that George Eliot was no different from John Stuart Mill and Karl Marx, "both of them seemed to have believed that such ideas as liberty, representative government, and individual happiness must not be applied in the Orient for reasons that today we would call racist."[130] Marxists, such as Said himself, can grapple with their Savior's feet of clay, but Mill is well worth defending. I hope these few remarks will go someway towards fulfilling that task, pointing readers to fuller discussions in some recent studies.

All his life, John Stuart Mill [1806-1873] was guided by his principles which led him to fight for the emancipation of women, for a secular, democratic and egalitarian society. He was hostile "to privilege and injustice and to the moral callousness he took to underlie these evils."[131] On the subject of race, three of Mill's concerns are of particular importance, "The Negro Question" [1850], his rebuttal to Carlyle's polemical tract in *Fraser's Magazine*; "The Contest in America" [1862] his essay on slavery and the

---

129 *Ibid.*, p. 403.

130 Edward Said, *The Question of Palestine*, New York: Vintage Books, 1980 [Ist published 1979] p. 65.

131 John Stuart Mill, *The Collected Works of John Stuart Mill, Volume XXI - Essays on Equality, Law, and Education,* ed. John M. Robson, Introduction by Stefan Collini (Toronto: University of Toronto Press, London: Routledge and Kegan Paul, 1984). Chapter: Introduction
Accessed from http://oll.libertyfund.org/title/255/21629 on 2013-07-15

American Civil War; and his distress over the acts of Governor Eyre of Jamaica, expressed in the papers of the Jamaica Committee.

Mill vehemently rejected his opponents' belief in natural inequalities, whether of women, or so-called "lower classes" or "lower races"—all individuals should be treated equally unless good cause can be shown to do otherwise. "The course of history," wrote Mill, "and the tendencies of progressive human society, afford not only no presumption in favor of this system of inequality of rights, but a strong one against it; and . . . so far as the whole course of human improvement up to this time, the whole stream of modern tendencies, warrants any inference on the subject, it is, that this relic of the past is discordant with the future, and must necessarily disappear."[132]

I. THE NEGRO QUESTION

Those who still insist on his racism should ponder Mill's spirited response to Thomas Carlyle's pamphlet, "Occasional Discourse on the Negro Question." As Collini summarizes, "what Carlyle takes as the distinctive and self-evidently inferior 'nature' of the negro is in fact the result of the historical circumstances of subjection under which that character has been formed, and it is the distinctive mark of the modern age to be bent on mitigating or abolishing such subjection. Both science and history, therefore, tell against the view that the negro—'Quashee,' to use Carlyle's mischievously provocative term—must perpetually work under the lash of a white master."[133]

First, Mill wrote of the slave trade "I have yet to learn that anything more detestable than this has been done by human beings towards human beings in any part of the earth." Mill then charges Carlyle with a vulgar error, "he would have escaped the vulgar error of imputing every difference which he finds among human beings to an original difference of nature. As well might it be said, that of two trees, sprung from the same stock, one cannot be taller than another but from greater vigour in the original seedling. Is nothing to be attributed to soil, nothing to climate, nothing to difference of exposure—has no storm swept over the one and not the other, no lightning scathed it, no beast browsed on it, no insects preyed on it, no passing stranger stript off its leaves or its bark? If the trees grew near together, may not the one which, by whatever accident, grew up first,

---

132 John Stuart Mill, *op.cit.*, Chapter I
Accessed from http://oll.libertyfund.org/title/255/21686/809608 on 2013-07-15
133 *Ibid.*, Stefan Collini, Introduction.

have retarded the other's developement by its shade? Human beings are subject to an infinitely greater variety of accidents and external influences than trees, and have infinitely more operation in impairing the growth of one another; since those who begin by being strongest, have almost always hitherto used their strength to keep the others weak."[134]

Mill even anticipates Martin Bernal's *Black Athena*[135] argument, which is not accepted by many eminent classicists[136]—but this is not the point here as we shall see. Mill reasoned, "It is curious withal, that the earliest known civilization was, we have the strongest reason to believe, a negro civilization. The original Egyptians are inferred, from the evidence of their sculptures, to have been a negro race: it was from negroes, therefore, that the Greeks learnt their first lessons in civilization; and to the records and traditions of these negroes did the Greek philosophers to the very end of their career resort (I do not say with much fruit) as a treasury of mysterious wisdom."[137]

The above is a staggering admission for a nineteenth century intellectual reared on Greek from the age of three, having read six dialogues of Plato in Greek by the age of seven,[138] and for whom Greek civilization was the *fons et origo* of Western Civilization, and all those concerns that he so passionately defended all his life, rationalism, democracy, scientific history, and so on.

As Mill wrote in his review of his friend George Grote's *History of Greece* of "the permanent gifts bequeathed by Greece to the world, and constituting the foundation of all subsequent intellectual achievements.... And considering what the short period of Athenian greatness has done for the world, it is painful to think in how much more advanced a stage human

---

134 John Stuart Mill, *op.cit., Chapter: THE NEGRO QUESTION 1850* Accessed from http://oll.libertyfund.org/title/255/21686/809608 on 2013-07-15

135 Martin Bernal, Black *Athena: Afroasiatic Roots of Classical Civilization, Volume I: The Fabrication of Ancient Greece, 1785-1985.* Rutgers University Press, 1987; *Black Athena: Afroasiatic Roots of Classical Civilization, Volume II: The Archaeological and Documentary Evidence.* Rutgers University Press, 1991.

136 See especially, Mary Lefkowitz, *Not Out Of Africa: How "Afrocentrism" Became An Excuse To Teach Myth As History*, New York: Basic Books, 1997.

137 John Stuart Mill, *op.cit., Chapter: THE NEGRO QUESTION 1850* Accessed from http://oll.libertyfund.org/title/255/21686/809608 on 2013-07-15

138 John Stuart Mill, *The Collected Works of John Stuart Mill, Volume I - Autobiography and Literary Essays*, ed. John M. Robson and Jack Stillinger, Introduction by Lord Robbins (Toronto: University of Toronto Press, London: Routledge and Kegan Paul, 1981). Chapter: [EARLY DRAFT]
Accessed from http://oll.libertyfund.org/title/242/7718/716254 on 2013-07-15

improvement might now have been, if the Athens of Pericles could have lived on in undiminished spirit and energy for but one century more."[139]

This citation alone should be sufficient to exonerate any charges of racism so carelessly, casually, and irresponsibly hurled at Mill, who was ready to acknowledge that all he held dear was ultimately due to "negroes."

Mill remonstrates to Carlyle in the most serious terms the great vulgar errors he was guilty of. Carlyle's so-called 'eternal Act of Parliament' "is no new law, but the old law of the strongest,—a law against which the great teachers of mankind have in all ages protested:—it is the law of force and cunning; the law that whoever is more powerful than another, is 'born lord' of that other, the other being born his 'servant,' who must be 'compelled to work' for him by 'beneficent whip,' if 'other methods avail not.' I see nothing divine in this injunction. If 'the gods' will this, it is the first duty of human beings to resist such gods. Omnipotent these 'gods' are not, for powers which demand human tyranny and injustice cannot accomplish their purpose unless human beings co-operate. The history of human improvement is the record of a struggle by which inch after inch of ground has been wrung from these maleficent powers, and more and more of human life rescued from the iniquitous dominion of the law of might. Much, very much of this work still remains to do, but the progress made in it is the best and greatest achievement yet performed by mankind, and it was hardly to be expected at this period of the world that we should be enjoined, by way of a great reform in human affairs, to begin *un*doing it." [140]

British Christian philanthropy was indeed responsible for "the great national revolt of the conscience of this country against slavery and the slave-trade....It triumphed because it was the cause of justice; and, in the estimation of the great majority of its supporters, religion." Black slaves have suffered for two centuries: "For nearly two centuries had negroes, many thousands annually, been seized by force or treachery and carried off to the West Indies to be worked to death, literally to death; for it was the received maxim, the acknowledged dictate of good economy, to wear them out quickly and import more. In this fact every other possible cruelty, tyranny, and wanton oppression was by implication included. And the motive on the part of the slave-owners was the love of gold; or, to speak more

139 John Stuart Mill, *The Collected Works of John Stuart Mill, Volume XI - Essays on Philosophy and the Classics*, ed. John M. Robson, Introduction by F. E. Sparshott (Toronto: University of Toronto Press, London: Routledge and Kegan Paul, 1978). Chapter: GROTE'S HISTORY OF GREECE [II] 1853.
Accessed from http://oll.libertyfund.org/title/248/21773/766011 on 2013-07-16
140 *Ibid.*

truly, of vulgar and puerile ostentation. I have yet to learn that anything more detestable than this has been done by human beings towards human beings in any part of the earth."

Carlyle misunderstands totally the situation in the West Indies, and his notions of justice are wanting: "Your [Carlyle's] contributor's notions of justice and proprietary right are of another kind than these. According to him, the whole West Indies belong to the whites: the negroes have no claim there, to either land or food, but by their sufferance. 'It was not Black Quashee, or those he represents, that made those West India islands what they are.' [*Ibid.*] I submit, that those who furnished the thews and sinews[*] really had something to do with the matter. 'Under the soil of Jamaica the bones of many thousand British men'—'brave Colonel Fortescue, brave Colonel Sedgwick, brave Colonel Brayne,' and divers others, 'had to be laid.' [P. 676] How many hundred thousand African men laid their bones there, after having had their lives pressed out by slow or fierce torture? They could have better done without Colonel Fortescue, than Colonel Fortescue could have done without them. But he was the stronger, and could 'compel;' what they did [p. 674] and suffered therefore goes for nothing. Not only they did not, but it seems they could not have cultivated those islands. 'Never by art of his' (the negro) 'could one pumpkin have grown there to solace any human throat.' [P. 675] They grow pumpkins, however, and more than pumpkins, in a very similar country, their native Africa. We are told to look at Haiti: what does your contributor know of Haiti? 'Little or no sugar growing, black Peter exterminating black Paul, and where a garden of the Hesperides might be, nothing but a tropical dog-kennel and pestiferous jungle.' [*Ibid.*] Are we to listen to arguments grounded on hearsays like these? In what is black Haiti worse than white Mexico? If the truth were known, how much worse is it than white Spain?"

Carlyle's moral failings do not end there, "But the great ethical doctrine of the Discourse, than which a doctrine more damnable, I should think, never was propounded by a professed moral reformer, is, that one kind of human beings are born servants to another kind. 'You will have to be servants,' he tells the negroes, 'to those that are born *wiser* than you, that are born lords of you—servants to the whites, if they are (as what mortal can doubt that they are?) born wiser than you.' I do not hold him to the absurd letter of his dictum; it belongs to the mannerism in which he is enthralled like a child in swaddling clothes. By 'born wiser,' I will suppose him to mean, born more capable of wisdom: a proposition which, he says, no mortal can doubt, but which I will make bold to say, that a full moiety of all thinking persons, who have attended to the subject, either doubt or positively deny."

Surely the greatest achievement of the present age is the abolition of slavery, "But (however it be with pain in general) the abolition of the infliction of pain by the mere will of a human being, the abolition, in short, of despotism, seems to be, in a peculiar degree, the occupation of this age; and it would be difficult to shew that any age had undertaken a worthier. Though we cannot extirpate all pain, we can, if we are sufficiently determined upon it, abolish all tyranny, one of the greatest victories yet gained over that enemy is slave-emancipation, and all Europe is struggling, with various success, towards further conquests over it. If, in the pursuit of this, we lose sight of any object equally important; if we forget that freedom is not the only thing necessary for human beings, let us be thankful to any one who points out what is wanting; but let us not consent to turn back"[141]

II. THE CONTEST IN AMERICA

Mill was gravely concerned that Carlyle's tract, given his considerable reputation, would give support to "the owners of human flesh" in the United States. Mill had always followed closely "the great democratic experiment" of the United States, and the Civil War, therefore, to quote Collini, "touched several nerves in Mill's moral physiology; not only did it involve the most blatant case of institutionalized inequality in the civilized world and the whole question of popular government's ability to combine freedom with stability, but, always powerfully active in determining Mill's interest in public issues, it provided a thermometer with which to take the moral temperature of English society as a whole....Mill, to whom the real issue at stake in the war had from the outset been the continued existence of slavery, considered that much of this sympathy for the South rested on ignorance or, even more culpably, moral insensibility, and 'The Contest in America' (1862) was his attempt to educate English opinion on both counts....Slavery is thus treated by Mill as the extreme form of undemocracy, a kind of Toryism of race to match the 'Toryism of sex' that he saw in women's exclusion from the franchise."[142]

---

141 John Stuart Mill, *The Collected Works of John Stuart Mill, Volume XXI - Essays on Equality, Law, and Education*, ed. John M. Robson, Introduction by Stefan Collini (Toronto: University of Toronto Press, London: Routledge and Kegan Paul, 1984). Chapter: THE NEGRO QUESTION 1850.
Accessed from http://oll.libertyfund.org/title/255/21657 on 2013-07-15
142 *Ibid.*, Stefan Collini, Introduction.

III. THE JAMAICA COMMITTEE

Edward John Eyre, the English Governor of Jamaica, fearing a far-reaching rebellion, introduced martial law, which gave his subordinates power to suppress the Morant Bay Rebellion very harshly, brutal acts included the execution of George William Gordon, a mixed race member of the Jamaica Assembly, suspected of being involved.

Mill was the driving force behind the prosecution of Governor Eyre. Mill was able to gather enough support and encouragement from Herbert Spencer, Frederic Harrison, T. H. Huxley, Charles Darwin, and Charles Lyell, to form the Jamaica Committee which published two reports, one in 1866 and a progress report in 1868. The former expressed the desire that the execution of British citizens be governed by law, and not be subject to the whims of the executive branch. Members of the committee hoped to limit the jurisdiction of martial law. The report of 1868 summed up the aims of the committee: "To obtain a judicial inquiry into the conduct of Mr Eyre and his subordinates; to settle the law in the interest of justice, liberty, and humanity; and to arouse public morality against oppression generally, and particularly against the oppression of subject and dependent races."[143]

IV. MISCELLANEOUS

Of all vulgar modes of escaping from the consideration of the effect of social and moral influences on the human mind, the most vulgar is that of attributing the diversities of conduct and character to inherent natural differences.
—J.S. Mill, *Principles of Political Economy*[144]

It is not in China only that a homogeneous community is naturally a stationary community…. It is profoundly remarked by M. Guizot, that the short duration or stunted growth of the earlier civilizations arose from this, that in each of them some one element of human improvement existed exclusively,

---

143 *Ibid.*

144 John Stuart Mill, *The Collected Works of John Stuart Mill, Volume II - The Principles of Political Economy with Some of Their Applications to Social Philosophy* (Books I-II), ed. John M. Robson, introduction by V.W. Bladen (Toronto: University of Toronto Press, London: Routledge and Kegan Paul, 1965). CHAPTER IX: Of Cottiers. Accessed from http://oll.libertyfund.org/title/102/9731/723113 on 2013-07-15

or so preponderatingly as to overpower all the others, whereby the community, after accomplishing rapidly all which that one element could do, either perished for want of what it could not do, or came to a halt, and became immoveable. It would be an error to suppose that such could not possibly be our fate. In the generalization which pronounces the "law of progress" to be an inherent attribute of human nature, it is forgotten that, among the inhabitants of our earth, the European family of nations is the only one which has ever shown any capability of spontaneous improvement, beyond a certain low level. *Let us beware of supposing that we owe this peculiarity to any necessity of nature*, and *not* rather to combinations of circumstances, which have existed nowhere else, and may not exist for ever among ourselves.

—J.S. Mill, *De Tocqueville on Democracy in America II*[145]
[Emphasis added]

Georgios Varouxakis, Lecturer in Politics at Aston University, Birmingham (UK), in a spirited, and surely definitive, defense of Mill on the subject of race,[146] points out that the word "race," in the nineteenth century, was sometimes "used in the sense that the term "culture" has today, without that is, necessarily implying any belief in the doctrine of biological and hereditary transmission of mental and cultural traits."[147] It is well to bear this in mind in any discussion of Mill's writings.

Mill being a child of the Enlightenment always stressed the the importance of rationality, which undergirded his views on morality, virtue and the good life, and led him to discredit the deterministic implications of racial theories. "Mind over matter" was his motto, rejecting any "necessity of nature." Humans were malleable, and what mattered was institutions, customs, education, and cultural, not innate racial, dispositions. Europe's success was not due to any innate or natural qualities in Europeans but the result of historical circumstances. For Mill, history has taught us that

---

145 John Stuart Mill, *The Collected Works of John Stuart Mill, Volume XVIII - Essays on Politics and Society Part I*, ed. John M. Robson, Introduction by Alexander Brady (Toronto: University of Toronto Press, London: Routledge and Kegan Paul, 1977). Chapter: DE TOCQUEVILLE ON DEMOCRACY IN AMERICA [II] 1840. Accessed from http://oll.libertyfund.org/title/233/16544/799700 on 2013-07-15

146 Georgios Varouxakis, *Mill on Nationality*, London & New York, Routledge, 2002, pp. 38-52.

147 *Ibid.*, p. 39.

human nature is moulded by external influences: "Of all difficulties which impede the progress of thought, and the formation of well-grounded opinions on life and social arrangements, the greatest is now the unspeakable ignorance and inattention of mankind in respect to the influences which form human character. Whatever any portion of the human species now are, or seem to be, such, it is supposed, they have a natural tendency to be: even when the most elementary knowledge of the circumstances in which they have been placed, clearly points out the causes that made them what they are. Because a cottier deeply in arrears to his landlord is not industrious, there are people who think that the Irish are naturally idle. Because constitutions can be overthrown when the authorities appointed to execute them turn their arms against them, there are people who think the French incapable of free government. Because the Greeks cheated the Turks, and the Turks only plundered the Greeks, there are persons who think that the Turks are naturally more sincere: and because women, as is often said, care nothing about politics except their personalities, it is supposed that the general good is naturally less interesting to women than to men. History, which is now so much better understood than formerly, teaches another lesson, if only by showing the extraordinary susceptibility of human nature to external influences, and the extreme variableness of those of its manifestations which are supposed to be most universal and uniform. But in history, as in travelling, men usually see only what they already had in their own minds; and few learn much from history, who do not bring much with them to its study."[148]

In his review, written in 1844, of the first five volumes of Michelet's *Histoire de France*, Mill disagreed with the French historian's tendency to explain cultural differences between the French, and their passion for equality, and Germans, with their sense of loyalty to one another, leading to a feudal society, to race. Mill wrote, "*We think that M. Michelet has here carried the influence of Race too far*, and that the difference is better explained by diversity of position, than by diversity of character in the Races. The conquerors, a small body scattered over a large territory, could not sever their interests, could not relax the bonds which held them together. They were for many generations encamped in the country, rather than settled in it; they were a military band, requiring a military discipline,

---

148 John Stuart Mill, *The Collected Works of John Stuart Mill, Volume XXI - Essays on Equality, Law, and Education*, ed. John M. Robson, Introduction by Stefan Collini (Toronto: University of Toronto Press, London: Routledge and Kegan Paul, 1984). Chapter I
Accessed from http://oll.libertyfund.org/title/255/21686/809615 on 2013-07-15

and the separate members could not venture to detach themselves from each other, or from their chief. *Similar circumstances would have produced similar results among the Gauls themselves.* They were by no means without something analogous to the German *comitatus* (as the voluntary bond of adherence, of the most sacred kind, between followers and a leader of their choice, is called by the Roman historians). The *devoti* of the Gauls and Aquitanians, mentioned by M. Michelet himself, on the authority of Caesar and Athenaeus, were evidently not clansmen. Some such relation may be traced in many other warlike tribes. We find it even among the most obstinately personal of all the races of antiquity, the Iberians of Spain; witness the Roman Sertorius and his Spanish body-guard, who slew themselves, to the last man, before his funeral pile. '*Ce principe d'attachement à un chef, ce dévouement personnel, cette religion de l'homme envers l'homme,*' is thus by no means peculiar to the Teutonic races. And our author's favourite idea of the '*profonde impersonnalité*' inherent in the Germanic genius, though we are far from saying that there is no foundation for it, surely requires some limitation. It will hardly, for example, be held true of the English, yet the English are a Germanic people. They, indeed, have rather (or at least had) the characteristic which M. Michelet predicates of the Celts (thinking apparently rather of the Kymri than of the Gaels), '*le génie de la personnalité libre*;' a tendency to revolt against compulsion, to hold fast to their own, and assert the claims of individuality against those of society and authority. But though many of M. Michelet's speculations on the characteristics of Races appear to us contestable, they are always suggestive of thought."[149]

In a letter to Charles Dupont-White, who had criticized him for denying the influence of race, Mill put forward his argument, deploring once again the tendency of their times: "I simply wish to censure a tendency which has always existed but especially in these present times (as a consequence of the reaction of the nineteenth century against the eighteenth), that of attributing all the differences in the character of peoples and individuals to indelible differences of nature, without asking if the influences of education and the social and political circumstances did not give an adequate explanation….In the case that concerns us, that is the differences of character between the Celts and Anglo-Saxons…and their propensity

149 John Stuart Mill, *The Collected Works of John Stuart Mill, Volume XX - Essays on French History and Historians*, ed. John M. Robson, Introduction by John C. Cairns (Toronto: University of Toronto Press, London: Routledge and Kegan Paul, 1985). Chapter: MICHELET'S HISTORY OF FRANCE 1844. Accessed from http://oll.libertyfund.org/title/235/21601/803988 on 2013-07-15 [Emphasis added]

for or against centralisation, I ask you if the difference in the historical development of France and England, of which you have given such a true and instructive sketch, does not alone suffise as an explanation."[150]

In his article on Michelet, Mill praises the French historian for recognizing the influence of human institutions in the disappearance of local peculiarities, "We say even, because M. Michelet is not unaware of the tendency of provincial and local peculiarities to disappear. A strenuous asserter of the power of mind over matter, of will over spontaneous propensities, culture over nature, he holds that local characteristics lose their importance as history advances. In a rude age the 'fatalities' of race and geographical position are absolute. In the progress of society, human forethought and purpose, acting by means of uniform institutions and modes of culture, tend more and more to efface the pristine differences. And he attributes, in no small degree, the greatness of France to the absence of any marked local peculiarities in the predominant part of her population."[151]

As Georgios Varouxakis brings out clearly, from the late 1840s onwards, Mill "went out of his way to stress how little importance race had. This shift was probably due to his growing realization of the uses to which racial theories were being put."[152] For such theories had grave consequences for those issues that made up the very core of Mill's moral being, "such as slavery, international relations, the government of dependencies, as well as women's rights."[153] And as a reformer, rationalist, and believer in the human capacity for improvement, he could not accept the consequence of determinism, or as Mill would put it, "fatalism."

150 John Stuart Mill, *The Collected Works of John Stuart Mill, Volume XV - The Later Letters of John Stuart Mill 1849-1873 Part II*, ed. Francis E. Mineka and Dwight N. Lindley (Toronto: University of Toronto Press, London: Routledge and Kegan Paul, 1972). Chapter: 1860
Accessed from http://oll.libertyfund.org/title/252/44724/783802 on 2013-07-15

151 John Stuart Mill, *The Collected Works of John Stuart Mill, Volume XX - Essays on French History and Historians*, ed. John M. Robson, Introduction by John C. Cairns (Toronto: University of Toronto Press, London: Routledge and Kegan Paul, 1985). Chapter: MICHELET'S HISTORY OF FRANCE 1844.
Accessed from http://oll.libertyfund.org/title/235/21601/803989 on 2013-07-15

152 George Varouxakis, *op.cit.*, p. 47.

153 *Ibid.*

6
South Park, Islam and Self-Censorship

INTRODUCTION

The *South Park* Affair,—yes, the incident has acquired the status of an affair—is of wider import than what many journalists and sundry pundits have made of it. First, to argue that the episode of *South Park* showing Muhammad in a bear suit was not really offensive, or even more fatuously that it was not funny, is to miss the point altogether. The artistic merit, or its potential power to offend Muslims, of the animated show is not the issue. The issue is freedom of expression, and free speech in general. In other words, even if the cartoon were offensive, and un-funny, we should still defend the right of the artists to continue with their indispensable vocation. Second, the cowardice of Comedy Central, and Yale University Press, and The Metropolitan Museum of Art, in their acts of self-censorship must, of course, be held up to public scorn, but surely the real blame lies squarely with the failure of successive administrations, including and above all, the present Obama Administration, to stand up for freedom of speech, to reassure the artists—filmmakers, poets, novel-ists—that the Federal government will not tolerate the curtailment of the liberties of American citizens guaranteed in the U.S. Constitution, and that the various federal agencies—F.B.I., police, Homeland Security—will provide all the protection necessary, indefinitely. Third, the media, intellectuals, artists, and other colleagues have also failed in their duties in not displaying greater solidarity; at least at the height of the Rushdie Af-fair, fellow writers had the courage to mount public readings of *The Satanic Verses.*

REPRESENTATION IN ISLAM

The Islamic law concerning human representation in Islam became a Western problem in September 2005 when the Danish newspaper *Jyllands-Posten* published twelve cartoons of Muhammad, the Prophet of Islam. The debates in the West about self-censorship re-surfaced when one learnt, in August 2009, of the decision by Yale University Press not to publish the cartoons in a book that discussed the original controversy, and their political and social consequences around the Islamic world. *South Park*, the television weekly animated feature that also mocked Muhammad, albeit in a rather mild manner, re-ignited the issue when Comedy Central censored the episode concerned.

The Arabic terms *Awthan* (XXII.30; XXIX.17, 25) and *asnam* (VI.74; VII.138; XIV.35; XXI.57; XXVI.71) appear in stories about past peoples, stories recounting, for example, Abraham's relationship with his father. There both words designate idols. *Nusub* (V.3; LXX.43) and *ansab* (V.90) are explained in a variety of ways, and uncertainty surrounds their meaning and usage; nonetheless, there is a marked tendency to also associate these words with idols. Idolatry is thus clearly condemned in the Koran. Though there are no explicit interdictions on the representations of human figures, verses cited above using terms such as *asnam* and *ansab* have been narrowly interpreted by some theologians to mean that sculpture is forbidden in Islam.

There are also numerous Traditions, in Arabic, *Hadiths* (the sayings and deeds of the Prophet) that are often interpreted as prohibiting the depiction of living creatures. Though sculpture is rare in some parts of the Islamic world there are remarkable exceptions throughout the history of Islam. For example, Khumarawayh, the Tulunid ruler of Egypt and Syria [died 896 C.E.] had statues of himself, his wives, and singing girls made; while in Spain, Abd al-Rahman III [912-961 C.E.] erected a statue of his favourite wife, al-Zahra; and the marble lions commissioned by Muhammad V in the second half of the fourteenth century for the Alhambra are still extant. The Seljuk princes of Asia Minor, in the thirteenth century, employed sculptors to carve stone figures both human and animal that were used to decorate their capital, Konya, and can still be viewed in the museum of that city. Ismail Pasha [1830-1895] of Egypt was the first ruler to erect statues of Muslim dignitaries in public places, in Cairo. Under the Egyptian dynasty of the Fatimids [909-1171], many bronze ewers and perfume burners in the form of birds and animals were made. Muslim princes in Persia, Syria and Egypt, paying no heed to the theologians, often engaged Christian metal workers, who made vivid representations of court life, even showing the monarch drinking among his servants, or hunting, and so on. There is a similar lively disregard of the theologians to be found on the pottery of Raiy, Iran, of the twelfth and thirteenth centuries, with colorful depictions of princes, musicians, and dancing girls. There are also carvings in wood which date from the Fatimid and Mamluk [1250-1517] periods in Egypt, and which represent humans and animals. Figures have also formed a part of the decoration of carpets, ivories and glass. In fact, one suspects that such objects were far more numerous once upon a time but were destroyed by fanatical iconoclasts.[1]

For one final example, I should like to refer to the rather anthropomorphic Ottoman gravestones. These gravestones do suggest, however vaguely, the human figure especially the head, without facial features, usually shown wearing some form of headgear, most often a turban. For this reason, many beautiful Ottoman gravestones were destroyed in the Balkans following the break-up of Yugoslavia by the many more zealous and bigoted Muslims who poured in from the outside.

Yet a story contradicting the *Hadith* prohibiting the depiction of living things is to be found in an equally revered account of the life of the Prophet, the *Sira* of Ibn Ishaq, as preserved by Azraqi (died 858 C.E.),

---

1 T.W. Arnold. article "TaSwīr" in *Encyclopaedia of Islam*, Ist Edn. Leiden: E.J. Brill, 1993 [Reprint, Ist edn., 1913-1938] Vol. VIII, pp. 692-693. I have leaned heavily on this article for much in this paragraph.

which recounts how Muhammad preserved portraits of Jesus and Mary from destruction, and the *Tabaqat* of Ibn Sa'd (died ca. 845 C.E.), which tells us that on one occasion the Prophet Muhammad found his young bride Aisha playing with her dolls. He asked her what they were, and, on being told they were King Solomon's horsemen, made no adverse observations and allowed her to continue playing with them.

Despite these latter examples, artists depicting humans were accused by certain schools of Islamic law of trying to imitate God's creative function. Some added a more subtle touch by saying that what was important was the artist's intent and that Muhammad only objected to full-size human figures that could be mistaken for real persons; hence, miniatures or small dolls were permissible.

"Hadrat messenger of the merciful – may God bless him [Muhammad] and his family – in his youth, when he used to be a shepherd." by Muhammad Tadjwīdī, dated 1352 AHŠ (1971 C.E.)

A series of Eastern painters derived their inspiration for their portrait of the Prophet Muhammad from the photograph published by the company Lehnert and Landrock. The latter Europeans named the subject of their photograph, Muhammad. The photograph seems to have been reproduced in a book published in Turkey in the 1960s. It was then taken as a model by many Eastern artists, and Muslim Sarlak (see below) drew his inspiration from them—it is unlikely he ever saw the original Lehnert-photograph himself.

Lehnert and Landrock, portrait of a young man—modern print taken from an original negative, 22 x 16 cm. 1905-1906, in the collection of Musée de l'Elysée, Lausanne, Switzerland.

The two Germans, Rudolf Franz Lehnert (1878-1948) and Ernst Heinrich Landrock (1878-1966) first met in Switzerland, and formed a partnership, with Lehnert as the photographer, and Landrock as the manager and publisher. The company was first based in Tunis, then in Cairo in the early 1920s, and was responsible for producing thousands of photographs and postcards of Tunisia, Egypt and other countries in the Near East.

* * *

Islam is not monolithic. At the very least we can speak of "Islam 1" —the Qur'an; "Islam 2"—Islamic Law and the teachings developed by theologians from the deeds and saying of the Prophet; and "Islam 3"— the actual behavior of believing Muslims, the things that are actually said and done across Islamic civilization. As is often the case, Islam 3 has behaved quite differently than it should have as prescribed by Islam 1 and Islam 2. For in fact Islamic history is full of examples of paintings, particularly miniatures—one of the glories of Islamic art—that depict human beings, including the Prophet. According to Priscilla Soucek, the earliest representation of the Prophet Muhammad known to us appears in a mid-thirteenth century illustrated manuscript in Persian entitled, "The Poem of Warqa and Gulsha."[2] But as Grabar and Natif also point out, "Several Arabic texts dated as early as the tenth century mention the existence of painted portraits of Muhammad, as well as of Jesus and several figures from the Old Testament. The setting for these paintings is the Byzantine realm at the time of the emperor Heraclius (r. 610-641) and during the lifetime of the Prophet (d. 632) when Islam took over most of the Near East."[3]

Illustrated Qur'ans depicting Muhammad are also known to exist. Some of the humans have a distinct line drawn over their necks, symbolically defying them to come to life and thereby demonstrating the artist's denial of his intent to compete with God in creating life. Other paintings clearly show the Prophet's face, and attendant details of eyes, lips and beard; others draw his body but leave his face blank, or depict the head as being veiled. The tradition of representing Muhammad in Islamic art is apparent in many Persian miniatures, but it is not, therefore, confined

---

2 Priscilla Soucek, "The Life of the Prophet", in P. Soucek ed., *Content and Context of the Visual Arts in the Islamic World*, University Park, 1988, referred to by Oleg Grabar, & Mika Natif, "The Story of Portraits of the Prophet Muhammad" in *Studia Islamica*, No. 96, Écriture, Calligraphie et Peinture (2003), pp. 19-38+VI-IX, p. 19.

3 Oleg Grabar & Mika Natif, "The Story of Portraits of the Prophet Muhammad" in *Studia Islamica*, No. 96, Écriture, Calligraphie et Peinture (2003), pp. 19-38+VI-IX, p. 19.

only to Shi'ism, since we have many examples from Turkey, and Mughal India. Even the tradition of veiling Muhammad's face may have nothing to do with any prohibition on representational art, but rather refer to a tradition that the face of Muhammad, since he was exceptionally holy, radiated such light that it would blind a normal person, hence the need to cover the Prophet's face.

In other words, the attitude to representational art varied enormously from region to region and period to period. For example, in the western part of the Islamic world, the Maghrib, one finds very rarely any depictions of living beings, whereas in Persia and surrounding areas the strictures against representational art seemed to have been, on the whole, ignored. Nonetheless, there seems to have developed a difference in attitude to representational art between the private and public spheres; one finds figural sculpture, painting and mosaic in private residences, and even figural wall-paintings under the Abbasids. Illustrations to the stirring stories in the *Shah-nama*, considered the national epic of Persia, composed by Firdawsi [940-1020 C.E.] played an enormous part in popularising the use of wall-paintings and book illustrations in Persia.

Persia has had perhaps the longest tradition of representing human figures in the Islamic world. The Ilkhanid Dynasty [1256-1353] was founded by Hulagu, a descendent of Chingiz Khan, and included Persia. One of the earliest representations of Muhammad comes from an Arabic version of Rashid al-Din's universal history commissioned by Mahmud Ghazan Khan, one of the Ilkhanid rulers based in Tabriz; it is usually dated to 1307. In it the Prophet is depicted replacing the Black Stone in the Ka'aba, in Mecca. The subsequent Timurid Dynasty [1370-1506] also produced illustrated works such as the *Miraj Name*, dated to 1436. Here Muhammad has clearly Chinese features.

In the late sixteenth century Persia, wandering dervishes would go from town to town telling stories of the Holy Family, that is Muhammad, Fatima, Ali, Hassan and Hussain,[4] and illustrating them with "curtains" or canvasses painted with representations of the four. We also have the evidence of murals, and paintings on tiles, depicting Ali and Muhammad during Qajar times [1794-1925]. In modern times, with the advent of printing, we had illustrated biographies of Muhammad, and posters of the Holy Family, easily available in poster shops in bazaars, or from hawkers in the streets. Ironically, for their poster art, the Persian artists were forced to draw on the Western Christian tradition, and many of the post-

---

4 Fatima was Muhammad's daughter who married Ali, by whom she had three children, Hassan, Hussain, and Muhsin. The latter died in infancy.

ers of Muhammad and Ali are essentially copies of scenes illustrating Old or New Testament stories by a minor Bible illustrator, Harold Copping [1863-1932].

The poster of the young Muhammad, originally painted by Iranian artist Muslim Sarlak in 1999, and printed not much later.

This contradictory tradition continues in the present day. Across the Muslim world, we can find portraits, including portraits of religious leaders, on banknotes, coins, and posters as well as in magazines and journals. Strictly speaking, the interdiction on representation should place television and even photography off limits; in reality, of course, all Islamic societies are addicted to the cinema and to soaps on television.

The Shepherd Knows His Sheep by Harold Copping

The Sarlak poster can be traced back to an illustration of the parable of Christ as the Good Shepherd by Harold Copping (1863-1932), a British painter who had specialized in Bible illustrations.[5]

NEW YORK SUPREME COURT, 1955

On the north-east corner of Madison Avenue and 25th Street, one will find a Corinthian columned small marble palace built in 1899, designed by James Brown Lord. The roof balustrade is graced by a series of single standing statues of historical figures associated with law-giving: Zoroaster, Alfred the Great, Lycurgus, Solon, St Louis, Manu, Justinian, Confucius and Moses. Along with these one finds sculptures embodying more abstract notions: Peace (with a dove), flanked by Strength and Abundance; Justice flanked by Power and Study, and four caryatids representing four seasons, and implying law's universality.

Originally, there were ten law-givers honored, the tenth figure being Muhammad, an eight-foot marble statue by Charles Albert Lopez. This Muhammad statue held a Koran in one hand and a scimitar in the other. It was described by the *New York Times* as "of average height, but broad-shouldered, with thick, powerful hands. Under his turban, his brows are prominent and frowning. A long, heavy beard flows over his robe. In his left hand, he holds a book, symbolizing the new religion he founded, and in his right, a scimitar, connoting the Moslem conquest."

At the time of general renovation, in 1955, the statue came to the notice of the Egyptian, Indonesian, and Pakistani ambassadors to the United Nations, who immediately demanded the U.S. Department of State to use its influence to have the Muhammad statue removed altogether, despite the obvious fact that the original intent of the architect and sculptors was to generously honor the Muslim lawgiver, considering him the equal of such great figures as Confucius and Solon. (This despite the blunder of showing Muhammad holding the Koran in his left hand, if indeed that was what the sculpture truly showed. No devout Muslim, let alone Muhammad himself, would touch the Koran with a hand reserved for dirty chores.)

The State Department duly complied and sent two functionaries to

---

5 I owe a special word of thanks to Dr. Elisabeth Puin, a world authority on religious posters, which was the subject of her doctoral thesis. She provided me with the four photos reproduced above (that is, the poster of Muslim Sarlak, photo of the painting by Muhammad Tadjwīdī, and the photo of the painting by Harold Copping, and the Lehnert-Landrock photograph), and all the relevant information. She also directed me to the webpage of the two scholars who discovered the original of the poster of the young Muhammad, Pierre Centlivres and Micheline Centlivres-Demont. http://etudesphotographiques.revues.org/index747.html

persuade New York City's public works commissioner, Frederick H. Zurmuhlen, to give in to the demands of the ambassadors. The court also received, "a number of letters from Mohammedans about that time, all asking the court to get rid of the statue." All seven appellate justices recommended to Zurmuhlen that he take down the statue, he was forced to agree and the statue was carted off to a warehouse in New Jersey. Its ultimate fate is unknown. But Zurmuhlen then had to fill in the vacant spot, which he accomplished by replacing Muhammad with Zoroaster, and shifting around the remaining nine statues.

It would be perhaps anachronistic to call that incident as "appeasement in the face of Islamic fundamentalism," but it does show, first, that Muslims living here even temporarily had the temerity to dictate their values on a non-Islamic nation, and second these demands on the Western world pre-dates Islamist activism of the last twenty years. Third, despite the small number of Muslims in the USA, they were, nonetheless, able to succeed with the minimum of effort or lobbying. Soft Islamism, as Daniel Pipes, put it, "presents dangers as great as does violent Islamism."[6]

THE NEED TO DEFEND OUR VALUES

Some of the above examples reveal that the West, in its unwillingness to pass judgements on other cultures, is far too ready to accept as legitimate spokesmen for the entire world-wide Muslim community the most shrill and publicity-savvy on matters of Islamic doctrine. Some fringe group threatens *South Park* and Comedy Central, and the latter parrots and accepts uncritically that group's claim that human representation is forbidden in Islam. As I have shown above, that is far from the historical reality. Since I risk being misunderstood, I should like to clarify exactly what I am saying here: first, let us defend our own values; second we do not need to take at face value or uncritically what some minority group claims are the doctrinal principles of Islam. In this case, these principles are far from clear. However, even if human respresentation were unequivocally forbidden in Islam, we should still as unequivocally defend our right to freedom of speech, and expression.

I am often asked at the end of conferences in the context of discussions of reforming Islam, and combating Radical Islam, what we should

---

6 Daniel Pipes, "Destroying Sculptures of Muhammad," in *Jerusalem Post*, (February 28, 2008), also now available at http://www.meforum.org/pipes/5487/destroying-sculptures-of-muhammad. I am indebted to Pipes for the entire section on Muhammad sculpture in New York City.

do. I reply, first we should unabashedly defend, and if necessary fight for our values without apologies. We would thereby be encouraging the liberals in the Islamic world, who look with dismay at us each time we sacrifice one principle after another, in an orgy of self-doubt, cultural masochism, and self-censorhip. Not only liberal Muslims, but radical Muslims would have more to think about when we put up some resistance in the form of defending our values; for every time we cave into their demands we are merely reinforcing their cruel certainties. By standing firm, we are at least offering an alternative viewpoint, an alternative set of values that may perhaps give some of them pause for reflection. It is certainly not by folding like some third rate poker player who throws in the cards at the first aggressive bluff when he is in fact holding the winning hand that we are likely to change the world. Yes, simply by defending our freedoms, and not by appeasement and some specious arguments about "engagement, and mutual respect and need," we shall bring about a reformation or even an enlightenment in the Islamic world. Even if we do not bring about overnight change in the Islamic world, we would at least remind our supporters, and those fighting for us abroad and at home, what it is we are fighting for.

ISLAMIC ART IN AMERICAN MUSEUMS SHOWING REPRESENTATIONS OF MUHAMMAD

There are numerous miniatures depicting Muhammad in many museums throughout Europe, [*e.g.* London, Vienna, Dublin, Edinburgh, Berlin] and the United States [Los Angeles, New York, Washington, D.C.] Three are to be found in the Freer Gallery of Art, and the fourth in the Arthur M. Sackler Gallery, in Washington, D.C. According to the *Washington Post*, "For reasons that include 'cultural sensitivity,' and today's bloody news, none of these old paintings is currently on view."[7]

Several websites have sprung up in recent years which have many such illustrations from many countries and many periods, *e.g.* http://zombietime.com/mohammed_image_archive/.

Dr. Gary Hull founded Voltaire Press at Duke University in 2009, and has just published *Muhammad: The Banned Images*, under its imprint. The book includes all the images omitted by Yale University Press from Jytte Klausen's *The Cartoons That Shook the World*, including the twelve Muhammad cartoons. There are fine reproductions of Persian and Mughal miniatures, and others by Western artists such as William Blake.

---

7 Paul Richard, "In Art Museums, Portraits Illuminate A Religious Taboo," in *Washington Post*, (February 14, 2006).

Young Muhammad meets the monk Bahira. From *Jami' al-Tavarikh* ("The Universal History" or "Compendium of Chronicles") written by Rashid Al-Din and illustrated in Tabriz, Persia, c. 1315 (Library of the University of Edinburgh).

CENSORSHIP UNDER ISLAM: THE CASE OF TAHA HUSSEIN

Al-Ma'arri [973-1058], sometimes known as the Eastern Lucretius, is one of the great freethinkers of Islam, and no true Muslim feels comfortable in his poetic presence because of his skepticism toward positive religion in general, and Islam in particular. For al-Ma'arri, religion is a fable invented by the ancients, worthless except for those who exploit the credulous, superstitious masses. All men accept the creed of their fathers out of habit, incapable of distinguishing the true from the false. Prophets were no better than the lying clergy, and he did not believe in any of their putative miracles. He did not believe in the resurrection, and preferred the Hindu practice of cremation to burial. And yet he was able to carry on writing unmolested.

Taha Hussein [Husayn][1889-1973], the eminent Egyptian man of letters—novelist, essayist, literary critic, educator—became the first graduate of what eventually became Cairo University, with a doctoral dissertation on al-Ma'arri. Hussein found himself in great difficulties when he published, in 1926, his *On Pre-Islamic Poetry* in which he argued that the bulk of this much-revered corpus had been forged, and that religious considerations were among the most important motives for the fraud. He also wrote, "The Torah is capable of talking to us of Abraham and Ismail, and the Koran is equally capable of talking of them. However, the presence of these two names in the Torah or the Koran is not sufficient to establish their historical existence; not to mention the historicity of the account that speaks to us of the migration of Ismail, son of Abraham, to Mecca...."[8] Hussein was accused of heresy by the traditionalists at al-Azhar Islamic University, and the book banned. However, he was not convicted and the book was republished in an edited form under the title, *On Pre-Islamic Literature*.

WESTERN APPEASEMENT IN MODERN TIMES: THE RUSHDIE AFFAIR

In February 1989, the Ayatollah Khomeini delivered his fatwa on Salman Rushdie. Immediately in its wake came articles or interviews with western intellectuals, Arabists and Islamologists, many of whom blamed Rushdie for bringing the barbarous sentence unto himself. Astonishingly, Professor Hugh Trevor-Roper (Baron Dacre) even seemed to encourage violence against Rushdie: "I wonder how Salman Rushdie is faring these days under the benevolent protection of British law and British police, about whom he has been so rude. Not too comfortably I hope ... I would not shed a tear if some British Muslims, deploring his manners, should waylay him in a dark street and seek to improve them. If that should cause him thereafter to control his pen, society would benefit and literature would not suffer."[9]

In many of the subsequent articles there was no unequivocal support for Rushdie or the principle of freedom of speech. Political and literary figures who were critical of Rushdie included Jimmy Carter, who wrote[10] that *The Satanic Verses* vilified Muhammad and defamed the Koran, "The author, a well-versed analyst of Moslem beliefs, must have anticipated a horrified reaction throughout the Islamic world." To his credit, Carter condemned the death sentence and affirmed Rushdie's right to freedom of speech, but went on to argue that "we have tended to promote him and his book with little acknowledgment that it is a direct insult to those millions of Moslems whose sacred beliefs have been violated and are suffering in restrained silence the added embarrassment of the Ayatollah's irresponsibility." In effect Carter was tacitly calling for self-censorship to protect the tender sensibilities of Muslims.

---

8 Taha Hussein [Taha Husayn], *Fi' sh-Shi'r al-Jahili*, Cairo: Matba' a Dar al-Kutib al-Misriya, 1344/1926, p. 26.

9 Trevor Roper quoted in Salman Rushdie, *Joseph Anton: A Memoir*, New York: Random House, 2012, p. 260.

10 Jimmy Carter, "Rushdie's Book Is An Insult," in *The New York Times* (March, 1989).

John Berger writing in *The Guardian* in February 1989 advised Rushdie to withdraw the book because of the danger to the lives of those involved in its publication. In other words, Berger advocated giving in to intimidation. In a letter to *The Times of London*, Roald Dahl dubbed Rushdie "a dangerous opportunist," who "must have been totally aware of the deep and violent feelings his book would stir up among devout Muslims. In other words, he knew exactly what he was doing and cannot plead otherwise. This kind of sensationalism does indeed get an indifferent book on to the top of the best-seller list, but to my mind it is a cheap way of doing it." Dahl also advocated self-censorship. It "puts a severe strain on the very power principle that the writer has an absolute right to say what he likes," he wrote. "In a civilized world we all have a moral obligation to apply a modicum of censorship to our own work in order to reinforce this principle of free speech."[11] This is, of course, Orwellian double-speak: "Censorship is Freedom of Speech."

While John le Carré said in an interview, "I don't think it is given to any of us to be impertinent to great religions with impunity."[12] Another writer who refused to side with Rushdie was Germaine Greer, describing Rushdie as "a megalomaniac, an Englishman with a dark skin." She also said, "Jail is a good place for writers - they write...."[13]

There were also many intellectuals and politicians who supported Rushdie and his right to free speech, among them Fay Weldon, Christopher Hitchens, Harold Pinter, Susan Sontag, Norman Mailer, and Stephen Spender. I wrote my first book *Why I Am Not a Muslim* (most of it in 1993 but which did not appear until 1995) to add my name to the latter distinguished group, and as a response to the pusillanimous reaction of so many other western intellectuals, who seemed incapable of seeing the implications of the Rushdie Affair for the future of western freedoms, and democracy, achieved slowly over centuries after much philosophical debate, courageous struggles and great sacrifice.

At a meeting in November 1993 at MIT Salman Rushdie said that the shooting of his Norwegian publisher made him determined "to try and make sure that this is the last such atrocity. And for that, I'm afraid I need your help, because the only weapon that I have is public opinion..... [I]f this form of terrorism seems to be working, it will be repeated." [The only way to stop terrorism is] "to say 'I'm not scared of you.' The purpose of terrorism is to terrorize. The only defense against terrorism is to refuse

---

11 *The Times*, (February 28, 1989).
12 Le Carré, quoted in Salman Rushdie, *op.cit.* p. 260.
13 Greer quoted by Paul Lewis in *The Guardian*, (Friday July 28, 2006).

to be terrorized." At the same event, his friend Susan Sontag said, "The worst kind of censorship is self-censorship. [Rushdie's] case is a great test of where we stand on the issue of freedom and solidarity and the future of our culture."[14]

Following the visit to MIT, Rushdie met with President Clinton, who, according to *The New York Times* wanted to "convey America's abhorrence of Iran's refusal to lift the death threat against the novelist."[15]

Twenty years later, the West still seems unable to defend robustly its values which are more than ever under attack from militant, political Islam.

SUBSEQUENT DEVELOPMENTS: POST SATANIC VERSES[16]

A number of bookshops were firebombed both in Great Britain (Collets and Dillons) and the United States (Cody's Books and a branch of Waldenbooks in Berkeley, CA). The Italian translator of *The Satanic Verses* was stabbed, and the Japanese translator was stabbed to death. The Norwegian publisher of *The Satanic Verses* was shot and injured. In supposedly secular Turkey, a group of 37 intellectuals, among them Aziz Nesin, a translator of *The Satanic Verses*, was killed in July 1993.

The Council on American-Islamic Relations [CAIR] objected to Weinman's frieze of lawmakers in the Supreme Court, Washington, D.C., and requested its removal. Chief Justice Rehnquist replied that it was unlawful to remove or injure any architectural feature of the Supreme Court, but that the Supreme Court would change its tourist literature to be more sensitive to Muslim religious beliefs.[17]

In 2002, and again in April 2006, Italian police were able to foil a plot by fundamentalist Muslims to bomb the Cathedral of Bologna, which contains a fifteenth century fresco depicting Muhammad in Hell,[18] unfortunately, now, the section with the Muhammad frescoes is closed to the public. Islamists have, in a sense, won. On November 2, 2004, Dutch

---

14 Daniel C. Stevenson, "Rushdie Stuns Audience 26-100," in *The Tech* Online Edition: Tuesday, (November 30, 1993), http://tech.mit.edu/V113/N61/rushdie.61n.html

15 Douglas Jehl, "Clinton and Aides Meet Rushdie at White House in Rebuke to Iran," in *The New York Times*, (November 25, 1993).

16 Gary Hull, *Muhammad: The "Banned" Images*, Voltaire Press: USA, 2009, pp. 11-14. I am heavily indebted to Dr. Hull's book, and to the time line on the webpage: http://muhammadimages.com/

17 Gary Hull *op.cit.*, p. 42.

18 *Ibid.*, p. 20.

filmmaker, Theo Van Gogh, was murdered by Mohammed Bouyeri, a Dutch Moroccan. Van Gogh made a film with Ayaan Hirsi Ali, *Submission*, highlighting the position of women under Islam. Hirsi Ali said, "I absolutely wish that Theo had not been killed. But I don't regret that I made it. In fact, I'm proud of that film. To feel otherwise would be to deny everything I stand for."[19]

Flemming Rose, culture editor of the Danish newspaper *Jyllands-Posten*, published twelve cartoon renderings of Muhammad in 2005[20] and eloquently defended freedom of speech on the same page. He pointed out that intmidation and fear were leading to self-censorhip, with the result that "Artists, writers, illustrators, translators and theatre directors avoid the most important cultural encounter of our time, the one between Islam and the secular Western societies that grew out of the Christian world. The modern, secular society is rejected by some Muslims. They demand a special position, insisting on special consideration of their own religious feelings. This is incompatible with contemporary democracy and freedom of speech, where one must be ready to put up with insults, mockery and ridicule....It is no coincidence that people living in totalitarian societies are thrown into jail for telling jokes or depicting dictators in a critical way."[21]

FANATICISM, OR MUHAMMAD THE PROPHET

Voltaire spent nineteen years of his life [1759-1778] in Ferney, now called Ferney-Voltaire, which lies in the Ain department in eastern France. Three miles from Ferney-Voltaire, in the same department, is the little town of Saint-Genis Pouilly, which showed far greater courage than most metropolitan centers in the West by staging a public reading of Voltaire's *Le fanatisme, ou Mahomet le Prophète*, [written in 1736 but not performed until 1741] despite the fact that Muslims in the town claimed that the play constituted an insult to the entire Muslim community, and demanded the reading be cancelled in order to preserve peace. Mayor Hubert Bertrand's response was to call in police reinforcements, firmly upholding the principle of free speech guaranteed by the French constitution. Bertrand was justly proud that his town had refused to cave into pressure. "For a long time we have not confirmed our convictions," said Bertrand, "so lots of people think they can contest them."

19 David Cohen, "Violence is Inherent in Islam," in *Evening Standard*, February 7, 2007.

20 Hull, *op. cit.*, p. 45.

14 *Ibid.*, p. 44.

Herve Loichemol, the French theater director who produced the readings of Voltaire's play, said he was not trying to provoke but realised his production would anger Muslims. He had to carry it through, nonetheless. Banning blasphemy "admits private beliefs into public space," he says. "This is how catastrophe starts."[22]

DANISH CARTOONS

In the case of the Danish cartoons, the U.S. State Department, and various Western politicians instead of standing firm have become apologists of the Islamists, apologising over and over again to the fanatics for having hurt their tender feelings. For example, former President Bill Clinton said during a tour of Qatar, "None of us are totally free of stereotypes about people of different races, different ethnic groups, and different religions ... there was this appalling example in northern Europe, in Denmark ... these totally outrageous cartoons against Islam."[23] While Kurtis Cooper, of the U.S. State Department, used the classic tactic familiar with, for example, antisemites, "I have nothing against Jews but you must admit...", or in this case, "of course, I believe in freedom of speech but..." He said (using the giveaway "but"), "We all fully recognize and respect freedom of the press and expression but it must be coupled with press responsibility. Inciting religious or ethnic hatreds in this manner is not acceptable."[24] British Foreign Secretary Jack Straw was no better, "I believe that the republication of these cartoons has been unnecessary. It has been insensitive. It has been disrespectful and it has been wrong."[25] And *The New York Times* revealed its cowardice, which it tried to cover up with feeble arguments, "*The New York Times* and much of the rest of the nation's news media have reported on the cartoons but refrained from showing them. That seems a reasonable choice for news organizations that usually refrain from gratuitous assaults on religious symbols, especially since the cartoons are so easy to describe in words."[26]

And yet, we must not paint a gratuitously pessimistic scenario.

22 Andrew Higgins, "Muslims ask French to cancel 1741 play by Voltaire," in *The Wall Street Journal* (Monday, March 06, 2006).

23 Quoted by Reuel Marc Gerecht, "Selling Out Moderate Islam," *Weekly Standard* (February 20, 2006).

24 http://www.religionnewsblog.com/13485/us-backs-muslims-in-european-cartoon-dispute

25 Jack Straw quoted in *The Guardian* (Friday February 3, 2006).

26 *New York Times*, (February 7, 2006).

There were a number of defiant gestures by individuals and institutions who did support the Danish cartoonists. Italian Minister Roberto Calderoli appeared on television wearing a T-shirt depicting one of the Danish cartoons. Prime Minister Silvio Berlusconi demanded his resignation. Calderoli quite rightly declared before resigning that what was "at stake is Western civilization."[27] By March 2006, 28 American periodicals had published some or all of the cartoons; ten of these were university newspapers. In February 2008, seventeen Danish newspapers showed courage and much needed solidarity by reprinting Westergaard's cartoon.

Despite these acts of courage, the overall picture remains bleak as institution after institution crumbles in the face of Islamic terrorism, real or implied. From bookshops refusing to stock *Free Inquiry* magazine containing the cartoons, to art galleries removing paintings, or miniatures because they offended Muslims [Metropolitan Museum of Art in New York; Whitechapel Art Gallery in London], to cutting short artistic productions [Berlin Opera's production of Mozart's *Idomeneo*], to publishers submitting their manuscripts to Muslims before publication, it is a but a litany of abject capitulation. And appeasement was followed by apologies: in March 2006, *Studi Cattolici* published a cartoon satirizing Italian politicians who give in to Muslim pressure. Even though Muhammad was not portrayed, Italian Muslims were outraged, and the Catholic organization Opus Dei (one of whose members publishes *Studi Cattolici*) promptly issued an apology. In September, 2006, Pope Benedict XVI apologized to Muslims[28] twice in two days for quoting (in a discussion of reason versus violence) a fourteenth century comment by Byzantine emperor Manuel II Paleologus: "Show me just what Muhammad brought that was new, and there you will find things only evil and inhuman, such as his command to spread by the sword the faith he preached."

Perhaps the most disgraceful surrender came from the very institution that was created to defend freedom of expression, the journal *Index on Censorship*, which boasts of being "Britain's leading organisation promoting freedom of expression. With its global profile, its website provides up-to-the-minute news and information on free expression from around the world. Our events and projects put our causes into action. Our award-winning magazine shines a light on these vital issues through original, challenging and intelligent writing." If only they would live up to their aspirations. Their reasons for not re-publishing the Danish cartoons in

---

27 http://slashnews.co.uk/news/2006/02/18/3355/10-Killed-in-Libya-Protest-Italian-Minister-Unrepentant

28 *New York Times*, (September 7, 2006).

an interview with the author Jytte Klausen can be summed up as: that publication would have put the lives of the staff in danger, and that it was "unnecessary" and, indeed, "gratuitous." As dissenting board member Kenan Malik put it, "As for the suggestion that publication would have been 'unnecessary' or 'gratuitous', I cannot see what could be less unnecessary or gratuitous than using cartoons to illustrate an interview with the author of a book that was censored by a refusal to publish those very cartoons. Almost every case of pre-emptive censorship, including that of Yale University Press, has been rationalised on the grounds that the censored material was not necessary anyway. Once we accept that it is legitimate to censor that which is 'unnecessary' or 'gratuitous', then we have effectively lost the argument for free speech."[29]

OBAMA AND SELF-CENSORSHIP: OR THE IMPORTANCE OF SAYING ISLAMIC, ISLAMIC, ISLAMIC, OVER AND OVER AGAIN

Even journalists normally sympathetic to him and his administration have noticed an undemocratic trend in Obama's recent decisions which amount to acts of self-censorship. For instance, the Obama administration is trying to eliminate certain words and phrases from American policy documents and statements concerning Islam, so that analysts, experts and advisors cannot use expressions such as "radical Islam," "Islamic extremists," "Islamists," and "Islamic terrorists." While it is true that such a policy of avoiding terms such as "Islamic terrorism" began under Bush, and in Britain under Tony Blair, they were confined to public statements. Now Obama's policy applies to internal government documents as well, which can only have disastrous consequences for our understanding of political groups and events in the Middle East, Afghanistan, Pakistan, and South and South East Asia. As Barry Rubin said, "Suppose I'm an intelligence analyst in the State Department, Defense Department, armed forces, or CIA, and I'm writing about one of these groups or this ideology. How can one possibly analyze the power and appeal of this ideology, the way that ideas set its strategy and tactics, why it is such a huge menace if any reference to the Islamic religion and its texts or doctrines isn't permitted?"[30]

President Obama is determined to appease Muslims at all costs to

---

29 http://www.indexoncensorship.org/2009/12/kenan-malik/

30 http://rubinreports.blogspot.com/ *The Rubin Report*, Tuesday, April 27, 2010.

the extent of denying the role of Islam, even if we restrict it to Radical Islam or Political Islam, in the wars the United States is at present engaged in. This mind set will not solve problems in the Middle East, and makes him unwilling to take unequivocal stands for freedoms guaranteed under the U.S.Constitution. A firm declaration in support of artists in whatever medium would send a clear message to all Islamic, yes Islamic, terrorists, and easily offended Muslims that we are proud of our values, and we will defend them at all costs, and that we shall not be terrorised.

SOUTH PARK AND THE IMPORTANCE OF COMEDY

Comedy is an indispensable ingredient in every culture.[31] Humour can be seen as a form of self-criticism, a defining virtue of the West, and has been present from the dawn of Greek civilization—from Aristophanes, Eupolis, and Cratinus to Menander; in Roman Civilization (Plautus and Terence), and ever since. It is also a necessary safety valve that allows us to laugh at each other's foibles and failures, an act of conciliation that enables us to laugh off our differences and live in relative harmony. The ethnic joke if not invented in New York was certainly given a new life there as Jews, and the Irish, the Poles and the Italians, all competing for space in a bustling, teeming metropolis, developed self-deprecating humour, the necessary oil to run a complex social organism. The Jews are particularly gifted for self-mockery, and the rabbinical tradition is full of jokes pointing to the irony of God's chosen people having to fight harder than most in order to survive. Let us beware of any civilization that cannot laugh at it-self—such a civilization is in a state of decline and dangerous. Despite the irreverent humour of poets like al-Ma'arri [died 1058], and the tradition in, for example, Punjabi poetry and music of questioning God and even ridiculing his claims, modern day Islam is singularly devoid of humour: as the Ayatollah Khomeini once said, "there are no jokes in Islam." Muslims are ever ready to take offence, and in fact, Muslims seem to have invented a new right, the right not to be offended, and the European Union seems determined not to allow any humorous remarks about Islam, promulgat-ing laws designed to silence criticism, and those indispensable social crit-ics, the comedians.

South Park's creators, Trey Parker and Matt Stone have been quite fearless when criticizing the Catholic Church, Buddhists, and Scientolo-

---

31 Roger Scruton, *Culture Counts*, New York: Brief Encounters 2007, pp. 6-8, 10-11, 45-48. and also R. Scruton, "The Decline of Laughter," *The American Spectator*. (June, 2007).

gists. The latter "church" has succeeded in silencing many a critic with intimidatory and expensive lawsuits, and hence *South Park* showed a great deal of courage in going ahead with their jokes. No institution, it seems, was safe from their satire, often in the most crude form imaginable—scatological even. But the fear of Islamic extremists was enough to send Comedy Central scurrying for cover. The offending episode satirized the fear pervading any discussion of Islam, and showed Muhammad hiding inside a bear costume. Though, eventually, we learn that it is not Muhammad after all, but Santa Claus in the costume. Comedy Central bleeped out every mention of the Prophet, and even a speech on intimidation which did not mention him. A group calling itself Revolution Muslim claimed on its website that the Prophet and hence all Muslims had been insulted, and the creators, Parker and Stone would "probably wind up like Theo van Gogh..." The statement went on to say, "This is not a threat but a warning of the reality of what will likely happen to them," thus perhaps, covering themselves legally.

There was thankfully some show of solidarity: there are now a small number of websites devoted entirely to displaying images of Muhammad, both from Islamic and Western sources. The one best known to me is http://www.zombietime.com/mohammed_image_archive/. There are also some books that have reproduced the banned images. Gary Hull founded Voltaire Press and then published *Muhammad: The "Banned" Images*, under its imprint; easily found on Amazon. Artists, writers, and intellectuals threatened by Islamists should demand a public statement from law-enforcement agencies such as the F.B.I., and politicians clearly promising every protection necessary. The second course of action is to take legal action against those making such threats even if they are based abroad. Daniel Pipes has established The Legal Project in order to protect, "researchers and analysts working on the topics of terrorism, terrorist funding, and radical Islam from predatory legal actions designed to silence them. The site tracks ongoing threats to free speech and reports on the LP's efforts to defend the rights of those who investigate and combat Islamism."

Finally, we need to hold a conference on Freedom of Speech that would have readings of Voltaire's play, *Le fanatisme, ou Mahomet le Prophète*, show Geert Wilders' *Fitna*, and project images of Muhammad taken from Gary Hull's book, *Muhammad: The "Banned" Images*, and, of course, speeches in defense of freedom of speech from, if possible, Salman Rushdie, Ayaan Hirsi Ali, Trey Parker and Matt Stone, among others.

CONCLUSION

While it is commendable and understandable to wish to protect, for example, the personnel of a publishing house, if the decision of a publisher to publish material considered blasphemous by Muslims leads to widespread violence, this violence cannot possibly be considered morally or legally the responsibility of the said publisher. The publisher, writer, comedian, cartoonist is exercising his or her constitutional right, and if threatened, the state should give, unbegrudgingly, every protection possible. Publishers must stand by their writers, newspapers with their cartoonists, Comedy Central with *South Park* artists, and intellectuals with their fellow intellectuals. But where was Hollywood when fellow filmmaker, Theo Van Gogh, was killed? The "Draw Mohammed Day" initiative by a Seattle cartoonist, far from being frivolous was a magnificent show of solidarity, exactly in the manner of public readings of *The Satanic Verses*, already mentioned. Unless we show greater solidarity, massive, public, noisy solidarity and show that we care for our freedoms, we risk losing all to Islamist thuggery.

INDEX

Palestine (continued)
  The Talisman set in 16
  Travelers in 195-205
  Uncultivated 196-200, 207
Palmerston, Lord (Prime Minister) 181-2
Parable of the Three Rings, The 119
Parker, Trey 243-4
Pasha Ahmad al-Jazzar 204
Paulicianism 48
Pearson, Hesketh 41
Pentateuch 175, 177
Peter (the Hermit) 43, 46, 47, 156
Phelan, Captain George 183
Pinter, Harold 237
Pipes, Daniel 233, 244
Poliakov, Léon 21, 148-9, 156-8
Pope Benedict XVI 241
Pope Eugenius III 158
Pope Innocent III 26
Pope Urban II 49-50, 125, 135
Porges, Nathan 150
Portugal 193
Posidonius [died c. 51 BCE] 158
Potter, Beatrix 124
Prague 156
Prawer, Joshua 89, 93, 112
Prince Reynald of Chatillon 65-6
Principles of Political Economy 218
Psalms 175-7
pseudo-Tatian 175
Ptolemy Lagos 192
Puin, Elisabeth 232
Purvey, John 177

Q
Qajar 229
Queen Elizabeth 175

R
Rabbi Nathan 27
Ramerupt 158
Raymond of Aguilers 49
Raymond of Jubail 116
Raymond of Toulouse 43, 45, 49
Rebecca 20-1, 24-5, 28-39
Restorationism 173, 181
Rhineland 29, 46, 147, 151-2, 154, 156
Richard the Lionheart 16, 20, 26, 34-5, 39, 41, 51-5, 59, 61-2, 66-7, 76-9, 101, 106-7, 110, 121-3, 173, 185
Richard, Jean. 153
Richards, D.S. 64, 73, 85-8, 94, 97
Rider Haggard, H. 123
Riley-Smith, Jonathan 16-17, 40, 59, 88, 139-41
Robertson, William 16, 82, 136
Robinson, Chase xii
Rolle, Richard 176
Rose, Flemming 239
Rosenberg, Edgar 21, 34-36, 39
Rowena 30-1, 33, 39
Rubin, Barry 242
Runciman, Sir Steven 44-6, 48, 62, 124, 137, 142, 152, 154, 156-7
Rushdie, Salman 223, 236-8, 244

S
Sackler Gallery (Washington, D.C.) 234
Said, Edward xii-xiii, 15-17, 40, 57, 59, 171-2, 187-91, 194, 200, 202, 206, 210-12
Saint Gildas 175
Saint-Genis Pouilly 239